TERENCE: *The Self - Tormentor*

D1595963

THE CHARACTERS OF *THE SELF—TORMENTOR*

Woodcut from *Terentius Comico Carmine*, Johann Grüninger, Strasbourg, 1503, in the Old Library of St David's University College, Lampeter.

(The lines indicate the relationships between the characters.)

TERENCE

THE SELF-TORMENTOR

Edited with translation and commentary by

A. J. Brothers

© A. J. Brothers 1988. All rights reserved. No part of this publication may be reproduced, stored in a retrieval system or transmitted by any means or in any form including photocopying without the prior permission of the publishers in writing.

 British Library Cataloguing in Publication Data

Terence
  [Heautontimorumenos. *English & Latin*].
  The Self-Tormentor. —— (Classical texts).
  I. [Heautontimorumenos. *English & Latin*]
  II. Title   III. Brothers, A.J.   IV. Series
872'.01   PA6756.H4

ISBN 0 85668 302 7 *cloth*
ISBN 0 85668 303 5 *limp*

Reprinted with corrections 1998

Printed and Published in England by Aris & Phillips Ltd, Teddington House, Warminster, Wiltshire, BA12 8PQ.

CONTENTS

FOR JOHN AND WENDY
IN MEMORY OF MUM AND DAD,
AND FOR DOROTHY
IN MEMORY OF HAROLD

PREFACE

Terence's *The Self—Tormentor* is the most neglected of the dramatist's six comedies. No new full—scale edition of the play has appeared in Britain this century, nor in the English—speaking world for over seventy five years, and such older commentaries as do exist are largely concerned with narrow linguistic and philological matters. It is perhaps the absence, for this play alone, of Donatus' commentary on Terence which may explain — though not excuse — this fact. Yet *The Self—Tormentor*, for all its occasional imperfections, in many ways 'shows Terence at his best; its plot is ingenious, complex, fast—moving and extremely skilfully constructed, its characters are excellently drawn, and the whole is full of delightful dramatic irony. It deserves to be better known.

This edition differs slightly from most others in the series in that its commentary contains a small proportion of notes which are geared to the Latin text; these are placed within square brackets in order to distinguish them from the great majority which are geared to the translation. In the main such notes are concerned with the more complex textual matters, and with explanation of pre—classical Latin forms and elucidation of the syntax; they are therefore necessarily spaced unevenly through the commentary. I am grateful to the publishers for their ready agreement to their inclusion, and I hope that by including them I have not fallen too far between two stools.

I first became interested in *The Self—Tormentor* while working for the degree of Bachelor of Philosophy at Oxford over twenty years ago, but this edition is of a far different nature from the mainly metrical study which I then produced. I am grateful to Professor Christopher Collard of University College, Swansea for his commendation of this new project, and to Mr John Aris and Mr Philip Mudd of Aris and Phillips Ltd for their great help and encouragement at all stages of its production and for their stoical acceptance of delays along the way. My colleague at Lampeter, Mr I.M. Barton, willingly took on the burden of reading large parts of the work, and I have benefited greatly from his acute judgement on many points. But my greatest debt is to Aris and Phillips' Editorial Adviser, Professor M.M. Willcock, whose careful reading of the draft has purged the final version of many imperfections, infelicities and errors. All such as remain are, of course, my own.

I must also express my thanks to the authorities of St David's University College, Lampeter for permission to reproduce the illustration which I have used as a frontispiece, and for granting me study leave in Michaelmas Term, 1985, during which a sizeable proportion of the work was done. I am also extremely grateful to the British Academy, whose award of a grant under their scheme for research in the humanities enabled me to spend my study leave in Oxford.

I thank Mrs Diana Catley of the Department of Classics at Lampeter and Mr C.P. Gibson of Oxford for their invaluable assistance with the typing at various stages; but in this connection I am primarily and particularly indebted to Mrs Maureen Hunwicks of Lampeter's Department of Geography, who typed the great bulk of the work in her leisure time with almost unbelievable speed and with extreme accuracy.

The fact that this book is dedicated to my brother and sister—in—law in memory of my late parents needs no explanation; the fact that it is also dedicated to Mrs Dorothy N. Harris in memory of her husband, the late Professor H.A. Harris, is an expression of my love for her and an inadequate repayment of the debt which I owe to a fine scholar and gentleman.

A.J. Brothers

INTRODUCTION

I   GREEK NEW COMEDY[1]

Terence's comedies are adaptations into Latin of Greek plays of the type known as New Comedy. Greek Comedy is conventionally divided into three periods called Old, Middle and New, though there was gradual and continuous development of the genre throughout. Old Comedy (to which most of Aristophanes' eleven surviving comedies belong) is the name for the type of comic drama produced at Athens down to about 400 B.C., Middle Comedy (of which Aristophanes' last two plays are our only examples) for that produced for about the first 75 years of the fourth century. New Comedy is "the name we give ... to the Greek plays (other than tragedies) written in the period following the death of Alexander the Great"[2] (323 B.C.).

By the New Comedy period Athens was no longer great and influential, but a city of comparatively little independent political importance in the empires of Alexander's successors, and the old democratic freedom of speech which is such a feature of much of Aristophanes had gone forever. Accordingly, comedy became less and less concerned with satirical comment on prominent figures in public life and criticism of important topics of the moment, and more and more concerned with the less obviously appealing but much safer problems continually but timelessly raised in the fictional lives of ordinary people. New Comedy also dispensed with the scurrility and obscenity which had been features of Old Comedy, and the chorus, which had also featured prominently, was reduced to a role of virtual insignificance. Unfortunately, because of the absence of any texts worth speaking of between Arisophanes' last play (388 B.C.) and our earliest datable example of New Comedy (317 B.C.), we know little of the rate of these changes or the stages by which they occurred.

Until the beginning of this century our knowledge of New Comedy was almost exclusively derived from brief quotations preserved out of context by ancient grammarians and commentators, and from the Latin adaptations made by Plautus and Terence of lost originals from the period. But this situation began to change radically with the first substantial discovery of papyrus texts in 1905, and the discoveries have continued in fits and starts since.[3] The result has been one virtually complete play (Menander's *Dyskolos* "The Bad—Tempered Man"), substantial portions of half a dozen others (particularly Menander's *Samia* "The Girl from Samos", where the gaps in our text do not prevent an appreciation of the play as a whole), and passages of a reasonable length from yet more. We are beginning to form a first—hand, rather than a second—hand, impression of what New Comedy was like.

1

None of the really big discoveries so far made come from comedies which Plautus and Terence adapted.[4] But all of the major ones do at least come from the pen of the same writer of New Comedy as provided models for four of Terence's six plays — Menander. Of over 70 comic dramatists of whom we have evidence in this period, Menander is by far the most famous. An Athenian who lived from c. 342 to c. 291 B.C., he began his dramatic career in 321, and wrote, according to one account, 108 plays altogether. During his lifetime his reputation did not stand all that high, with eight first prizes in dramatic competition — a respectable, but not a spectacular, record. Later in antiquity, however, he was regarded with an admiration which almost amounted to veneration, being particularly renowned for his excellence in character—drawing, his good plots and his mastery of language. Thus the learned scholar Aristophanes of Byzantium could say: "O Menander, o life, which of you imitated the other?", while Plutarch asked what any educated man would go to the theatre for except to see Menander.[5]

Of the other writers of New Comedy we know much less than we do of Menander, and we possess few substantial passages from their works. Mention need only be made of one other, if only because he provided the originals for the other two of Terence's plays. He is Apollodorus of Carystus, a town on the island of Euboea.[6] We are told he wrote 47 plays and won five victories; he probably became an Athenian citizen, and produced his first play about 285 B.C.

The most important aspect of New Comedy for the student of Terence is the nature of the plays themselves. In form[7] these had five acts separated by song—and—dance routines performed by a chorus which otherwise took no part in the action of the play; the words it sang do not appear in our texts, the place for the songs merely being indicated by the presence of the Greek word meaning "(a performance) of the chorus" at the appropriate points. The number of speaking actors was probably limited to three, though some small parts could be taken by additional players.[8] The action was preceded (or interrupted early on, after one or two scenes) by an explanatory prologue which set the scene, introduced some of the principal characters, filled in some of the background to the plot and sometimes hinted at its outcome; the prologue—speaker was often some kind of divine or semi—divine figure who took no other part in the action, but whose privileged position enabled him (or her) to see the plot, and the misunderstandings and complications it usually involved, from the viewpoint of all the different characters at once.[9] As anyone who reads Roman comedy will quickly see, the chief alteration made to this form by Plautus and Terence in their adaptations is that they both dispensed with the chorus;[10] and, though Plautus retained the prologue in something like its New Comedy form, Terence substituted a prologue of a very different kind.[11]

More significant than the form of the plays is their content. They

2

were normally set in Athens or one of the townships of Attica, and the scene usually represented a street backed by houses.[12] The action revolved around the fortunes of one or more middle–class families, with a love–affair almost invariably at the centre of the plot. All the characters were fictional, and the dialogue was almost entirely free of topical references except of the most innocent and incidental kind. In the plays stock motifs are frequently repeated, the same proper names for characters crop up again and again, and the characters themselves are generally variations on a number of stock 'types'. Prominent is the often impecunious free–born young man, around the difficulties of whose love–affair the plot revolves, and he may be assisted by a friend of similar age and class. In a society where marriages are arranged and young men and women do not mix freely before they marry, the object of his affections is often a young girl who is supposedly a slave, or else a money–grabbing *hetaira* "courtesan". The young girl, sometimes already pregnant by the young man, is often during the course of the play discovered — through the not uncommon motif of a 'recognition scene' — to be of free birth (having been exposed as a baby or captured by pirates at an early age), and the required happy ending is assured; the *hetaira*, by contrast, is disposed of by parental decree and a more acceptable substitute provided to be the young man's wife. The young man's father opposes his son's affair unless and until the way is cleared for marriage, and is frequently represented as ill–tempered, disapproving, and mean with his considerable amount of money; he, too, often has a peer in the form of an elderly neighbour. But the son generally has an ally in the form of one of his father's slaves who has a particular attachment to his young master and shows great ingenuity in furthering the romance with the young girl or securing money (often from the unwitting father himself) to satisfy the expensive tastes of the *hetaira*; as a contrast to this smart city slave there is sometimes also a rather stupid but more conventionally loyal slave, often from the family's country estate. And so the list continues, with boastful soldiers who are often the young man's rivals in love, cooks continually talking about food, hard–bitten slave dealers or brothel keepers who have the young heroine in their clutches, parasites and flatterers, mothers who attempt a reconciliation between father and son, elderly family nurses who prove critical in the recognition scene, and so on.

It might be thought that such plays, with stock characters, frequently recurring motifs and situations, and a prologue which often hinted at what the ending would be, might be repetitious, dull and boring; but that, as Sandbach says,[13] is to misunderstand the nature of Greek art. What mattered to a Greek audience was not the playwright's destination (they knew anyway since they were watching a comedy, that everyone would live happily ever after), but how he got there; the interest would be in the variations on the themes which he introduced on the journey.[14] Even leaving aside the plays of Plautus and Terence, where the possible presence of alterations makes judgement difficult, there is in what remains of New Comedy itself ample evidence of the variety and novelty, often of a most subtle kind, which a dramatist of the calibre of Menander could impart to character and to situation. Perhaps some writers of New Comedy did indeed produce dreary and predictable drama; but this would only serve to show how correct was antiquity's opinion of Menander's genius.

II COMEDY AT ROME

Terence's adaptations of Greek New Comedy are known by the technical name (*fabulae*) *palliatae* "Greek−cloak plays", *palliatae* being coined from *pallium* "Greek cloak", and typifying the Greek setting and dress taken over with the originals. But Terence was not the first Latin writer to produce this type of play; for a proper picture of comedy at Rome, we need to look at his predecessors in the genre, and at the precursors of that genre in Italy.

The classic ancient account of the growth of drama (including comedy) at Rome is given by Livy (7.2.3−13), but it is generally accepted that this forms part of a fairly late tradition based on Greek antiquarian models, and is not to be trusted. However, Livy does mention in that account certain native forms which are at least akin to comic drama, and which probably antedate the production of the first *palliatae* and prepared the ground for the acceptance of that type of play. [1]

Most significant among these are (*fabulae*) *Atellanae* "Atellan farces", [2] which were later included with other forms of entertainment as *exodia* "tail−pieces" after more substantial dramatic performances. These took their name from Atella, one of the Oscan towns of Campania where they first appeared in Italy, having perhaps developed from the Doric farces of the Greek colonies of the south. They achieved popularity early at Rome, where performances were in the hands of amateurs; later, however, they attained literary form. We hear of two writers, L. Pomponius Bononiensis "of Bononia" (*fl. c.* 100−85 B.C.) and Novius (*fl. c.* 95−80 B.C.); surviving fragments of their work illustrate the coarseness of the genre. The plays seem to have been farcical masked performances, mainly illustrating provincial life, with stock characters such as Maccus ("the fool"), Pappus ("greybeard"), Bucco ("fat−cheeks") and Manducus ("champ−jaws").

There is another early form of dramatic expression, not mentioned in Livy's account − mime. [3] Like Atellan farce, this probably became widespread in southern Italy because of Greek influence, and this, too, later achieved literary form. Macrobius [4] preserves several anecdotes about its two chief writers, D. Laberius (*c.* 115−43 B.C.) and his contemporary Publilius Syrus, together with short passages of their work. We hear of troupes of *mimi* "mime actors" performing mimes, which soon rivalled

Atellan farces in popularity as tail—pieces.

It was into a Rome where, according to most scholars, these forms of drama were already known that adaptations of Greek plays were introduced in 240 B.C. That is the date of the first *palliata* (and of the first tragedy) of L. Livius Andronicus (*c.* 284—*c.* 204 B.C.),[5] a Greek from Tarentum taken to Rome as a captive in 272 B.C. and subsequently freed. It is generally assumed that the timing of this innovation was connected with the desire for a particularly memorable festival to celebrate the end of the First Punic War the previous year. After 240 B.C. Livius, who was also renowned for his Latin version of Homer's *Odyssey*, wrote other such plays, but we know the names of only three of his *palliatae*, and possess only about half a dozen lines, most of them incomplete.

Rome's second dramatist, Cn. Naevius (before 260—*c.* 200 B.C.), perhaps Campanian by birth, produced his first plays in 235 B.C.[6] He too adapted both tragedies and comedies for the Roman stage, and also wrote the first native drama on Roman mythical or historical themes, and an epic poem on the First Punic War in which he had fought. We know the names of 35 of his *palliatae* and a number of short fragments survive. Naevius is said to have run into trouble as a result of attacks on prominent Romans — particularly the Metelli — which he included in his plays;[7] these led to imprisonment and later to exile. We are told he died in exile at Utica in North Africa.

The lessons of Naevius' punishment, if true, were not lost on the next dramatist, T. Maccius Plautus (*c.* 254—184 B.C.),[8] whose plays contain only innocent contemporary allusions, one of which is actually to Naevius' imprisonment;[9] he wrote only *palliatae*, and was the first Roman writer so to specialize. Besides fragments, we possess twenty complete plays of his and an incomplete twenty—first. These are the 21 thought by the antiquarian M. Terentius Varro (116—27 B.C.) to be undoubtedly Plautine,[10] though he also ascribed others to him on grounds of style, and some plays not in Varro's list are said elsewhere to be by Plautus.[11]

Plautus took his models from Greek New Comedy,[12] using plays — where we know enough to say so — by Menander, Diphilus and Philemon among others; his choice shows considerable variety, embracing mythological burlesque, sentimental tragi—comedy, farce and domestic comedy. As far as we can tell without possessing his originals, he treated them with considerable freedom, sometimes seemingly almost as raw material, living from scene to scene and on occasion having little regard for the play as a whole. His plays contain frequent Roman puns and allusions, crudities and somewhat laboured clowning; slave roles are expanded, existing scenes lengthened and even occasionally new scenes inserted, causing inconsistencies and hold—ups in the action unthinkable in the Greek original. In this, his approach is very different from the one Terence was to adopt later.

Plautus also differed from Terence in that, as if to compensate for his removal of the chorus, he included in many of his plays elaborate sung lyric passages, making the plays seem, as has often been suggested,[13] more like operas or musicals; there is evidence, necessarily small, that in this he was following Livius and Naevius, but, except for some short passages, Terence did not imitate him.[14]

The great Q. Ennius (239−169 B.C.), famous for his tragedies and his epic poem on Rome's history, seems to have had little taste for comedy, since we only possess a very few fragments from the small number of *palliatae* he wrote, and the next comic poet of note is Caecilius Statius (*c.* 230−168 B.C.). Like Plautus, Caecilius wrote only *palliatae*, and, like Terence, he had difficulty at the start of his career;[15] he may also have begun a movement, followed by Terence and excessively vigorously advocated by Terence's critics,[16] towards greater faithfulness to the spirit of the Greek originals by cutting down on the puns, topical references etc. which are so typical of Plautus. We know the titles of over 40 of his comedies, and are fortunate to have preserved a comparison of three passages from his *Plocium* with the relevant sections of its original by Menander.[17] Caecilius' successor was Terence, and after Terence we only hear of one other composer of *palliatae*, Sextus Turpilius (*c.* 180−103 B.C.).

About the time of Terence, another type of comedy arose at Rome, its plays known as (*fabulae*) *togatae* (from *toga*, the typical Roman dress, because their setting was purely Italian) or *tabernariae* (from *taberna*, a poor man's house, because they mainly portrayed lower−class life). The theory that the emergence of *togatae* was a reaction against the increasingly Greek tone of *palliatae* is now largely discredited,[18] if only because both types existed side by side for over half a century; they are now seen as complementary, being parallel developments from the Romanized Greek plays of Plautus. Some 70 titles and about 600 lines have survived, the work of three dramatists, Titinius (perhaps Terence's contemporary), L. Afranius (born *c.* 150 B.C., the most important of the three) and T. Quinctius Atta (died 77 B.C.); however, we cannot reconstruct a single plot. The Italian flavour of *togatae* is seen in the prominence of women, reflecting their higher status in Roman society, the absence of the clever slave, and the appearance of certain themes, such as paederasty, not found in Greek New Comedy. In one fragment Afranius expresses his indebtedness to Menander, and in another his admiration for Terence; these sentiments, coupled with his use of Greek proper names, may indicate the inability of the writers of *togatae* to break free from the influence of *palliatae*.

No more *palliatae* were written after the death of Turpilius, and no more *togatae* after that of Quinctius Atta, but the age of the theatre was not yet over. Literary *Atellanae* were being written in Sulla's day, and literary mimes in Caesar's; and the age of Cicero was in many ways the golden age of Roman drama, when the audience knew its 'classics' and comic actors like the great Roscius could make fortunes in their profession. References by writers like Quintilian[19] indicate that *palliatae* were occasionally revived under the early empire, but it was really only *Atellanae* and mimes, and by the end of the first century A.D. only the latter, which remained in vogue as regular entertainment. However, as theatre−goers' attentions were attracted elsewhere, a reading public arose for the more weighty drama, particularly in the so−called 'archaising age' of the second century A.D., while during the next two centuries after that reading copies of the old dramatists continued to be made, especially for use in schools; it is significant that our earliest MSS of Plautus and Terence, and Donatus' commentaries on the latter's plays, all date from the fourth century A.D.

PRODUCTION

Terence's plays were produced[20] at public festivals or "games" (*ludi*), either regular ones of a religious character, or ones arranged for special occasions such as victories or funerals. They were organised by magistrates, usually the aediles, and they or other prominent figures would often augment the money given to them by the state for the purpose, doubtless hoping to further their political careers thereby. The magistrates would negotiate for plays with the *dux* (or *dominus*) *gregis* "leader of the company" of actors, who would himself negotiate with the author, and also make all other arrangements, about costumes, masks[21] etc., necessary for the production. The *dux gregis* was a freedman, and in charge of the all−male company, whose actors were not necessarily, as is sometimes said, slaves.[22]

Theatres in Terence's day were temporary wooden structures erected for the occasion; the first permanent stone theatre in Rome was that of Pompey in 55 B.C.[23] Unfortunately we know little about the design of these early structures (though doubtless they were fairly simple) and so it is impossible to be sure how Terence's plays were originally staged; what ancient writers say about production is often confused and sometimes misleading. It is of little help to look at later permanent theatres, since they were built with the design of Greek theatres very much in mind; the only certain clues are almost casual hints in the plays themselves, which, however, contain nothing like our modern stage directions.[24]

It seems that in early theatres the wooden stage was wide and shallow,[25] as befitted the 'normal' setting of a street; this arrangement facilitated the activities of the *servus currens* "running slave",[26] and made more plausible the frequent stage−devices of eavesdropping,[27] asides[28] and failure to notice another character's presence.[29] Behind the stage stood the actors' accommodation, the front of which, containing three sets of doors representing the 'normal' three houses fronting the street, formed the back—scene; the building was presumably a flimsy wood—and—canvas construction, but the doors were probably stout and heavy.[30] There were also two entrances from the 'wings', that to the spectators' left conventionally leading to the country and/or the harbour, that to their right to the centre of town.[31] There was probably little or no attempt to have realistic scenery, and there was no curtain; the only other feature was an altar on stage.[32] In the earliest times spectators may have stood or sat on the ground, but by Plautus' day there were benches;[33] the spectators' area must have been fairly open, since it could easily be invaded by people expecting rival attractions.[34] The audience, admitted free, was very mixed; there is evidence that the less attentive and intelligent had to have tricky points spelled out carefully,[35] but, equally, a play such as *The Self—Tormentor*, with many twists and turns in a fast—moving plot, needs concentration and a quick mind if it is to be properly appreciated.

III THE LIFE AND WORKS OF TERENCE

A brief summary of Terence's life and career would run as follows. Born in Africa some time in the first quarter of the second century B.C., he became a slave at Rome but attained his freedom. Under the name Publius Terentius Afer, he embarked — some said at a precociously early age — on a career as a writer of *palliatae*; in this career he enjoyed the support — according to some the active creative assistance — of a number of highly—placed Romans interested in Greek literature and culture. This fact, and certain aspects of his handling of his Greek originals, led to attacks on his methods by at least one other comic dramatist, against which he vigorously defended himself in the prologues of his plays. After a short, but by no means uniformly successful, career of no more than seven or eight years, he died early in the 150s B.C.; the circumstances of his death were unknown.

Our principal sources for the details of this are three: Suetonius' *Vita Terenti "Life of Terence"*,[1] what Terence himself says in his prologues, and the *didascaliae* "production notices" of his plays.[2] Unfortunately the first two of these must be handled carefully. As far as the *Life* is concerned, ancient biography is notoriously anecdotal, and much of what this one contains could, on a sceptical view, be held to be little more than fabrication based on vague hints found in the prologues and elsewhere;[3] moreover, Suetonius himself admits that there is little agreement about some of what he says.[4] As for the prologues, much of the material in them which is relevant to Terence's career is given when he is defending himself against the attacks on his methods; since this defence will obviously be subject to special pleading, the information it contains will be suspect. Only with the production notices are we on surer ground, since their authenticity is undoubted; yet even here the record of the original production has suffered from accretion of details about subsequent performances. [5]

According to the *Life* (5), Terence died while on a trip to Greece undertaken in his 25th year, shortly after his last plays were produced in 160 B.C.; he will therefore have been born *c.* 185 B.C. and have died *c.* 159 B.C. Both these dates can be disputed, since some of our Suetonius MSS say '35th year', not '25th year', and the timing of his death could merely be an inference from the known date of the last plays. But such an inference is probably justified, given that Terence had produced six plays in the previous seven years and that after 160 B.C. no more appeared; and the MS reading '25th' certainly gives more weight than '35th' to the jibe of Terence's principal critic that he was a young upstart. [6]

Terence is said (*Life* 1) to have been born at Carthage in North Africa and to have subsequently become a slave at Rome of the senator Terentius Lucanus, who educated him and gave him his freedom. The senator's name provides circumstantial detail, so this may well be true; but the sceptical view holds that it could equally well be guesswork based on Terence's full Latin name, Publius Terentius Afer. [7] Afer is a good Roman *cognomen* "surname", but it also means "African"; and, so the argument runs, since a freed slave customarily took his erstwhile master's *nomen* "gentile name", what could be more tempting to a biographer searching for material than to suggest that this Afer should have been African and slave to a Terentius? [8] Moreover, Terence's renowned skill with the Latin language might militate against the idea of foreign birth. On the other hand, as Sandbach says when drawing a comparison with the modern world: "Men who have won literary fame in languages not their own are not common ... but some can be named." [9]

The *Life* (3) tells how, when Terence presented his first play, *Andria* "*The Girl from Andros*", to the aediles for consideration, they told him to read it first to Caecilius, who was then doyen of Roman comic poets. This he did, at first, because of his shabby appearance, seated on a stool beside Caecilius as he reclined at dinner; but when he had read a few lines he was asked to join the meal, after which he read out the rest of the play, which was much admired. This time the disbelief of the sceptics does seem correct, since there is considerable difficulty with the story. Firstly, the anecdotal connection of a comic poet with his immediate predecessor is suspiciously neat; we are reminded of the tale connecting two of the great tragic poets of Rome, Pacuvius and Accius. [10] More seriously, there are chronological difficulties. According to Jerome's *Chronicle*, Caecilius died the year after Ennius, that is in 168 B.C., when Terence was probably only 17; and why, if Caecilius so admired *Andria*, was it not produced until 166 B.C.? [11] But the story is nevertheless additional testimony to Terence's youth when he embarked upon his dramatic career.

9

About the details of that career there is now general agreement among scholars, based on the evidence of the production notices, though some individual points are still disputed.[12]   The following is the accepted picture:

Date	Title	Greek original	Occasion of production
166 B.C.	*Andria (An.)* 'The Girl from Andros'	Menander, *Andria*	Megalensian Games, April
165 B.C.	*Hecyra (Hec.)* 'The Mother-in-law' (a failure)	Apollodorus of Carystus, *Hekyra*	Megalensian Games, April
163 B.C.	*Heautontimorumenos (Hau.)* 'The Self-Tormentor'	Menander, *Heautontimorumenos*	Megalensian Games, April
161 B.C.	*Eunuchus (Eu.)* 'The Eunuch'	Menander, *Eunouchos*	Megalensian Games, April
161 B.C.	*Phormio (Ph.)* 'Phormio'	Apollodorus of Carystus, *Epidikazomenos* 'The Claimant at Law'	Roman Games, September
160 B.C.	*Hecyra* (a second failure)		Funeral Games for L. Aemilius Paullus
160 B.C.	*Adelphi (Ad.)* 'The Brothers'	Menander, *Adelphoi B*[13]	Funeral Games for L. Aemilius Paullus
160 B.C.	*Hecyra* (third, and successful, production)		Roman Games, September (?)

The chief dispute here is over the relative positions of our play and *Eunuchus* "*The Eunuch*".   The production notices tell us that the former was *facta III* "written third", the latter *facta II* "written second",[14] but the dates given in the same production notices are at variance with this. Some have therefore posited an unsuccessful production of *Eunuchus* in 165 or 164 B.C.,[15] but this idea sits badly beside evidence that the play was an unprecedented success in 161.[16]   Alternatively it could be that *Eunuchus* was written second but produced third,[17] but a two−year delay before production again seems unlikely.

This list exhibits certain interesting features: the slow start to Terence's career, possibly implying difficulty in getting himself established and accepted, his problems with *Hecyra*, his fondness for Menander, and his predilection for retaining the titles of his Greek originals.   The first point may have been due as much to opposition from rivals as to Terence's own abilities; the problems with *Hecyra* are explained more fully in the two prologues to that play (1ff., 21ff.).   Over the final two points,

10

Terence stands out in great contrast to Plautus. Perhaps as few as four of Plautus' 21 plays are from originals by Menander,[18] as opposed to Terence's four out of six; and, while Terence only changed the title of one play,[19] Plautus not infrequently adopted Latin titles.[20] Does this reflect a desire by Terence to preserve the spirit and atmosphere of his originals, as opposed to Plautus' rather less obvious concern for faithfulness to the spirit of his models?

It was believed in antiquity that Terence was encouraged in his career by some famous and noble Romans.[21] The favourite candidates for this role were P. Cornelius Scipio Aemilianus (Africanus Minor, 185/4−129 B.C.), C. Laelius and L. Furius Philus, the leading lights of the so−called 'Scipionic Circle';[22] some even went so far as to say that Scipio and Laelius had actually written at least part of what was passed off as Terence's work. In the *Life* (4), for instance, Laelius is said, on the testimony of the biographer C. Cornelius Nepos (*c.* 99−*c.* 24 B.C.), to have written a passage which included *Hau.* 723. This tradition of actual help persisted, though the careful words of Cicero[23] and Quintilian[24] seem to cast doubts on its reliability. It was probably mere gossip, the inevitable consequence of Terence's known friendship with these highly−placed Romans. But of the fact that Terence did enjoy the friendship of the great (as opposed to being a front for their creative activity), there seems little doubt; the very fact that, when he mentions the accusation of receiving help in two of his prologues, he makes evasive replies instead of denying it (*Hau.* 22ff.; *Ad.* 15ff.) is tantamount to proof. Moreover, the involvement of the Scipionic Circle is rendered highly likely by the fact that two of Terence's plays were put on at the funeral games for Scipio's father, L. Aemilius Paullus.[25]

The only point of agreement about Terence's death[26] is that he was journeying abroad at the time, probably to Greece. There is no agreement about the reason for his journey (to escape talk that he was not the real author of his plays, or to study Greek customs and character), the place of his death (at sea, in Arcadia or on Leucadia) or the cause (shipwreck, disease or grief at the loss of his baggage, including plays, sent on home ahead). Some authorities mentioned the year 159 B.C.; this could be correct, or merely a date chosen as the year after his last plays were known to have appeared. Clearly Terence's end was largely a mystery, and therefore the subject of much guesswork.

IV   TERENCE AND HIS CRITICS

As already mentioned, throughout his career Terence was attacked on several counts; therefore, though he dispensed with the explanatory prologues of his Greek originals,[1] he chose to substitute 'literary' or 'polemical' ones,[2] in which to reply to the criticisms of his work.[3] These prologues therefore provide a unique insight into the specialized debate about dramatic aims and methods which was going on at the time.[4] They are, however, partisan and biased; not only do we not know whether Terence is making an honest defence against the charges laid against him, but we do not even know whether he is fairly representing what those charges were. We are in the position of people able to read a defence lawyer's speech, but not able to read the speech for the prosecution and not knowing exactly on what charge the defendant is arraigned.

Terence sometimes refers to critics in the plural, calling them *malevoli* "spiteful individuals" (*Hau.* 16), *isti malevoli* "those spiteful characters" (*Ad.* 15), *advorsarii* "enemies" (*Ad.* 2), or simply *isti* or *illi* "those people" (*An.* 15, 21; *Ad.* 17); at other times he singles out one man, whom he calls *malevolus vetus poeta* "a spiteful old poet" (*An.* 6–7; *Hau.* 22), *poeta vetus* "an old poet" (*Ph.* 1, 13), or simply *ille* or *is* "that chap" (*Hau.* 30, 33; *Ph.* 18, 22; *Eu.* 16). Ancient commentators say that this individual critic was the dramatist Luscius Lanuvinus "of Lanuvium"; the plurality of critics were probably the lesser associates of this one real opponent.[5] Unfortunately, apart from what is said in Terence's prologues and in Donatus' commentary, we know only one fact about Luscius which is independent of the context of this debate — he appears ninth in a canon ranking ten writers of *palliatae*, compiled by Volcacius Sedigitus *c.* 100 B.C.[6]

As for Terence and Donatus, Terence tells us (*Eu.* 7ff.) that Luscius "by good translation and bad writing produced poor Latin plays from good Greek originals", that he produced a version of Menander's *Phasma* "*The Ghost*", and that in *Thesaurus* "*The Treasure*"[7] he made the defendant in a dispute over ownership of some gold speak before the plaintiff; commenting on the passage, Donatus gives the plots of Menander's *Phasma* and Luscius' *Thesaurus*.[8] In *Ph.* 6ff. Terence implies that Luscius depicted a youngster crazed (by love?) and seeing a doe chased by hounds and begging his help; Donatus merely adds that such scenes are more appropriate in tragedy.[9] Lastly, at *Hau.* 31ff. Terence criticizes Luscius for a scene of "a crowd making way for a slave running down the street".[10] He also more than once threatens to expose more of Luscius' faults if his attacks do not stop.[11] In this meagre supply of information, much of it probably distorted as part of Terence's counter–attack, it is, as Duckworth says,[12] the comment that Luscius is a good translator but a bad writer that is the most enlightening in connection with the quarrel between the two men.

Before turning to the central issue, it is best to deal first with two other charges made by Luscius. The first (*Hau.* 22ff.; *Ad.* 15ff.) is that Terence had embarked on his career without adequate preparation (and, by implication, when too young) and had received help from his influential friends; Luscius believes, or tries to make out, that the only explanation of this sudden new arrival on the dramatic scene must be that Terence's work was not really his. We have seen that Terence was very young at the start of his career, and that he did have friends in high places; we have also seen that such friendships, coupled with his youth, would inevitably bring accusations of collaboration. Terence's defence is no defence at all, but evasion, probably because of the embarrassing position in which he found himself.[13] In *Heautontimorumenos* he tells the audience to decide, and in *Adelphi* he says that while his critics regard it as "a reproach" (*maledictum*), he considers it "the greatest compliment" (*laudem ... maxumam*) to find favour with such men; and he counters the implication of immaturity by calling Luscius old.

The second 'minor' charge (*Ph.* 4–5) is that Terence's plays were slight in content and stylistically thin.[14] It is at once the easiest and the hardest to assess — easiest because we can read Terence for ourselves, hardest because such judgements are necessarily subjective. It is also the cleverest from Luscius' point of view, because its subjectivity makes it as difficult to disprove as to prove. P. Fabia[15] considers Terence guilty, and the charge "une accusation fondée". He does this by comparing Terence with Plautus and by referring to some ancient opinions, particularly the famous ones of Cicero and Caesar.[16] Cicero says of Terence *Menandrum in medium nobis sedatis vocibus effers* "you make Menander known among us with quietened utterance", Caesar *lenibus atque utinam scriptis adiuncta foret vis* "would that vigour had been combined with your smooth writing"; but what these statements mean is much discussed and much disputed.[17] Decision is, of course, impossible. It was perhaps because of this that Terence did not even try to reply; instead he launched into the attack on Luscius' scene of the mad youngster, already mentioned.

Luscius' most important charges refer to Terence's treatment of his originals. In the first two prologues (*An.* 16; *Hau.* 17) Terence, quoting his critics, uses the phrase *contaminare fabulas* "to mess about with, spoil plays" in describing what he is supposed to have done; in the prologue to *Eunuchus* (19ff.) he says that, when Luscius saw the play during a preliminary performance before the aediles, he accused him of *furtum* "plagiarism". Concerning the first point Terence admits (*An.* 9ff.) to transferring into his version of *Andria* suitable elements from a similar play by Menander, *Perinthia* "*The Girl from Perinthos*"; in answer to the second (*Eu.* 27ff.) he agrees he transferred into his version of Menander's *Eunouchos* two characters from Menander's *Kolax* "*The Flatterer*", but denies that he has plagiarized the work of Roman writers, saying that he was unaware that Naevius and Plautus had already produced versions of *Kolax*. In addition, in the prologue to *Adelphi* (6ff.) he says that he has incorporated into his version of Menander's play a scene from Diphilus' *Synapothneskontes* "*Joined in Death*", which Plautus had omitted in his version of that play, *Commorientes* (also "*Joined in Death*").

All this has led to immense debate from the time of Donatus onwards, to which justice cannot be done here.[18] Since Terence uses the verb *contaminare*, scholars have adopted the noun *contaminatio*[19] to describe what Terence is supposed to have done, and argued about what that is. Some have said that the word signifies only 'combination', referring to combining more than one original into one Latin play; but the prevalent opinion inclines to 'spoiling' − which is the normal and obvious meaning of the word.[20]

This approach seems to contain two faults. Firstly it overlooks the fact that *contaminare* appears in only the first two prologues and that thereafter attention switches to *furtum* (*Eunuchus*) or making use of scenes discarded by earlier Roman playwrights in their adaptations (*Adelphi*); secondly it seeks to limit *contaminatio* to one precise and identifiable procedure. To take the second point first, A.S. Gratwick has already pointed out[21] that *contaminatio* might have no such specific reference, but might be "merely the quotation of Luscius' abusive description of Terence's particular procedure". It could equally be that the word is not Luscius', but Terence's, description of what Luscius had accused him of doing, and a deliberately vague and evasive one at that. It would therefore be profitless to try to discover what the word referred to, since Terence was deliberately using it to cover all or any of Luscius' criticisms about his handling of his originals, with no precise reference in mind. As for the first point, we can now see why Terence only uses the world *contaminare* in the first two prologues: he was being purposely vague there, but, when Luscius charged him semi−publicly before the aediles with something definite and precise, plagiarism, he could no longer use his umbrella−word, but had to reply more directly.

But whatever the answer to that particular problem, Terence certainly sometimes altered his originals in adaptation, and sometimes used elements from more than one play. Twice (*An.* 18ff.; *Hau.* 20−1) he claims he has precedents; once (*An.* 18) he lists these as Naevius, Plautus and Ennius,[22] and adds that he prefers their *neglegentia* "carelessness of approach" to his critics' *obscura diligentia* "incomprehensible exactitude". Why then does Luscius criticize Terence for what others have done before? The answer may lie in a change of fashion and ideas, possibly linked to the emergence of *fabulae togatae*.[23] Since Plautus' day there had been a swing away from ready incorporation of Roman elements into adaptations of Greek plays; such elements could now find their outlet in *togatae*, and so some writers of *palliatae* advocated closer adherence to Greek originals. Foremost among these purists was Luscius, but he demanded faithfulness to the letter, as well as the spirit, of Greek plays, and was willing to use his theories in a campaign to oust a young rival. The rival, however, felt that Luscius was going too far; Terence believed in reflecting the spirit of originals, but felt that adherence to their letter was *obscura diligentia* which produced bad plays. That is why he called Luscius a good translator but a bad writer, and why he criticized him for translating without alteration scenes more suitable for tragedy and scenes where defendants spoke before plaintiffs.

14

V THE SELF-TORMENTOR AND ITS RELATIONSHIP TO MENANDER'S PLAY[1]

It has long been part of scholarly practice to attempt to understand the relationship of the Roman comedies to their lost Greek originals, and to try to pinpoint the additions, omissions and alterations of the Roman dramatists and recover the original Greek form − to play, in fact, 'hunt the New Comedy' with the text of a Terence (or Plautus) play. Though this type of activity has its limitations, particularly if carried out to the exclusion of other studies,[2] it is nevertheless not merely legitimate but interesting and valuable.

Such investigations are always difficult, because we have so little to go on. With our play, the problem is perhaps worse than usual, since we do not have Donatus' commentary and so do not possess, as we do for the other five of Terence's plays, the rather sparse information, varying greatly in quality, which he can provide about Terentian workmanship;[3] we do, however, have the less helpful commentary of Eugraphius.[4] We have some fragments of Menander's play, preserved (not as are most of the fragments of the other originals) by Donatus, but by chance quotation elsewhere; however, not all of these obviously match up with the Latin text.[5] We also have the prologue, where lines 4−6 are crucial, but we have seen that that evidence may not be straightforward. Lastly, we have the play itself, which we can examine for internal evidence of change − though as I have said elsewhere,[6] "we must at all times beware of assuming that Terence was so unskilled that his points of alteration will always be obvious to us if only we look for them hard enough".

In the prologue (6) Terence says of his version of the play *duplex quae ex argumento facta est simplici* "which from being a single plot has been turned into a double play".[7] The seemingly inescapable interpretation of this (especially since all of Terence's other plays except *Hecyra* involve the love affairs of two couples) is that the Roman poet has 'doubled' the play by increasing the pairs of lovers from one to two; attempts to interpret the line without assuming that it entails some such 'doubling' do not succeed.[8] However, if one attempts to remove one of the pairs (presumably Clitipho and Bacchis, since Clinia, as son of the self−tormentor of the title, and Antiphila, for whose sake he incurred his father's displeasure, must have been in Menander), the entire fabric of the play falls apart. Two themes in particular, the pretence that Bacchis is Clinia's and not Clitipho's, and the cock−and−bull story that Antiphila is surety for a debt owed to Bacchis, ensure that the affairs of Clitipho and Bacchis are so closely interwoven with those of Clinia and Antiphila that they cannot be divorced from one another without the plot totally disintegrating.[9] And if the plot does disintegrate in this way, it means that all elements involving Bacchis (and possibly Clitipho and Chremes

15

too)[10] would derive from Terence and not Menander's *Heautontimorumenos*;[11] and this in turn means that Terence largely rewrote the play from line 223 onwards (if he introduced Bacchis) or totally (if he introduced the other two as well). Quite apart from the nature of the existing Menander fragments making this extremely unlikely,[12] it would mean that Menander's *Heautontimorumenos*, containing only the Menedemus/Clinia/Antiphila element, would have been dramatically very thin. It is the virtual certainty that this hypothesis of almost total re−writing by Terence is therefore wrong which has led scholars to try to interpret line 6 in such a way that they need not say that Terence has 'doubled' the play. This, as I have said, seems quite impossible, and so the argument returns to its starting point.

However, there is another way of looking at the 'doubling' of a play.[13] It concerns the introduction of extra characters, not into the plot, but into the action of the play as presented on stage. There seems to be good internal evidence for believing that in his adaptation Terence has made Antiphila and Bacchis speaking characters, when in Menander they either did not appear on stage at all or were non−speaking parts. If this is true, then in the Greek original there were two pairs of lovers in the plot, but only the young men were given full roles in the action; Terence, however, for reasons of his own, decided to give the women something to say as well. He therefore took from Menander a single plot in the sense that he only used one play and did not add characters from his own head or from another original; but he 'doubled' the play in the sense that he showed all four lovers with speaking parts, whereas Menander had shown only two. Clearly, this is not 'doubling' in the obvious sense; the additions are to the action only and not to the plot, the chief change is not a second pair of lovers but two women provided for the two men, and the extra writing consists of just two short scenes not half the play. But the statement in line 6 is not absolutely untrue, though it is exaggerated and misleading − perhaps deliberately so. R.C. Flickinger[14] mentions "the deliberate policy of teasing and bewilderment which is pursued throughout the prologue". Perhaps by saying that he had made a single plot double, Terence was hoping to trap Luscius; he had 'doubled', but not in the way he hoped his critic would think.

Briefly,[15] arguments for suspecting the change are that Bacchis only appears in two short scenes (381ff., 723ff.), Antiphila only in the former, and that there are grounds for thinking that Terence, not Menander, was the author of these.

381ff. divides easily into two (381−97; 398−409). The first part consists largely of a monologue by Bacchis which shows her to be much more respectable and considerate than previous description (223ff.) has led us to expect and than the picture of her given later (455ff.) will show; the second part, where Bacchis makes little contribution, is the reunion of Clinia and Antiphila (awkwardly delayed by Bacchis' speech). It seems

16

that Terence wanted to depict this reunion on stage, and felt that in doing so he could give Bacchis something to say which would reinforce the audience's high opinion of Antiphila — even though what she said was out of keeping with her character. This view of the scene entails that Terence must also have altered the end of the previous scene (376ff.).

In 723ff. nothing essential is done apart from what is said will happen at the end of the previous scene and what we are told has happened at the start of the next — the transfer of Bacchis and her *grex ancillarum* "retinue of maids" from Clitipho's house to Clinia's. The rest is merely a humorous threat by Bacchis to leave, which is immediately averted by Syrus' assurance that he will obtain the money Bacchis wants. The scene is also awkward dramatically, with doubts about Clinia's exit[16] and an impossibly short time allowed for the transfer of the *grex*.[17] If this scene is Terentian, then Terence created Phrygia, Bacchis' maid, who only appears here.

Both scenes involve movements by Bacchis and her *grex*. It is probable that in Menander these movements were 'masked' by choral interludes.[18] When Terence dispensed with the chorus, for two of its four appearances he substituted these scenes.

Other changes have been suspected. If Menander's original had an explanatory prologue, the long exposition scene in Terence (53ff.) may have been expanded with some information originally there.[19] Chremes' supposed exit at 170 to visit his neighbour Phania, where the Oxford Text marks a *saltatio convivarum* "dance of supper—guests", has been thought by some to mark the place of a Greek choral interlude or deferred prologue;[20] his hurried exit to put off some business with neighbours (502) and his rapid return (508) have seemed so odd to others that they have been held to mark Terentian alteration.[21] Another difficulty has been found in the spread of the action over two days with a night interval, which has been though un—Greek and therefore Terentian;[22] and yet another has been the ending, which some have felt too untypical. Other theories about change, based on scenes where in Terence more than three characters speak, are now seen to have less force than was thought.[23] Finally, the fact that Menedemus, the self—tormentor of the title, is not for long the centre of attention and the focus for intrigue in the play[24] has been taken by some as evidence of wholesale rewriting by Terence of the type already indicated. This has been seen to be unlikely; and the argument from the title of Menander's and Terence's plays is in fact spurious, since in this type of drama titles are not necessarily good guides to content.[25]

VI THE SELF—TORMENTOR AS A ROMAN COMEDY

In the early part of this century, the attention paid to the relationship of the plays of Terence (and Plautus) to their Greek originals took precedence over appreciation of the plays as they stand. The Roman dramas were regarded merely as pale reflections of their Greek predecessors, useful mainly as a means of learning about Greek New Comedy, and they were not given full consideration as independent art. More recently, however, the emphasis has shifted, and this imbalance is being corrected; no doubt this change has been assisted by the discovery of enough New Comedy to provide a basis for fruitful first—hand study. It has been rightly said that "research could be more profitably directed into what the comedies of Plautus and Terence have themselves to offer than into their uncertain relationships with lost sources."[1] We must always remember that Terence wrote for the Roman stage and that his audience regarded *The Self—Tormentor* as a Roman play.

In the prologue (36) Terence calls his play *stataria*, "containing more talk than action".[2] But, though it does not contain vigorous action like the siege in *Eunuchus* (771ff.) or exaggerated cameos like the pimp or the "running slave" in *Adelphi* (155ff., 299ff.), the "talk" nevertheless produces a fast—moving and complicated play. The twists and turns of the plot, as Syrus proves ever more inventive about getting money for Clitipho's mistress each time he is thwarted, leave the audience (or reader) breathless and perhaps confused. Such confusion is deliberate. The spectator is meant to be amazed by the frequent changes of direction brought about by Syrus' unending ingenuity; he is not necessarily meant to keep up with him every step of the way. One is reminded of Sandbach's comment that "close attention was necessary to follow Menander's dramas";[3] this is no less true of Terence's adaptation of this Menander play.

The "talk" also produces excellent character—drawing. The chief example is Chremes; but, apart from the interest centred on him, Menedemus, Syrus, Clitipho, Clinia and Sostrata are also characters fully, sensitively and sympathetically drawn.

It is Chremes, rather than the 'self—tormentor' Menedemus, who is the central character of the play and the victim of deception and trickery by Syrus, Clitipho and Clinia for much of its duration. Menedemus' problems begin to be resolved as early as 182, when the audience learns that his son Clinia has returned from abroad; and, but for Chremes' snap decision (199) not to reveal Menedemus' true feelings to his own son Clitipho, who is Clinia's close friend, they would have been swiftly settled. By contrast, Chremes' problems are only just beginning with the first mention of Clitipho's affair with the courtesan Bacchis (223) and Syrus' sudden revelation that Bacchis is on her way to Chremes' house (311). Thereafter the gradual but steady resolution of Menedemus' worries (assisted by the recognition of Clinia's love, Antiphila, as Chremes' daughter) becomes almost a sub—plot[4] as interest centres on the increasing state of self—deception into which Chremes drifts[5] until he is finally forced to confront the truth about his son's affair (908), and tries to salvage what he can of his self—sought reputation for sound judgement at the end of the play.

There are several ways of looking at Chremes' character. One, now largely discredited,[6] regards him as someone whose genuine interest in and regard for others, typified by the sentiments of 77,[7] is a model of human sympathy. Another[8] sees him as a busybody, too anxious to take a hand in other people's affairs[9] and to preach to them,[10] when he cannot even keep his own house in order. A third sees him as something of both: "inquisitive, opinionated, self—satisfied, and insensitive, yet genuinely moved by the other man's situation and ready to extend his unwanted help".[11]

The first view, at least, cannot be right. It is surely the essence of the comedy that a rather unpleasant man gets his 'comeuppance', not that a good one comes to grief through honest refusal to believe ill of his son. And the whole irony of the situation is that Chremes is too busy intervening in other people's affairs to notice what is going on under his nose,[12] not that his genuine concern for others does not leave him time to see what is happening. The unattractive side to his character is underlined by his treatment of his wife Sostrata, whose words he mockingly imitates (622), and to whom he is rude and overbearing (624, 630, 632ff., 1006ff., 1018ff.). Moreover, his judgement, on which he prides himself, is unsure; his decision to keep Clitipho (199) and Clinia (436) in the dark about Menedemus' feelings is misconceived and prolongs his neighbour's unhappiness, while his encouragement of Syrus' mischief (533ff.) merely rebounds on himself. Only when he has been made to look a complete fool at the end of the play and his moral authority has been seriously impaired, does he allow himself (with rather bad grace, 1053) to be persuaded to forgive his son.

How far one accepts the view which combines both traits depends upon the interpretation put on several passages. For example, are Chremes' words at 159—60 genuine encouragement or empty platitude? Is his dinner invitation (161ff.) anything more than a desire to play Lord Bountiful? Is his expression of sorrow at 167—8 sincere or perhaps a little too perfunctory? Is his wish to be first to tell Menedemus (184ff., 410ff.) prompted by concern for his neighbour or eagerness for credit as a bringer of good news? I tend to take the less charitable, more jaundiced view; but the reader must decide, and even Chremes' sternest critic must accept that the complaints he makes about Clitipho at 1039ff. are fully justified.

Menedemus is altogether more attractive. His vivid accounts of how he drove Clinia away (96ff.) and afterwards in remorse chose a life of hard labour and rejected all pleasure and relaxation (121ff.) combine with the picture of his continued misery (420ff.) to excite our sympathy; his ready acknowledgement of how wrong he was (99ff., 134, 158) arouses respect for his candour and creates an impression of his essential good nature. And towards the end of the play this impression is reinforced by a contrast drawn with Chremes: whereas Menedemus behaved as he did towards Clinia with nobody to advise him otherwise, Chremes acts in precisely the same manner towards Clitipho even though he has the lesson of Menedemus before him[13] and even though Menedemus (932) and Sostrata (1013) warn him of the trouble he will cause. It is only with difficulty that Chremes is persuaded to relent — and it is fair and honest Menedemus, wiser for his recent sufferings, who in his new—found happiness finds time to come outside and reconcile his neighbour with his son (1045ff.). It is small wonder that we earlier shared this appealing character's resentment at Chremes' curiosity (75—6), just as later (897, 914) we felt we could allow him to have a little fun at the expense of his discomfited *adiutor ... monitor et praemonstrator* "helper, counsellor and guide".[14]

Syrus, one of Chremes' slaves particularly attached to Clitipho, is the next most important figure in the action after Chremes; from him stems all the intrigue aimed at securing for his young master enough money for him to continue to enjoy Bacchis' favours. As in many plays of this type, the young men prove rather unimaginative and helpless when confronted with problems; it is the slaves who make all the running, and Syrus is the *servus callidus* "cunning slave" *par excellence*, quick—witted, bold, full of ideas and never downcast. In this he is contrasted to Clinia's slave Dromo, whom he calls *stolidus* "pretty stupid" (545) and whom earlier Clitipho had felt should be accompanied by Syrus when Clinia sent him to fetch Antiphila (191).

As a schemer, Syrus enjoys freedom of action, not waiting for instructions; it comes as a complete shock to Clitipho (311) that he has taken the amazingly bold step of bringing Bacchis along with Antiphila, intending to pretend to Chremes (332—3) that she is Clinia's. His task is now to find the wherewithal to keep Bacchis there, and this search, which occupies his mind until money is secured at 831, shows his ingenuity at its best. He starts (512—3), as is natural, by planning to get the money out of his own master Chremes, but is deflected from this by a golden opportunity presented by Chremes himself (546—7) into attempting to get it from Menedemus. He pretends (599ff.) that Antiphila is surety for a debt owed to Bacchis, and proposes (608ff.) to tell Menedemus that she is a captive from Caria and to persuade him to buy her from the courtesan. When Chremes tells him that Menedemus will not agree, Syrus replies that there is no need for him to; but, although pressed to explain, he does not (610ff.). This is one of a number of occasions where the exact nature of what Syrus has in mind is not explained.[15] Such instances are devices intended to boost our opinion of the slave's cleverness. There is no need to suppose that Terence (or Menander) worked out what these unexpressed plans were, and the audience had no need to know; it is sufficient to be told that Syrus' fertile brain has produced them.

The discovery that Antiphila is Chremes' daughter ruins Syrus' plan of

20

getting Menedemus to purchase her. We are amused to see his despair as it collapses (659−60, 663) and vastly impressed by the speed with which he thinks up another (668−78). This one, he boasts (709ff.), is his masterpiece, because he will achieve his aim simply by telling the truth. He persuades Clinia to allow Bacchis, still supposedly Clinia's, to transfer to Menedemus' house, and gets him to tell his father the truth − that Bacchis is Clitipho's and that he himself wants to marry Antiphila. When Menedemus later duly tells this to his neighbour (847, 852−3), Chremes does not believe it; he has already been duped by Syrus (767ff.), and thinks it is a ruse for Clinia to get money for Bacchis out of Menedemus under the pretence that it is needed for his wedding. However, Syrus' plan again fails, because Chremes refuses to cooperate (779) in pretending to betroth Antiphila to Clinia. But in an instant the slave comes bouncing back; he returns (790ff.) to the story of the debt and says that Chremes must pay it since his newly−discovered daughter is surety. Without a murmur Chremes agrees; Syrus has at last got money for Clitipho to give to Bacchis, and he has got it from Chremes himself, the person he had originally intended to defraud. And his crowning glory is that he persuades Chremes to let Clitipho take it to Bacchis himself (799−800).[16]

The complexities of all this are enormous, but the plot construction which brings them about is masterly. In the end we have a situation where Chremes is confronted with the truth and refuses to believe it;[17] but when presented with the nonsense about Antiphila and the debt, he swallows it whole and pays up. Syrus' triumph is complete.

When the truth eventually comes out and Chremes' anger erupts, another side to this likeable rascal emerges; he is genuinely sorry for getting Clitipho into such trouble (970), and attempts to take his share of the blame (973−4). When this is brushed aside, there is one more service his cleverness can do for his young master, and his final trick plays a major part in bringing about a reconciliation between father and son. By suggesting to Clitipho that the extent of Chremes' anger is due to the fact that he is not his parents' real son (985ff.), and by prompting him to ask Chremes and Sostrata what his true parentage is (994−6), Syrus ensures that Sostrata will be shocked into helping her son obtain his father's pardon. We have seen that Menedemus is influential in achieving this; but so is Sostrata, and it is Syrus' ingenious move (cf. 996−7) which though it causes Clitipho some short−term pain, nevertheless helps to ensure that his father does forgive.

Clinia and Clitipho are not so instrumental in the advancement of the plot; young men in this type of comedy tend to protest at the actions or plans of their slaves (Clitipho 311ff., 589, 810ff.; Clinia 699, 713), or be exaggeratedly grateful for them (Clitipho 825),[18] rather than be initiators themselves. Standing in awe of their fathers (Clinia 189, 433−5) and complaining − but not doing much − about them (Clitipho 213ff.), they entrust the resolution of their troubles entirely to their slaves (Clitipho 350−1). Our two young men provide good examples of the extremes of despair and elation between which they can swiftly alternate (Clinia 230ff., 244, 246ff., 308; Clitipho 805ff., 825). They are also appealing characters, particularly in their mutual friendship (182ff.) and support (358−60) − facets upon which Syrus plays (688ff.).

Perhaps the most attractive figure of all, despite her comparatively small role, is Sostrata, who is excellently drawn. Devout (1038), endearingly superstitious (650−2, 1015), self−deprecatory (649−50) and devoted to her family (1029ff., 1060−1), she has to put up with a lot from her husband, but not without protest (1003ff., 1010−1), and she knows how to handle him (623−4, 631−2, 644ff.). And she takes equal credit with Menedemus for reconciling Chremes and Clitipho at the end of the play.

The complexities of the plot, with its frequent changes of direction, make for a fast−moving play, which in turn combines with the skilfully−executed character drawing to produce good theatre. But there are some weaknesses in the construction, many of which have been held, rightly or wrongly, to be evidence of Terentian workmanship;[19] some of these have been mentioned in the preceding section. Among others which have been identified are the contrast between the two older men's only recent acquaintance (53ff.) and their sons' long friendship (183−4), the awkwardness of the empty stage at 873−4, and the contrast between Chremes' threats against Syrus (950ff.) and his actual words to his face (974ff.). It need hardly be said that such comparatively minor inconsistencies and awkwardnesses, though evident to a careful reader, would have been scarcely noticeable to the audience as it was swept along by the quickly changing pattern of events being enacted on the stage.

VII THE TEXT[1]

The manuscripts of Terence − the number of which has been put as high as 650, with more than 100 dating from the ninth to thirteenth centuries − are divided into two main groups. In the first group there is just one representative, the codex Bembinus (A). This has the distinction of being one of our earliest manuscripts of a Latin writer, dating from the late fourth or early fifth century A.D., and it presents the plays in the order given in the production notices (*An., Eu., Hau., Ph., Hec., Ad.*). The second group, commonly known as 'Calliopian' because some of them bear witness to a recension by a certain Calliopius,[2] embraces the medieval manuscripts. It is itself divided into three sub−groups. Two of these, the large γ class and smaller δ class, go back to lost archetypes known as Γ and Δ respectively, which themselves in turn go back to a common lost archetype designated Σ. The third Calliopian class, which is by far the largest, is the so-called 'mixed' manuscripts, which appear to share, to differing extents, the characteristics now of γ, now of δ, and do not go directly back to either Γ or Δ; given the availability of manuscripts for copyists to consult in the middle ages and the frequent copying which must have been done, it is hardly surprising that such a mixed group should arise, though it is sometimes difficult to establish exactly what has happened to individual manuscripts in this area of the tradition.

The relationship of the lost Calliopian archetype Σ to A has been much discussed. It is now generally accepted that the presence of errors common to them both ensures that they both go back to a lost archetype of their own designated Φ, and are not, as Marouzeau holds,[3] independent of one another in separate descent from Terence. The associated matter of the date of Σ, and its relation to the date of A and of Φ, cannot be known with certainty, though there are some clues;[4] neither can the date of the division of Σ into the Γ and Δ traditions.

The division into the γ and δ classes is based upon three principal differences: omissions and errors common to one group and not the other; the order of the plays (in both cases different from that in A) — in δ an alphabetic sequence (An., Ad., Eu., Ph.(=F.), Hau., Hec.),[5] and in γ An., Eu., Hau., Ad., Hec., Ph.;[6] and thirdly the presence in some γ manuscripts of miniature illustrations at the head of scenes, depicting the characters featured. Jachmann showed that these illustrations are based upon reading of the text, and not, as was once thought, upon memories of actual performances (and therefore in origin antedating the demise of Terence in the theatres). The date the miniatures arose within the tradition is uncertain, as is their precise provenance.[7]

Although, as has been said A and Σ contain a number of common errors, and although A has others which are not found in Σ, A is nevertheless in general superior. This is not necessarily because of its considerably greater age, but because the tradition of which it is the sole representative is, relatively speaking, purer and less subject to emendation and interpolation than that represented by Σ. The latter contains more such changes, many of them probably designed to make Terence easier to read in schools. As to the Σ manuscripts themselves, it had long been accepted that the δ class was superior to the γ class, but this is yet another of the traditional views about the transmission of Terence's text which has been seen not to have the force it was once believed to have.[8]

In the apparatus criticus of this edition the following manuscripts are cited:

1	A	Codex Bembinus (Vatican lat. 3226).	4th/5th cent.
2	Sa	St Gall 912, pp. 299-300, 313-14.[9]	5th cent.
		A palimpsest containing fragments of	
		Hau. 857-63 and 875-8.	
3		δ manuscripts:	

23

D	Codex Victorianus (Florence, Laur. 38 24). Lacking *Hau*. 466–517, which are supplied by a 15th–century hand.[10]	10th cent.
G	Codex Decurtatus (Vatican lat. 1640). Lacking *Hau. periocha*, 1–313, 1049–67.	10th cent.
p	Codex Parisinus (Paris lat. 10304).	10th cent.
L	Codex Lipsiensis (Leipzig 1 4 37). (L is classed by some as 'mixed'.)	10th cent.

4   γ manuscripts:

P	Codex Parisinus (Paris lat. 7899). Illustrated.	9th cent.
C	Codex Vaticanus (Vatican lat. 3868). Illustrated.	9th cent.
F	Codex Ambrosianus (Milan, Ambr. H 75 inf.). Illustrated.	10th cent.
E	Codex Riccardianus (Florence, Ricc. 528).	11th cent.
λ	Fragmentum Lugdunense (Lyon 788). Containing *Hau*. 522–904 only.	9th cent.
η	Codex Einsidlensis I (Einsiedeln 362). Lacking *Hau*. 1–16, 310–822, 903–981.	10th cent.
ε	Codex Einsidlensis II (Einsiedeln 362).	10th cent.
v	Codex Valentiennensis (Valenciennes 448 [420]).	11th cent.

(F and E are classed by some as 'mixed')

The manuscripts contain corrections by later hands (D^2 E^2 etc. in the apparatus). In the case of A particularly important is a certain Jovialis or Joviales, who corrected the Bembinus and introduced changes from the Calliopian tradition.[11] The precise extent of his reponsibility for the alterations in A is the subject of disagreement;[12] I use the abbreviation 'Iov.' in the wider way in which it is employed in the Oxford Text.

It is traditional, following the manuscripts, to mark act— and scene—divisions in the plays. It seems certain that the division of the plays into five acts was not the work of Terence, who wrote them for continuous performance, but was introduced afterwards by Roman scholars who knew that the Greek originals had been so divided; Donatus affirms that Varro knew of such divisions, but admits to the difficulty of dividing them.[13] Division into scenes is marked in the manuscripts where characters enter (or sometimes where they leave) by a scene heading indicating the names and often the roles of the characters in that scene; it is at these points that some manuscripts have the miniature illustrations.

To the evidence of the manuscripts we can sometimes add the testimony of Donatus since, although his commentary does not exist for our play, quotations from *The Self—Tormentor* appear in other parts of his work (cf. apparatus 61, 69). There are also Eugraphius' commentary (cf.

24

136, 185), the work of scholiasts, especially that in A, the scholia Bembina (cf. 143, 185),[14] and quotations, not only in ancient grammarians (cf. 94, 136) but also in writers like Cicero (cf. 69). The problem with such quotations is, of course, that those who used them may have been employing a text which was already corrupt, quoting from memory or even altering Terence to suit their own Latinity. One further source is *glossae* "glossaries", collections of unfamiliar words. One of these, indicated by the abbreviation 'gl. II' in the Oxford Text (and in this edition), was a collection of words from a lost manuscript of Terence which came to be incorporated in a larger glossary called the Abolita glossary (such works being usually known by the first word appearing in them).[15] In our play it provides the correct reading once (471) and lends decisive support to a minority view twice (408, 836).

In spite of — perhaps because of — the existence of so many manuscripts, no really comprehensive critical edition of the text of Terence has yet appeared. The best is still that of F. Umpfenbach (Berlin, 1870), followed by the Oxford Text of R. Kauer and W.M. Lindsay (2nd edn, Oxford, 1926; additions to the apparatus[16] by O. Skutsch, 1958) and the Budé edition of J. Marouzeau (3 vols, Paris, 1942−9). The elaborate edition of S. Prete (Heidelberg, 1954) contains many errors.[17]

NOTE ON THE TEXT AND APPARATUS CRITICUS OF THIS EDITION

The text of this edition is printed without the marks employed in the Oxford Text to facilitate scansion in accordance with the practices of early Latin verse. In addition, I have not followed that text's practice of indicating by an apostrophe the dropping of final −s after a short vowel and before an initial consonant (whether or not a particular instance might be deemed metrically 'necessary'); I have, however, written *ill'* not *ille* (197, 515) and *und'* not *unde* (978) on the much rarer occasions when final −e is dropped. I have written −um est, −a est, −o est etc. rather than −umst, −ast, −ost, since it is perfectly possible for a reader to scan a line with either form before him; but I have where necessary written −ust not −us est, −u's not −us es etc., since not to do so could seriously mislead the reader interested in scansion. The aim of this (perhaps not entirely consistent) procedure has been to present as uncluttered and easily readable a Latin text as possible; my excuse must be that the commentary is not primarily concerned with metrical considerations.

In matters of spelling — *quoi / cui; tuos / tuus* etc. — sometimes connected with metrical matters — *mihi / mi; nihil / nil* — I have generally followed the Oxford Text. But I have considerably altered that text's punctuation to bring it more into line with modern English practice.

The apparatus criticus makes no claims to completeness or originality, but is highly selective and taken wholly from published sources. Since, for example, "neither Δ nor Γ anywhere seems to preserve the truth significantly against the agreement of the other with the Bembinus",[18] I have not generally included instances where A and the δ manuscripts agree against γ, or where A and γ agree against δ; exceptions are occasions where the Oxford Text accepts the minority view. Where the reading I adopt has manuscript support, I have not quoted the conjectures of those who find all the manuscript readings unsatisfactory − with the exception of conjectures appearing in the Oxford Text; where I accept a conjecture, I cite its source, but do not give rival conjectures − with the same exceptions.

Of the manuscripts listed above, I regularly cite seven, A, D and G from δ, and P, C, F and E from γ , in that order; only occasionally do I cite the others. Σ indicates the consensus of the Calliopian manuscripts, and I use 'Don.' for Donatus and 'Eugr.' for Eugraphius. Where I use editors' names, details of their editions are to be found in the bibliography.

I have adopted a reading different from that of the Oxford Text, or differ from it significantly in matters of punctuation, at the following points:

5, 21, 32, 69, 71−2, 94, 129, 130, 165, 185, 192, 199, 210, 211, 217, 245, 258, 290, 333, 336, 339, 390, 408, 437, 496, 570, 579, 589−90, 626, 678, 689, 693, 712, 724, 725, 736, 786, 825, 848, 851, 853, 854, 869, 870, 910, 950, 954, 960, 978, 996, 997, 1008, 1019, 1020, 1023, 1027.

NOTES TO INTRODUCTION

Section I

1. Our knowledge of New Comedy has been revolutionized by the discoveries of the last twenty or thirty years, and older works on the subject are best avoided. The best short introduction is Sandbach, chs 4 and 5.

2. Sandbach 55.

3. Gomme and Sandbach 3−4.

4. The largest is a fragment of Menander's *Dis Exapatōn* corresponding to Plautus' *Bacchides* 494−562. It contains 112 lines, about half of which are too incomplete to be intelligible, and is the first passage of any real length where comparison of the Latin adaptation with its original is possible. It reveals considerable changes made by Plautus in his version, and serves as a warning of the perils of working back from adaptation to model. Text and translation: W.G. Arnott, *Menander* I (London and Cambridge, Mass., 1979), 140ff.; comparison with Plautus: Sandbach 128ff.

5. Körte II 7 (*testimonium* 32) and 9 (*testimonium* 41) respectively; the latter = Plutarch, *Moralia* 854B. Ter., for all his brilliance, was apostrophized by Caesar as only *dimidiate Menander* "half−sized Menander" (Suetonius, *Life of Terence* 7).

6. So called to distinguish him from another Apollodorus who wrote New Comedies, but came from Gela in Sicily.

7. With only one complete play, it is clearly impossible to be dogmatic about the form of a New Comedy. But the general picture given by that play, on which my summary is based, has not been contradicted by any of the other texts which have been found.

8. This point is still disputed; cf. Sandbach 78−80. For the problem as it applies to our one complete play, see E.W. Handley (ed.), *The Dyskolos of Menander* (London, 1965), 25ff. This much at any rate seems clear: the so−called 'three−actor rule', if it existed, was not so inflexible as to enable us to assume automatically that, where a scene in a Latin adaptation of a Greek New Comedy contains more than three speaking actors, the Roman dramatist has altered his original by inserting extra characters.

9. In the presence of this type of prologue, as in other features of New Comedy such as the monologue, it is usual to see the influence of Greek tragedy, especially Euripides, at work.

10. Traces of the Greek chorus are still held by some to be present at places in Plautus, e.g. the flute player in *Pseudolus* (573−3a) and the chorus of fishermen in *Rudens* (290ff.). See also *Hau.* 170−1n.

11. Cf. *An.* 5ff., *Ad.* 22ff., and see further p. 11.

12. There are exceptions. For example, the original of Plautus' *Rudens*, if Plautus has followed it faithfully in this respect, was set on the coast of Africa, with a cottage and a temple, while his *Captivi* was set in Aetolia; Menander's *Dyskolos*, set in the country, requires two farmhouses and a shrine.

13. 62.

14. Whether the majority of a Roman audience, watching a Latin adaptation of one of these plays, would feel the same is another matter.

Section II

1. That is not to say that they are in any sense ancestors of drama proper at Rome, though the ancients certainly felt that they were, and they certainly coexisted with

it. Much of our evidence for these native forms is late. See further Beare 10ff.

2. Beare 137ff., 143ff.

3. Beare 149ff.

4. 2.7.

5. Date: Cic. *Brut.* 72, *Sen.* 50, *Tusc.* 1.3; Gel. 17.21.42. A comedy and a tragedy: Cassiodorus' *Chronica*, though under the year 239 B.C.

6. Gel. 17.21.45.

7. But see H.B. Mattingly, 'Naevius and the Metelli', *Historia* 9 (1960), 414−39.

8. There is some doubt whether Plautus' *nomen* was Maccius or Maccus; but as Maccius is a known gentile name and Maccus was a character in Atellan farces, the former seems more likely, with the latter being a pun on the correct version. But see A.S. Gratwick, 'TITVS MACCIVS PLAVTVS', *CQ* n.s. 23 (1973), 78−84.

9. *Miles Gloriosus* 210−12.

10. This so−called 'Varronian recension' is dealt with at some length in Gel. 3.3.

11. E.g. Ter. mentions Plautus' *Colax* (*Eu.* 25) and *Commorientes* (*Ad.* 7), though neither appears in Varro's list.

12. It is possible that one or two may have been from Middle Comedy.

13. E.g. by Sandbach 120−1.

14. He seems to experiment with such lyrics in his first play (*An.* 481ff., 625ff.), then to give up; but he tries again in his last (*Ad.* 610ff.).

15. *Hec.* 14−27.

16. See p. 14.

17. Gel. 2.23.

18. Duckworth 68ff.; Beare 128ff.

19. *Inst.* 11.3.178−82; but the reference could equally well be to *togatae*.

20. For all matters connected with production and staging in the Roman theatre, see Beare 164ff. (and appendices) and Duckworth 73ff.

21. The question of whether masks were worn in Terence's day is much disputed, and a clear answer seems impossible. See Sandbach 111ff.; Beare 192ff., 303ff.; Duckworth 92ff.

22. See Beare 166ff.; Duckworth 75ff.

23. Earlier attempts to build permanent theatres at Rome were stopped by the Senate as guardian of public morals.

24. Phrases in the dialogue such as "Here comes Dromo, and Syrus too" (*Hau.* 241) or "She's coming outside herself now" (*Hau.* 722) are probably pointers for the audience, not stage directions; but they could be both.

25. When seen by the spectators. It is usually described as "long and narrow", presumably from the actors' point of view.

26. *Hau.* 30n., 37−9n.

27. E.g. *Hau.* 514ff., 615, 682.

28. E.g. *Hau.* 564, 659−60, 831−2, 844.

29. E.g. *Hau.* 242−55, 381−402, 614−21.

30. In some plays the doors have to stand a lot of knocking, and opening them made a considerable noise; cf. *Hau.* 173n., 613.

31. The evidence is discussed by Duckworth 85−7. For our play, see the commentary at the start of Act I Scene 1.

32. Duckworth 83−4. The altar features prominently as a place of refuge in Plautus' *Mostellaria* (1094ff.) and *Rudens* (688ff.), and in *An.* 726−7 leafy branches are taken from it to protect a new−born baby which is to be placed on the ground; cf. *Hau.* 975n.

33. Beare 171−2, 241ff.

34.   *Hec.* 1ff., 33ff.   For the correct interpretation of the second of these passages, which proves that theatres could also be used for other forms of entertainment, see F.H. Sandbach, 'How Terence's *Hecyra* failed', *CQ* n.s. 32 (1982), 134–5.

35.   E.g. the difference between Jupiter–disguised–as–Amphitruo and Amphitruo, and between Mercury–disguised–as–Sosia and Sosia (Plautus, *Amphitruo* 120ff., 142ff.), and the fact that master and slave had exchanged dress (Plautus, *Captivi* 35ff.).

Section III

1.   One of the lives of poets from a biographical work on literary figures, *De viris illustribus "On famous men"*, by C. Suetonius Tranquillus (c. A.D. 70–c. A.D. 140), this has been preserved, perhaps in an abbreviated form, by being prefaced to Donatus' commentaries on Ter.'s plays; to it Donatus has added a brief appendix of his own.   Text: Donatus I, 3–10; translation: Radice 389–94.

2.   These were probably compiled no later than the first century B.C., and introduced into the MSS of Ter. at that time.   The production notice of *An.* is not in our MSS, but can be reconstructed on the evidence of Donatus.

3.   For this sceptical view, see Beare 91ff.   Duckworth 56ff., though expressing doubt on some points, is more inclined to accept the broad outline of Suetonius' account.

4.   E.g. whether Ter. came to Rome as a prisoner of war (*Life* 1), who his influential friends were (2; 4), and how he met his death (5).

5.   In one MS the production notice of *Hau.* preserves traces of a performance some thirteen years after Ter.'s death; see commentary on production notice 5.

6.   *Hau.* 23 and n.

7.   See Beare 93; Sandbach 135.

8.   The same reason is given for the *nomen* of the first Roman playwright, L. Livius Andronicus, who is said to have been freed by his master M. Livius Salinator. Such anecdotes have a habit of recurring in Roman biography, and this is not the only one connected with Ter. which finds a parallel elsewhere.

9.   *Loc. cit.* in n. 7 above.

10.   Gel. 13.2.

11.   R.C. Flickinger ('The prologues of Terence', *PhQ* 6 (1927), 237–8) believes that the delay was partly due to the removal of Caecilius' backing when he died soon after the play had been read to him.

12.   See Arnott 47 and 60, n. 78.

13.   Menander wrote two plays with this title, conventionally known as *Adelphoi A* and *Adelphoi B*.   The former was the original for Plautus' *Stichus*, the latter for Ter.'s *Adelphi*.   See Körte II 14ff.

14.   The first unsuccessful production of *Hec.* is discounted in the numbering given by the production notices; the play is placed fifth.

15.   E.g. Duckworth 60 and n. 51; Radice 159 and 395.

16.   *Life* 3.

17.   E.g. Thierfelder 146–7.   Donatus (I 267) says *edita tertium est* "it was produced third".

18.   *Bacchides, Cistellaria* and *Stichus* are certainly adaptations of plays by Menander, and the original of *Aulularia* may also have been his; see Gomme and Sandbach 4ff.   There may be more, since the originals of several of Plautus' plays are unknown.

19.   *Ph.*, given the name of a character in the plot – see *Ph.* 24ff.   As well as the reason given there, Ter. may have felt that the participial title *Epidikazomenos "The Claimant at Law"*, describing a particular Greek legal process, was too obscure –

29

something he does not seem to have felt about *Heautontimorumenos*!

20.   E.g. *Captivi "The Prisoners", Mercator "The Merchant", Miles Gloriosus "The Swaggering Soldier", Rudens "The Rope"*, all employing good honest Latin words.

21.   *Life* 2; 4.   Suggestions there that it was Ter.'s physical attractions which appealed to his patrons can be dismissed as pure scandal—mongering.

22.   "A philosophic and literary coterie of mid—second—century philhellenes known as the 'Scipionic Circle' sought ... to promote the study of Greek at Rome and to develop the Latin language and literature." (T.F. Carney (ed.), *P. Terenti Afri Hecyra* (Salisbury, Rhodesia, 1963), 6); but see H. Strasburger, 'Der 'Scipionenkreis'', *Hermes* 94 (1966), 60—72.   Some ancient writers found the relative ages of Ter. and Scipio a problem, and other possibilities were suggested; particularly attractive is the learned ,C. Sulpicius Gallus, consul in the year *An.* was produced (*Life* 4).   It is not impossible that Sulpicius started Ter. off, and the Scipionic Cricle took him up later.

23.   *Att.* 7.3.10:   "Terence, whose plays ... were thought to be written by C. Laelius".   In *Amic.* 89 Cicero pictures Laelius calling Ter. his *familiaris* "intimate friend".

24.   *Inst.* 10.1.99:   "though the writings of Terence are ascribed to Scipio Africanus".

25.   Scipio was adopted into the family of the Scipiones, and his *cognomen* Aemilianus reveals his origin as an Aemilius.

26.   *Life* 5.

Section IV

1.   *Ad.* 22—4.

2.   *An.* 5—7.

3.   The two prologues to *Hec.* (for the second and third productions) are rather different from the rest, being 'literary' but not 'polemical'.   They are not concerned with replying to attacks, but solely with securing a hearing for the play.

4.   Although not the point at present under discussion, it is interesting to speculate how many of the audience would really be interested in this esoteric squabble, and what effect these specialist prologues had on their mood and receptivity as they prepared to watch the plays.   Ter. clearly felt the defence of his reputation important enough to risk boring at least some of them.

5.   See *Hau.* 16n.

6.   Gel. 15.24, where it is said to come from Volcacius' *De poetis "On poets"*. This famous list (which places Caecilius first, Plautus second, Naevius third, Ter. sixth, Turpilius seventh and Ennius last) is not as useful as it may seem, since we know nothing of the criteria used in compiling it.   Cf. Suetonius, *Life* 7.

7.   It is perhaps implied, but not explicitly stated, that this play was also by Menander; cf. Körte II 77—8.

8.   I 272—3; the description of *Thesaurus* contains our only fragment of Luscius' work.

9.   II 352.

10.   See *Hau.* 30n.

11.   *An.* 22—3; *Hau.* 33—4; *Eu.* 16—19.

12.   65.

13.   See *Hau.* 25n.

14.   *Ph.* 5:   *tenui esse oratione et scriptura levi*.   For the meaning of *oratio* "content" here, see *Hau.* 46n.

15.   *Les Prologues de Térence* (Paris and Avignon, 1888), 252—61.

16.   Quoted by Suetonius, *Life* 7.

17.   See Duckworth 385−6, and the bibliography in 385 n.4.   It is worth noting that Ritschl's alteration of *vocibus* "utterance" in the Cicero passage to *motibus* "emotions", "passions" has been widely accepted, and that in the Caesar passage *vis* "vigour" can become *vis comica* "comic vigour" by altering the punctuation at the end of the line.
18.   See, for example, Arnott 48ff.; Beare 98ff., 310ff.; Duckworth 63−4, 202ff.; Sandbach 139−40; W.R. Chalmers, 'Contaminatio', *CR* n.s. 7 (1957), 12−14; Beare, 'Contaminatio', *CR* n.s. 9 (1959), 7−11, with bibliography; O. Kujore, 'A note on *contaminatio* in Terence', *CPh* 69 (1974), 39−42; further bibliography in Marti (1963), 23−7.
19.   The noun does not appear in Latin until used by Ulpian (died A.D. 228) in the *Digest*; but scholars have found it helpful to employ it when discussing the process Ter. uses the verb *contaminare* to describe.
20.   As in the only other appearance of the word in Ter. (not in the so−called 'specialist literary' sense in a prologue, but in the body of a play) at *Eu.* 552.   It is surely wrong to assume that a word always otherwise used in the sense of "sully" could have the neutral sense "combine" when used in Ter.'s prologues.   See further *Hau.* 17n.
21.   *The Cambridge History of Classical Literature* II: *Latin Literature* (Cambridge, 1982), 117.
22.   It might seem odd for Ter. to appeal to the precedent of Ennius, who had so little to do with *palliatae* (see p. 6   above); but Ter. could equally well be thinking of the way Ennius handled the originals of his tragedies.
23.   See p. 6.

Section V

1.   For all matters discussed in this section, see A.J. Brothers, 'The construction of Terence's *Heautontimorumenos*', *CQ* n.s. 30 (1980), 94−119, with the references and bibliography given in the footnotes.   My views on the play have not changed since that was written, though my views on the use of the term *contaminatio* have.
2.   See the preliminary remarks in Section VI of the Introduction.
3.   The commentary of Aelius Donatus, a grammarian of the fourth century A.D. and tutor of St Jerome, has already been mentioned; it is not clear whether the section dealing with our play is lost or was never written.   In its present form the commentary appears to be a sixth−century combination of two versions found in MSS of Ter., incorporating later additions.   It probably relied heavily on the earlier commentary of Aemilius Asper (late second century A.D.), which is now lost.
4.   Eugraphius probably wrote his commentary in the late fifth or early sixth century A.D.   It is a work much inferior to that of Donatus, from which parts of it are drawn, and often merely paraphrases Ter.'s text; as with Donatus' commentary, it has two versions.   The section on *Hau.* is given in Donatus III i 151−210.
5.   Fragments: Körte II 55−8, frs 127−135; there are traces of another fragment on a piece of papyrus which possibly contained a synopsis of Menander's play − see 53ff. n.   Problems of matching are discussed at appropriate points in the commentary.   The existence of fragments which cannot be readily fitted to Ter.'s text shows how much we do not know about what he did in his adaptation.   See also n. 12 below and Webster 144ff.
6.   Brothers 103.
7.   For the reading adopted, see 6n.; for the fact that 6 does not contradict what is said in 4, see 4n.
8.   Brothers 105−8.   Since that was written, the idea that *duplex* "double" refers to the two−day duration of the action (cf. 170n., 410n.) has been further supported by

31

Thierfelder 148.

9. The idea of pretending that Bacchis belongs to Clinia is suggested by Syrus at 332−3 and Chremes is only convinced that it is a pretence and not the truth at 908; Syrus first mentions the ruse of the debt at 599ff. and Chremes hands over money in settlement of it at 831.

10. Radice (96) supports the idea that Chremes is Terentian, but he cannot be entirely so since he speaks 61ff., which is paralleled by Körte II 56, fr. 127. Though it seems improbable that Bacchis was invented by Ter., it seems even more improbable that Clitipho and/or Chremes were too.

11. Whether they would be Ter.'s own free invention (as Charinus and Byrria in *An.*) or borrowed from another Greek play (as Gnatho and Thraso in· *Eu.*) does not affect the argument.

12. For fr. 127, see n. 10 above. Frs 128−30 are concerned only with the Menedemus/Clinia/Antiphila element, but 131 may form part of Chremes' words to Menedemus at 440ff., and 133 may come from Chremes' description of the meal he gave to Bacchis (455ff.). Webster (144ff.) associates fr. 134 with 672 and fr. 135 with 968, but cannot suggest a parallel for fr. 132; he associates fr. 475, a passage of Menander not ascribed to any particular play (Körte II 164), with 77. Fr. 935, a line not even definitely by Menander (Körte II 268), has been connected by some with 675. It may, however, be significant that 293ff. of Ter. is the last passage of our play with which a Greek fragment (130) can definitely be associated.

13. See Brothers 109.

14. 'A study of Terence's prologues', *PhQ* 6 (1927), 254.

15. For a full discussion, see Brothers 108ff., 117ff.

16. See 729n.

17. See 745n.

18. That is not to say that Menander's chorus assumed the role of the *grex*. The extent to which a New Comedy chorus could take on a dramatic role is disputed; see Brothers 116.

19. See 93n. Webster (144−5) thinks that the vital fact given by the prologue would have been the truth about Antiphila's identity, which does not occur in this scene. See also E. Lefèvre, *Die Expositionstechnik in den Komödien des Terenz* (Darmstadt, 1969), 27−37.

20. In fact there is no need to suppose that in Ter. Chremes leaves the stage; see 170−1n., and cf. D. Gilula, 'Menander's XOPOY, and where not to find it in Terence', *Latomus* 39 (1980), 694−701, esp. 700. For the views of those who support the idea of a choral interlude or prologue here in Menander, see the bibliography in Brothers 94, n. 1, and cf. Radice 96; see also R.L. Hunter, *ZPE* 36 (1979), 27−8 and J.C.B. Lowe, *Hermes* 111 (1983), 450−1.

21. See Radice 96 and Marouzeau II 50, n. 1; the difficulty felt is clearly of long standing, since the lines are misplaced in the MSS − as if they had been excluded as spurious and put back in the wrong place. But the passage is satisfactory and serves further to characterize Chremes; see 498ff. n., 502n., 508n.

22. See 170n., 410n.

23. See p. 2 and n. 8 to Section I.

24. See p. 18.

25. See Brothers 104 and the instances cited there. Among *palliatae*, Plautus' *Rudens* "*The Rope*" is named from a rope which becomes the object of a tug−of−war in one incident in the play. It may be that our play, like Menander's *Epitrepontes*, Apollodorus' *Epidikazomenos* and others, is named from one scene, not the whole play − in this case the memorable scene with which it opens.

Section VI

1.   Arnott 4.
2.   See 36n.
3.   126.
4.   The point is accentuated by the fact that, when Clinia leaves the stage at 748, he does not reappear (though his father does talk back to him in the house at 842ff.). The problems between Menedemus and Clinia are by now largely resolved, and Menedemus' main role for the rest of the play is to attempt to influence Chremes and to assist in reconciling him with his son.
5.   Compare the way in which Demea is deceived about Ctesipho in *Ad.*
6.   But recently supported by D. Gilula, op. cit. in n. 20 to Section V, 701.
7.   The famous line *homo sum; humani nil a me alienum puto* "I'm a human being; I feel that nothing that affects any man is no concern of mine".
8.   Well put by Hunter 99−100. See also Jocelyn, esp. 21ff.; he calls Chremes (28) "a comic personage combining the vices of the impertinent busybody and those of the intellectual".
9.   And not only those of Menedemus (53ff.). His evident satisfaction that Simus and Crito have chosen him to arbitrate in their boundary dispute (498ff.) shows his self−importance.
10.   E.g. he preaches at Menedemus particularly insensitively at 119−20 and 151ff., and delivers him a long lecture at 439ff.
11.   Sandbach in *Ancient Writers: Greece and Rome* I (New York, 1982), 545.
12.   The irony is underlined by, for example, Menedemus' prophetic observations (502−5), his quoting back at Chremes (919) the very words the latter used to him in 70, his pointed comment (922−3) and his advice (924) that Chremes should do the very thing he had earlier said Menedemus was doing too little of.
13.   He does not practise what he preaches to his son at 210.
14.   Quoted from 875.
15.   In a similar way, Syrus says (335−6) that it would take too long to explain why Antiphila is to go to Sostrata when Bacchis is taken in to Chremes' house. Compare the fact that we are not told what the plans are which Syrus rejects (676ff.), and cf. Davos at *An.* 705ff., 733.
16.   The dramatist had, of course, intended all along that the plan directed against Chremes should be the one to succeed. In this type of drama, the proper person for the slave to defraud is his own master, not his master's neighbour. (At least one editor (Ashmore) thinks that Syrus never seriously intends to get the money from Menedemus, but all along aims to defraud Chremes − in other words that his avowed plans to cheat Menedemus are just a blind. Even granted that it is unusual for a slave to try to defraud anyone except his own master, it is extremely difficult to extract such an interpretation from Ter.'s text − which is perhaps why Ashmore offers no detailed evidence. But it is possible that things were different (and perhaps clearer) in Menander.)
17.   Similarly, Simo refuses to believe the truth about Glycerium's baby, *An.* 459ff., 834ff.
18.   Such protests and such unbounded gratitude serve to heighten the audience's impression of the outrageous boldness and ingenious abilities of the slave.
19.   It is at least questionable that all such weaknesses must be ascribed to Ter., and that none of them can be attributed to Menander.

1. The best short modern discussion is by M.D. Reeve in L.D. Reynolds (ed.), *Texts and Transmission* (Oxford, 1983), 412−20. The most detailed work, though one now superseded on some points, is G. Jachmann, *Die Geschichte des Terenztextes in Altertum* (Basle, 1924); for recent developments on Jachmann's work, see J.N. Grant, 'Γ and the miniatures of Terence', *CQ* n.s. 23 (1973), 88−103, and J.N. Grant 'Contamination in the mixed MSS of Terence: a partial solution?', *TAPhA* 105 (1975), 123−53.

2. "The identity of Calliopius and the extent of his influence on the tradition are problems that remain unsolved" (Grant (1975) 123, n. 1).

3. I 85ff.

4. For instance, since both A and the Calliopians contain the *periochae* "summaries" of the plays written by C. Sulpicius Apollinaris sometime in the middle of the second century A.D., it has been supposed that Φ must be later than that date. But "such an embellishment would be apt to spread" (Reeve 414, n. 18).

5. Grant (1975) 152 thinks that this alphabetical arrangement is "a secondary development within the δ branch", i.e. it may not have been a characteristic of Δ, but arose later.

6. Marouzeau I 81 gives the order in γ incorrectly. F. Leo, 'Die Uberlieferungsgeschichte der terenzischen Komödien und der Commentar des Donatus', *RhM* 38 (1883), 317−47 believes (319) that the order represents the four plays from Menander followed by the two from Apollodorus. Grant (1973) 102−3 finds this "not very convincing" and suggests an ingenious alternative.

7. Grant (1973) 100ff. feels that they were not directly designed for Γ; he has an interesting discussion in which the miniature at *Hau.* 381 (of which he provides an illustration) figures prominently.

8. See, for instance, Duckworth 438 and n.2, and Reeve 413.

9. See E.A. Lowe (ed.), *Codices Latini Antiquiores* VII (Oxford, 1956), 38, no. 974, and J.D. Craig, 'A palimpsest fragment of Terence', *CR* 45 (1931), 215−6.

10. Statements about omissions refer only to those in *Hau.*

11. E.g. in 6 he changes *duplici* "double" of A to *simplici* "single" of Σ.

12. Marti (1961) 124−6 summarizes the various views.

13. See Donatus' remarks in his prefaces to *An., Eu., Ad.* and *Hec.*: I 38, 40; I 266; II 4; II 192. For act− and scene−divisions in general, see Beare 196ff.; Duckworth 98ff.

14. For the scholia in A see Mountford; the scholia of D, G, C and E, and of a 'mixed' manuscript at Munich (M), are in Schlee.

15. See R. Weir, 'Terence glosses in the Abolita glossary' *CQ* 16 (1922), 44−50 and W.M. Lindsay, 'Two lost manuscripts of Terence', *CQ* 19 (1925), 101−2.

16. Including readings from the St Gall palimpsest for *Hau.*

17. See the review by O. Skutsch, *CR* n.s. 6 (1956), 129−33.

18. Reeve 413.

BIBLIOGRAPHY

A. Texts, editions and translations

(i) Terence

The following are cited by the surname(s) of the editor(s) or translator only.

S.G. Ashmore, *The Comedies of Terence*[2] (New York, 1908); introduction, critical text and commentary.
R. Bentley, *Publii Terenti Afri Comoediae* (Cambridge, 1726); critical text and Latin commentary.
K. Dziatzko, *P. Terenti Afri Comoediae* (Leipzig, 1884); critical text.
A. Fleckeisen, *P. Terenti Afri Comoediae*[2] (Leipzig, 1898); critical text.
J.H. Gray, *P. Terenti Hauton Timorumenos* (Cambridge, 1895); introduction, text and commentary.
R. Kauer and W.M. Lindsay, *P. Terenti Afri Comoediae*[2], with additions to the apparatus by O. Skutsch (Oxford, 1958); critical text.
J. Marouzeau, *Térence*, 3 vols (Paris, 1942−9); critical text, French translation and notes, with a general introduction in vol. 1; *Hau.* is in vol. 2.
S. Prete, *P. Terenti Afri Comoediae* (Heidelberg, 1954); critical text.
B. Radice, *Terence, The Comedies* (Harmondsworth, 1976); introduction and English translation, and including a translation of Suetonius, *Life of Terence*.
J. Sargeaunt, *Terence*, 2 vols (London and Cambridge, Mass., 1912); short introduction, text and English translation; *Hau.* is in vol. 1.
E.S. Shuckburgh, *The Hauton Timorumenos of Terence* (London, 1877); introduction, text, commentary and English translation, and including a translation of Suetonius, *Life of Terence*.
A. Thierfelder, *Terenz, Heautontimorumenos: Einer straft sich selbst* (Stuttgart, 1981); text, German translation, notes and *nachwort*.
F. Umpfenbach, *P. Terenti Comoediae* (Berlin, 1870); critical text.

(ii) Others

The following are cited by the surname(s) of the editor(s) only, with the exception of Wessner's text of Donatus and Eugraphius, which is cited as Donatus (Don.) or Eugraphius (Eugr.).

A.W. Gomme and F.H. Sandbach, *Menander, A Commentary* (Oxford, 1973).
A. Körte, *Menander, Reliquiae*[2], rev. A. Thierfelder, 2 vols (Leipzig,

1955−9); the fragments of Men.'s *Hau.* are in vol. 2.

J.F. Mountford, *The Scholia Bembina* (Liverpool and London, 1934).

F. Schlee, *Scholia Terentiana* (Leipzig, 1893).

P. Wessner, *Aeli Donati quod fertur Commentum Terenti. Accedunt Eugraphii Commentum et Scholia Bembina*, 3 vols (Leipzig, 1902−8); vols 1 and 2 contain Donatus' commentary, prefaced in vol. 1 by Suetonius, *Vita Terenti*, Evanthius, *De Fabula* and *Excerpta de Comoedia*; vol. 3, part 1, contains Eugraphius' commentary; vol. 3, part 2, to contain the Scholia Bembina, was never published.

B. Other works

Those of the works in the following list which are mentioned in the Introduction and Commentary are cited there by the surname of the author only. Other works (including additional works by authors in this list) are always cited in full.

J.T. Allardice, *The Syntax of Terence* (London, 1929).

J. Andrieu, *Le Dialogue Antique* (Paris, 1954).

W.G. Arnott, *Menander, Plautus, Terence* (Oxford, 1975).

W. Beare, *The Roman Stage* [3] (London, 1964).

O. Bianco, *Terenzio: Problemi e aspetti dell' originalità* (Rome, 1962).

M. Bieber, *The History of the Greek and Roman Theater* [2] (Princeton and London, 1961).

A.J. Brothers, 'The construction of Terence's *Heautontimorumenos*', *CQ* n.s. 30 (1980), 94−119.

B. Denzler, *Der Monolog bei Terenz* (Zurich, 1968).

T.A. Dorey and D.R. Dudley (eds), *Roman Drama* (London, 1965).

G.E. Duckworth, *The Nature of Roman Comedy* (Princeton, 1952).

E. Fantham, '*Heautontimorumenos* and *Adelphoe*: a study of fatherhood in Terence', *Latomus* 30 (1971), 970−998.

K. Gaiser, 'Zur Eigenart der römischen Komödie: Plautus und Terenz gegenüber ihren griechischen Vorbildern', *Aufstieg und Niedergang der römischen Welt* I, 2, 1027−1113.

R.L. Hunter, *The New Comedy of Greece and Rome* (Cambridge, 1985).

E.B. Jenkins, *Index Verborum Terentianus* (Chapel Hill, North Carolina, 1932).

H.D. Jocelyn, 'Homo sum: nil a me alienum puto (Terence, *Heauton timorumenos* 77)', *Antichthon* 7 (1973), 14−46.

W.A. Laidlaw, *The Prosody of Terence* (London, 1938).

E. Lefèvre (ed.), *Die römische Komödie: Plautus und Terenz* (Darmstadt, 1973).

R. Maltby, 'The last act of Terence's *Heautontimorumenos*', *Papers of the Liverpool Latin Seminar* 4 (1983), 27−41.

H. Marti, 'Terenz 1909−59', *Lustrum* 6 (1961), 114−238 and 8 (1963),

5−101 and 244−247.

P. McGlynn, *Lexicon Terentianum*, 2 vols (London and Glasgow, 1963−7).

H.J. Mette, 'Die περιεργία bei Menander', *Gymnasium* 69 (1962), 398−406.

G. Norwood, *The Art of Terence* (Oxford, 1923).

C. Questa, *Introduzione alla Metrica di Plauto* (Bologna, 1967).

F.H. Sandbach, *The Comic Theatre of Greece and Rome* (London, 1977).

T.B.L. Webster, *An Introduction to Menander* (Manchester, 1974).

Lefèvre, Radice and, particularly, Marti contain useful bibliographies. Subsequent work is listed each year in *L'Année Philologique*. In addition, M. Platnauer (ed.), *Fifty Years (and Twelve) of Classical Scholarship* (Oxford, 1968) discusses work on Terence in Chapter IX and its Appendix.

A note on abbreviations

For ancient sources I have followed the conventions set out in P.G.W. Glare (ed.), *Oxford Latin Dictionary* (Oxford, 1968−82) − a work here abbreviated to *OLD*. In addition, I use 'Eugr.' for Eugraphius and 'Men.' for Menander.

For modern periodicals I follow the conventions used in *L'Année Philologique*.

Additional Bibliography 1997

K. Büchner, *Das Theater des Terenz* (Heidelberg, 1972)

G. Cupaiuolo, *Bibliografia Terenziana (1470–1983)* (Naples, 1984)

S.M. Goldberg, *Understanding Terence* (Princeton, New Jersey, 1986)

E. Lefèvre, *Terenz' und Menanders Heautontimorumenos* (Munich, 1994)

LIST OF METRES

As has already been stated in the Introduction (p. 25), this edition is not primarily concerned with metrical matters; the text is very largely printed without the 'aids' to scansion which appear in some modern versions, and metre is only mentioned in the Commentary on a comparatively few occasions.

However, the reader who is interested in such topics may find it helpful to be able to refer to the following list of metres, as they relate to the text adopted in this edition.

Periocha	Iambic senarii.	574—578	Iambic octonarii.
1—174	Iambic senarii.	579	Trochaic septenarius.
175	Trochaic octonarius.	580—582	Trochaic octonarii.
176	Trochaic septenarius.	583—584	Trochaic septenarii.
177	Trochaic octonarius.	585—588	Iambic octonarii.
178	Trochaic dimeter catalectic.	589—590	Iambic senarii.
179—180	Trochaic septenarii.	591—613	Trochaic septenarii.
181—186	Iambic octonarii.	614—622	Iambic octonarii.
187	Trochaic septenarius.	623—667	Trochaic septenarii.
188—241	Iambic octonarii.	668—678	Iambic octonarii.
242—256	Trochaic septenarii.	679—707	Iambic septenarii.
257—264	Iambic octonarii.	708	Iambic senarius.
265—311	Iambic senarii.	709—722	Trochaic septenarii.
312—339	Trochaic septenarii.	723—748	Iambic septenarii.
340—380	Iambic senarii.	749—873	Iambic senarii.
381—397	Trochaic septenarii.	874—907	Trochaic septenarii.
398—404	Iambic octonarii.	908—939	Iambic senarii.
405—561	Iambic senarii.	940—979	Trochaic septenarii.
562—563	Trochaic octonarii.	980—999	Iambic octonarii.
564	Trochaic septenarius.	1000—1002	Iambic septenarii.
565	Iambic octonarius	1003	Iambic octonarius.
566	Iambic dimeter acatalectic.	1004	Iambic dimeter acatalectic.
567—569	Trochaic octonarii.	1005—1012	Iambic octonarii.
570	Trochaic septenarius.	1013—1016	Trochaic septenarii.
571	Iambic octonarius.	1017—1018	Iambic octonarii.
572	Trochaic octonarius.	1019	Iambic dimeter acatalectic.
573	Trochaic septenarius.	1020—1067	Trochaic septenarii.

TERENCE: *The Self - Tormentor*

DIDASCALIA

Incipit Heautontimorumenos Terenti. acta ludis Megalensibus,
L. Cornelio Lentulo L. Valerio Flacco aedilibus curulibus.
egit L. Ambivius Turpio. modos fecit Flaccus Claudi. acta
primum tibiis imparibus, deinde duabus dextris. Graeca est
Menandru. facta est tertia, M' Iuventio Ti. Sempronio   5
consulibus.

C. SVLPICI APOLLINARIS
PERIOCHA

In militiam proficisci gnatum Cliniam
amantem Antiphilam conpulit durus pater,
animique sese angebat facti paenitens.
mox ut reversust, clam patrem devortitur
ad Clitiphonem. is amabat scortum Bacchidem.   5
cum accerseret cupitam Antiphilam Clinia,
ut eius Bacchis venit amica ac servolae
habitum gerens Antiphila; factum id quo patrem
suum celaret Clitipho. hic technis Syri
decem minas meretriculae aufert a sene.   10
Antiphila Clitiphonis reperitur soror.
hanc Clinia, aliam Clitipho uxorem accipit.

DIDASCALIA

3   egit Ambivius Turpio A : egere L. Ambivius Turpio L. Atilius Praenestinus Σ.
5   Menandru A : Menandri Σ.
    tertia A : III PCF : IV D : II L : secunda Evϵ.
    M. Iunio T. Sempronio Σ(Tito P : Marco Tullio Iulio Simphronio E) :
      Cn. Cornelio Marco Iuvenio A.

PERIOCHA

4   patrem PC : patre ADFE.
8   factum AD[1] : fictum D[2]PCFE.

PRODUCTION NOTICE

Here begins Terence's *The Self-Tormentor*; put on at the
Megalensian Games, when Lucius Cornelius Lentulus and Lucius
Valerius Flaccus were curule aediles; produced by Lucius
Ambivius Turpio; music composed by Flaccus, slave of
Claudius; performed first on unequal pipes, then on two
right-hand pipes; Greek original by Menander; composed   5
third, when Manius Iuventius and Tiberius Sempronius were
consuls.

SUMMARY
BY GAIUS SULPICIUS APOLLINARIS

A stern father forced his son Clinia to go abroad on military
service, because he was in love with Antiphila; and he
mentally tormented himself in regret for what he had done.
Clinia, when he returned soon afterwards, without his father's
knowledge put up at Clitipho's. The latter was in love with   5
the harlot Bacchis. When Clinia sent for Antiphila, whom he
longed for, there came along both Bacchis, posing as his
mistress, and Antiphila, dressed as her servant-girl; this
was done so that Clitipho could conceal his mistress from his
father. Through Syrus' tricks, Clitipho extracts ten minae   10
from the old man for his mistress. Antiphila is discovered to
be Clitipho's sister. Clinia marries her, while Clitipho
takes a different woman as his wife.

41

PERSONAE

CHREMES senex

MENEDEMVS senex

CLITIPHO adulescens

CLINIA adulescens

SYRVS servos

DROMO servos

BACCHIS meretrix

ANTIPHILA virgo

SOSTRATA matrona

NVTRIX

PHRYGIA ancilla

CHARACTERS

CHREMES
                        elderly gentlemen of Attica
MENEDEMUS

CLITIPHO   Chremes' son

CLINIA   Menedemus' son

SYRUS   a slave in Chremes' household,
                           attached to Clitipho
DROMO   a slave in Menedemus' household,
                           attached to Clinia
BACCHIS   Clitipho's mistress

ANTIPHILA   a young girl with whom Clinia
                           is in love
SOSTRATA   Chremes' wife

A NURSE   a member of Chremes' household

PHRYGIA   Bacchis' maid

PROLOGVS

Ne quoi sit vostrum mirum quor partis seni
poeta dederit quae sunt adulescentium,
id primum dicam, deinde quod veni eloquar.
ex integra Graeca integram comoediam
hodie sum acturus Heautontimorumenon,   5
duplex quae ex argumento facta est simplici.
novam esse ostendi et quae esset; nunc qui scripserit
et quoia Graeca sit, ni partem maxumam
existumarem scire vostrum, id dicerem.
nunc quam ob rem has partis didicerim paucis dabo.   10
oratorem esse voluit me, non prologum;
vostrum iudicium fecit, me actorem dedit.
sed hic actor tantum poterit a facundia
quantum ille potuit cogitare commode
qui orationem hanc scripsit quam dicturus sum?   15
nam quod rumores distulerunt malevoli
multas contaminasse Graecas, dum facit
paucas Latinas, factum id esse hic non negat,
neque se pigere et deinde facturum autumat.
habet bonorum exemplum, quo exemplo sibi   20
licere id facere quod illi fecerunt putat.
tum quod malevolus vetus poeta dictitat
repente ad studium hunc se adplicasse musicum,
amicum ingenio fretum, haud natura sua,
arbitrium vostrum, vostra existumatio   25
valebit. quare omnis vos oratos volo
ne plus iniquom possit quam aequom oratio.

---

5   Heauton **codd.** : Hauton Kauer-Lindsay.
6   simplici Iov., Σ : duplici A.
18   factum id esse hic Fleckeisen, Kauer-Lindsay : factum hic esse id A : id esse
       factum hic D²PCF (hic **om.** D¹) : id factum esse E.
19   se A : se id DPCE : id se F.
21   licere id facere AD²PCFE : id **om.** D¹, Kauer-Lindsay.

44

PROLOGUE

So none of you should wonder why our author has given an old man like me
a role which properly belongs to young actors, I shall explain that
point first, then give the address I've really come to make.
It's a fresh comedy from a fresh Greek source I'm going to put on today,   5
The Self-Tormentor, which from being a single plot has been turned into
a double play. I've shown that it's new, and what play it is; now I'd
go on to say who's written it and whose Greek original it is, if I
didn't think the vast majority of you know.
I shall now briefly explain why I've taken on this role. The author   10
intended me to be an advocate, not a prologue-speaker; he's made you
the judges and produced me as his pleader. But will this pleader's
eloquence give him the power to match the power of the author's timely
thoughts when he wrote this plea I'm going to make?   15
Now, as for spiteful individuals having spread rumours that he's messed
about with many Greek models while producing few Latin plays, our author
doesn't deny this has been done, and affirms that he's not upset about
it and will do it again. He has the precedent of good playwrights, and   20
by that precedent he supposes he's allowed to do what they have done.
Then as for a spiteful old poet repeatedly saying that our author has
taken to the poetic art all of a sudden, relying on his friends'
talents, not on his own abilities, on that it's your verdict, your view   25
that will be decisive. So I want to ask you all not to let the talk of
the prejudiced have more effect on you than the words of the

45

facite aequi sitis, date crescendi copiam
novarum qui spectandi faciunt copiam
sine vitiis. ne ille pro se dictum existumet   3
qui nuper fecit servo currenti in via
decesse populum. quor insano serviat?
de illius peccatis plura dicet quom dabit
alias novas, nisi finem maledictis facit.
adeste aequo animo, date potestatem mihi   3
statariam agere ut liceat per silentium,
ne semper servos currens, iratus senex,
edax parasitus, sycophanta autem inpudens,
avarus leno adsidue agendi sint seni
clamore summo, cum labore maxumo.   4
mea causa causam hanc iustam esse animum inducite,
ut aliqua pars laboris minuatur mihi.
nam nunc novas qui scribunt nil parcunt seni;
si quae laboriosa est, ad me curritur;
si lenis est, ad alium defertur gregem.   4
in hac est pura oratio. experimini
in utramque partem ingenium quid possit meum.
[si numquam avare pretium statui arti meae
et eum esse quaestum in animum induxi maxumum
quam maxume servire vostris commodis,]   5
exemplum statuite in me, ut adulescentuli
vobis placere studeant potius quam sibi.

---

45   si AD^{2}E^1 : sin D^{1}PCFE^2.
48-50   = **Hec.** 49-51.
48-9   **om.** A.

fair-minded. Make sure you're fair, and, when people give you a chance
to see new plays which are free from faults, give them a chance to get
on. But that chap needn't think that this has been said by way of a   30
defence for him - the one, I mean, who just recently put on a scene of a
crowd making way for a slave running down the street. Why should our
author do a service for a madman? He'll say more about that fellow's
faults when he puts on other new plays - unless, that is, he puts an end
to his slanderous accusations.

Pay attention with an open mind; give me the chance to be allowed to   35
put on, without interruption, a play which contains more talk than
action. That way an old man won't for ever continually have to play the
running slave, the angry old man, the greedy parasite, the shameless
swindler and the grabbing pimp - at the top of his voice and with lots   40
of effort. Convince yourselves my cause is just, for my sake, to lessen
some of my exertions. You see, people who write new plays nowadays show
no consideration for an old man; if it's a taxing piece, they run to
me; if it's a light and easy one, they take it off to some other   45
company. In this play we've got talk, talk that is natural and
unaffected; so put my talents to the test - see what they can do in
either line. [If I've never been greedy and put a price on my art, but
made up my mind that my greatest profit is to serve your interests as   50
much as I can,] Set a precedent in my case, so that youngsters may be
keen to please you rather than themselves.

I i   CHREMES   MENEDEMVS

CH.   quamquam haec inter nos nuper notitia admodum est
        (inde adeo quod agrum in proxumo hic mercatus es),
        nec rei fere sane amplius quicquam fuit,   55
        tamen vel virtus tua me vel vicinitas,
        quod ego in propinqua parte amicitiae puto,
        facit ut te audacter moneam et familiariter
        quod mihi videre praeter aetatem tuam
        facere et praeter quam res te adhortatur tua.   60
        nam pro deum atque hominum fidem quid vis tibi aut
        quid quaeris? annos sexaginta natus es
        aut plus eo, ut conicio; agrum in his regionibus
        meliorem neque preti maioris nemo habet;
        servos compluris. proinde quasi nemo siet,   65
        ita attente tute illorum officia fungere.
        numquam tam mane egredior neque tam vesperi
        domum revortor quin te in fundo conspicer
        fodere aut arare aut aliquid ferre. denique
        nullum remittis tempus neque te respicis.   70
        haec non voluptati tibi esse satis certo scio.   "at
        enim," dices, "quantum hic operis fiat paenitet."
        quod in opere faciundo operae consumis tuae,
        si sumas in illis exercendis, plus agas.
ME.   Chreme, tantumne ab re tua est oti tibi   75
        aliena ut cures ea quae nil ad te attinent?
CH.   homo sum; humani nil a me alienum puto.
        vel me monere hoc vel percontari puta;
        rectum est, ego ut faciam; non est, te ut deterream.
ME.   mihi sic est usus; tibi ut opus facto est face.   80

---

61   aut Iov., ELp, Don. **Eu.** 45 : **om.** ADPCF.
69   **post** ferre **dist.** Eugr. : **post** denique Don. **Ph.** 121, Cic. **Fin.** 1.3, Kauer-Lindsay.

(The scene is a street in a country town, on to which face three houses, one belonging to Chremes, another to Menedemus, and the third to Phania. **CHREMES** *and* **MENEDEMUS** *walk on slowly from the audience's left, the latter carrying several large hoes.)*

I 1

CH.   Though this acquaintance of ours is quite recent (from the time, indeed, that you bought some land here right next door), and   55
though we've had almost no other contact at all - yet either your good qualities or the fact that you live close by (which I consider the nearest thing to friendship) makes me give you a bold yet friendly warning, because you seem to me to be active   60
beyond your years and beyond what your circumstances ask of you. In the name of gods and men, what do you mean by it? What are you up to? You're sixty years of age, or more than that, by my guess; nobody has land round here that's better or worth more; you've quite a few slaves. Yet you're carrying out their tasks   65
as intently as if you'd got no slave at all. I never go out so early in the morning nor return home so late in the evening that I don't see you on your farm digging or ploughing or carrying something about. In short, you don't relax for a single moment,   70
and don't show any consideration for yourself. I know for certain this isn't any pleasure for you. "But," you'll tell me, "I'm not satisfied with how much work gets done here." All that effort you spend on doing the work yourself - if you were to spend it on keeping those slaves of yours busy, you'd get more done.

ME.   Chremes, have you got so much time free from your own affairs   75
that you worry about things which are no concern of yours and have nothing to do with you?

CH.   I'm a human being; I feel that nothing that affects any man is "no concern" of mine. Regard this either as a warning I'm giving, or as a question - so that I can do it myself if it's right; so that I can put you off if it's not.

ME.   This is how it must be for me; you do as you must do.   80

49

CH. an quoiquam est usus homini se ut cruciet?
ME.   mihi.
CH. siquid laborist, nollem. sed quid istuc mali est?
     quaeso, quid de te tantum meruisti?
ME.   eheu!
CH. ne lacruma atque istuc, quidquid est, fac me ut sciam.
     ne retice, ne verere, crede, inquam, mihi;   85
     aut consolando aut consilio aut re iuvero.
ME. scire hoc vis?
CH.   hac quidem causa qua dixi tibi.
ME. dicetur.
CH.   at istos rastros interea tamen
     adpone; ne labora.
ME.   minime.
CH.   quam rem agis?
ME. sine me vocivom tempus nequod dem mihi   90
     laboris.
CH.   non sinam, inquam.
ME.   ah, non aequom facis.
CH. hui! tam gravis hos, quaeso?
ME.   sic meritum est meum.
CH. nunc loquere.
ME.   filium unicum adulescentulum
     habeo. at quid dixi habere me? immo habui, Chreme;
     nunc habeam necne incertum est.
CH.   quid ita istuc?
ME.   scies.   95
     est e Corintho hic advena anus paupercula;
     eius filiam ille amare coepit perdite,
     prope iam ut pro uxore haberet; haec clam me omnia.
     ubi rem rescivi, coepi non humanitus
     neque ut animum decuit aegrotum adulescentuli   100
     tractare, sed vi et via pervolgata patrum.

81   est usus homini E : hominis est usus A : est homini usus DPCF.
94   at Iov., D¹p¹CF, Sacerdos 468 : ac A : ut E¹ : ha E² : ah edd. plerique.

CH.	Must *any* man torment himself?

CH. Must *any* man torment himself?

ME. Yes, *I* must.

CH. If you're in any distress, I wouldn't want it so. But what is this trouble of yours? Tell me, what have you done to deserve so badly of yourself?

ME. Oh, dear! *(He starts to break down.)*

CH. Don't cry; just make sure I know what's the matter, whatever it is. Don't hold back, and don't be afraid; trust me, I tell you.   85
By comfort, advice or practical help, I'll assist.

ME. You really want to know the story?

CH. Yes, for the reason I gave you.

ME. Then I'll tell you.

CH. But while you do, put down those hoes; don't keep on exerting yourself.

ME. Certainly not!

CH. What are you doing?

ME. *(coldly)* Permit me to allow myself no time off from work.   90

CH. *(taking the hoes from him)* I won't, I tell you.

ME. Oh, you're not doing right.

CH. *(feeling the weight)* Phew! I ask you, as heavy as this?

ME. It's just what I deserve.

CH. *(putting the hoes out of Menedemus' reach)* Now, say on.

ME. I have an only son, quite a youngster. But why did I say I *have* one? Rather, I *had*, Chremes. Now it's not clear whether I've   95
got one or not.

CH. How so?

ME. I'll tell you. There's a stranger here from Corinth, an old lady of pretty slender means. That boy of mine began to fall hopelessly in love with her daughter, so that he practically considered her as his wife - all this without my knowing it. When I did get to know of the affair, I started to treat him, not in any kindly way, and not as one should treat the love-sick   100
feelings of a mere boy, but harshly and in the hackneyed way of

```
            cotidie accusabam:  "hem!  tibine haec diutius
            licere speras facere me vivo patre,
            amicam ut habeas prope iam in uxoris loco?
            erras, si id credis, et me ignoras, Clinia.                    105
            ego te meum esse dici tantisper volo
            dum quod te dignum est facies;  sed si id non facis,
            ego quod me in te sit facere dignum invenero.
            nulla adeo ex re istuc fit nisi ex nimio otio.
            ego istuc aetatis non amori operam dabam,                       110
            sed in Asiam hinc abii propter pauperiem atque ibi
            simul rem et gloriam armis belli repperi."
            postremo adeo res rediit:  adulescentulus
            saepe eadem et graviter audiendo victus est.
            putavit me et aetate et benevolentia                            115
            plus scire et providere quam se ipsum sibi;
            in Asiam ad regem militatum abiit, Chreme.
CH.        quid ais?
ME.               clam me profectus mensis tris abest.
CH.        ambo accusandi;  etsi illud inceptum tamen
            animi est pudentis signum et non instrenui.                     120
ME.        ubi comperi ex is qui ei fuere conscii,
            domum revortor maestus atque animo fere
            perturbato atque incerto prae aegritudine.
            adsido;  adcurrunt servi, soccos detrahunt;
            video alios festinare, lectos sternere,                         125
            cenam adparare;  pro se quisque sedulo
            faciebant quo illam mihi lenirent miseriam.
            ubi video, haec coepi cogitare:  "hem!  tot mea
            solius solliciti sunt causa, ut me unum expleant?
            ancillae tot me vestiant?  sumptus domi                         130
```

---

118   profectus A : est profectus Σ : profectus est Eugr.

121   ei fuere A : fuere ei Σ.

127   faciebant Ap[1] : faciebat DPCFE.

129   solius **codd.** : soli Kauer-Lindsay.

130   vestiant AD[2]PCFE : vestient D[1]p[2], Kauer-Lindsay.

fathers. Every day I used to scold him: "What? Do you expect
to be allowed to carry on like this any longer, while I, your
father, am still alive - so that you can keep your mistress in
what almost amounts to the position of a wife? If you believe   105
that, you're wrong, and you don't know me, Clinia. I'm willing
for you to be called my son for just as long as you do what's
proper for you; but if you don't do that, I'll find something
proper for me to do to you. This comes about, I tell you, as a
result of nothing but too much spare time. At your time of life   110
I wasn't bothering with love; because I was so poor, I went away
from here to Asia, and there found both fortune and fame in war
and under arms." In the end, things reached a critical point;
through hearing the same message time and again, and with
growing distress, the lad was beaten down. He thought that   115
because of my years and my concern for him I knew more than he
did and looked to his interests more; he went off to Asia to
serve for the king, Chremes.

CH.   What!
ME.   He set off without my knowing, and he's been away three months.
CH.   You're neither of you free from blame, though the step he's taken
        shows a turn of mind that's full of respect and certainly not   120
        lazy.
ME.   When I found out from his friends who were in the know, I came
        back home dejected, my mind upset and all confused from worry. I
        sat down; up ran some slaves, pulled off my boots; I saw others   125
        bustling about, making the couches up, getting the supper ready;
        each one was busily doing his best to relieve my misery. When I
        saw this, I began to think along these lines: "What? Are so
        many people kept busy for my sake alone, to satisfy just me? Am   130
        I to have so many maids to see to my clothes? Am I to incur so

53

tantos ego solus faciam? sed gnatum unicum,
quem pariter uti his decuit aut etiam amplius,
quod illa aetas magis ad haec utenda idonea est,
eum ego hinc eieci miserum iniustitia mea.
malo quidem me dignum quovis deputem,   135
si id faciam. nam usque dum ille vitam illam colet
inopem carens patria ob meas iniurias,
interea usque illi de me supplicium dabo,
laborans, parcens, quaerens, illi serviens."
ita facio prorsus; nil relinquo in aedibus,   140
nec vas nec vestimentum; conrasi omnia.
ancillas, servos, nisi eos qui opere rustico
faciundo facile sumptum exsercirent suom,
omnis produxi ac vendidi; inscripsi ilico
aedis mercede. quasi talenta ad quindecim   145
coegi; agrum hunc mercatus sum; hic me exerceo.
decrevi tantisper me minus iniuriae,
Chreme, meo gnato facere dum fiam miser,
nec fas esse ulla me voluptate hic frui,
nisi ubi ille huc salvos redierit meus particeps.   150
CH.   ingenio te esse in liberos leni puto,
et illum obsequentem siquis recte aut commode
tractaret. verum nec tu illum satis noveras,
nec te ille. hoc qui fit? ubi non vere vivitur.
tu illum numquam ostendisti quanti penderes,   155
nec tibi ille est credere ausus quae est aequom patri.
quod si esset factum, haec numquam evenissent tibi.
ME.   ita res est, fateor; peccatum a me maxume est.
CH.   Menedeme, at porro recte spero, et illum tibi
salvom adfuturum esse hic confido propediem.   160
ME.   utinam di ita faxint!

---

136   colet D^{1}PC, Eugr., Non. p.250M : incolet D^{2}F^{1}E : colit A.
139   parcens quaerens APCF : quaerens parcens DE.
143   exsercirent Paumier, cf. schol. Bemb. : exercerent ADPCF, Eugr. : exercent E.
158   maxume DE^1 : maximum APCFE^2, Eugr.

much expense at home all by myself? Yet my only son, who ought
to be enjoying all this as much as I am - or even more so,
because his time of life is more suited to enjoying it - poor
boy, I've thrown him out of here through my own unfair behaviour!
Why, I'd think myself deserving of every kind of misfortune if I   135
were to carry on like this. For all the time he lives his
penniless existence away from home because of the wrongs I did to
him, I'll make amends to him from my own life, by toiling,
penny-pinching, money-making, slaving away for him." That's   140
what I did, and a thorough job it was. I left nothing in the
house, not a cup nor a cushion; I got everything together. The
maids and the servants I put up for sale and sold - the whole lot
of them except for those who could easily earn their keep by
working in the fields. I immediately put the house on the   145
market. I raised a total of about fifteen talents and bought
this piece of land, and here I keep myself hard at it. I've
decided that I'm doing less wrong to my son, Chremes, as long as
I make myself wretched, and that it's just not right for me to
enjoy any pleasure in this life, except when my boy's come back   150
here safe and sound to share it with me.

CH.   I think you've got an indulgent attitude to children, and that
he'd be obedient if one handled him correctly and properly. But
you hadn't got to know him well enough, nor he you. And how does
this come about? When people don't live their lives truthfully.
You never showed how much you thought of him, and he didn't have   155
the courage to trust you with the secrets it's right to trust a
father with. If that had been done, this would never have
happened to you.

ME.   That's true, I admit; I've done great wrong.

CH.   But I expect things will turn out all right in the future,
Menedemus, and I'm confident he'll turn up here safe and sound   160
before too long.

ME.   The gods grant that he does!

CH.   facient. nunc, si commodum est -
         Dionysia hic sunt hodie - apud me sis volo.
ME.   non possum.
CH.   quor non? quaeso, tandem aliquantulum
         tibi parce; idem absens facere te hoc volt filius.
ME.   non convenit, qui illum ad laborem hinc pepulerim,   165
         nunc me ipsum fugere.
CH.   sicine est sententia?
ME.   sic.
CH.   bene vale.
ME.   et tu.
CH.   lacrumas excussit mihi,
         miseretque me eius. sed ut diei tempus est,
         tempust monere me hunc vicinum Phaniam
         ad cenam ut veniat; ibo, visam si domi est.   170
         nil opus fuit monitore; iamdudum domi
         praesto apud me esse aiunt. egomet convivas moror.
         ibo adeo hinc intro. sed quid crepuerunt fores
         hinc a me? quinam egreditur? huc concessero.

I ii   CLITIPHO   CHREMES

CLIT.   nil adhuc est quod vereare, Clinia; haudquaquam etiam cessant,   17
         et illam simul cum nuntio tibi hic adfuturam hodie scio.
         proin tu sollicitudinem istam falsam quae te excruciat mittas.
CH.   quicum loquitur filius?
CLIT.   pater adest, quem volui; adibo. pater, opportune advenis.
CH.   quid id est?
CLIT.   hunc Menedemum nostin nostrum vicinum?
CH.   probe.   18

---

165   hinc pepulerim Bentley : inpulerim codd. : inepepulerim Kauer-Lindsay.
169   tempust Bentley, cf. schol. Bemb. (?) : om. codd.
174   om. A (hinc a me om. $E^1\eta^1\epsilon$) : secl. Umpfenbach.
      quinam $D^2PCF^1E^1$: quisnam $D^1F^2E^2$.
180   nostin ADF^2E : nosti PCF^1.

CH.   They will. For the present, if it suits you - it's the Dionysia
      here today - I want you to spend it with me.
ME.   I can't.
CH.   Why not? Please, do give yourself a little bit of respite. Your
      son would want you to do just that, even though he's not here.
ME.   Since I drove him out of here to a life of hardship, it's not   165
      right for me to avoid hardship now myself.
CH.   Is that your final decision?
ME.   *(picking up his hoes)* Yes, it is.
CH.   Good-bye, then.
ME.   And good-bye to you. *(He goes into his house.)*
CH.   He's brought me to the verge of tears, and I feel sorry for him.
      But, seeing what hour of day it is, it's high time for me to
      remind Phania, my neighbour here, to come to supper; I'll go and   170
      see if he's at home.

*(He walks across to the third house and knocks. When the door is
opened, a brief feigned conversation takes place with someone inside,
after which the door is closed and Chremes returns to centre stage.)*

      He had no need of a reminder;   I'm told he's been waiting at my
      house for quite some time already. I'm the one who's keeping the
      guests waiting. I'll go inside. But why this creaking from my
      door? Who's coming out? I'll hide over here.

*(He withdraws slightly, just as **CLITIPHO** comes out of Chremes'
house, talking back to someone inside.)*

I 2

CLIT. There's nothing for you to be afraid of so far, Clinia; they're   175
       not at all late, and I know you'll have her here today just as the
       messenger returns. So stop that worrying - it's quite unjustified and it's
       torturing you.
CH.   *(aside)* Who's my son talking to?
CLIT. *(aside, on seeing Chremes)*   My father's here, just the man I
       wanted.   I'll have a word with him.   *(Aloud, to Chremes.)*
       Father, you're back - how convenient.
CH.   What is it?   180
CLIT. Have you got to know our neighbour Menedemus here?
CH.   Very well.

CLIT. huic filium scis esse?

CH.   audivi esse in Asia.

CLIT.   non est, pater;
       apud nos est.

CH.   quid ais?

CLIT.   advenientem, e navi egredientem ilico
       abduxi ad cenam; nam mihi cum eo iam inde usque a pueritia
       fuit semper familiaritas.

CH.   voluptatem magnam nuntias.
       quam vellem Menedemum invitatum ut nobiscum esset amplius,   18
       ut hanc laetitiam necopinanti primus obicerem ei domi!
       atque etiam nunc tempus est.

CLIT.   cave faxis; non opus est, pater.

CH.   quapropter?

CLIT.   quia enim incertum est etiam quid se faciat. modo venit;
       timet omnia, patris iram et animum amicae se erga ut sit suae.
       eam misere amat; propter eam haec turba atque abitio evenit.

CH.   scio.   19

CLIT. nunc servolum ad eam in urbem misit et ego nostrum una Syrum.

CH.   quid narrat?

CLIT.   quid ille? se miserum esse.

CH.   miserum? quem minus credere
                                                       [est?
       quid relicui est quin habeat quae quidem in homine dicuntur bona?
       parentis, patriam incolumem, amicos, genus, cognatos, ditias.
       atque haec perinde sunt ut illius animus qui ea possidet;   19
       qui uti scit, ei bona; illi qui non utitur recte, mala.

CLIT. immo ill' fuit senex importunus semper, et nunc nil magis
       vereor quam nequid in illum iratus plus satis faxit, pater.

CH.   illicine? sed reprimam me; nam in metu esse hunc illi est utile.

---

185 **ante** amplius **dist.** Eugr., schol. Bemb., Kauer-Lindsay.

192 se miserum esse AD : miserum se esse PC, Kauer-Lindsay : miserum sese esse F :
       miserum esse ait E[1].

195 animus AE : animus est DPCF : est animus Censor. **Di. Nat.** 1.

199 illicine Fleckeisen : illene **codd.**, Kauer-Lindsay.

CLIT. Do you know he's got a son?

CH. Yes; I've been told he's in Asia.

CLIT. He isn't, father; he's at our house.

CH. What!

CLIT. When he arrived and was disembarking from his ship, I dragged him off to supper straightaway - I've been a friend of his ever since we were boys.

CH. What really splendid news! How I wish I'd been more insistent in inviting Menedemus to be with us, so I could be the first to give him this lovely surprise in my own house, when he was least expecting it. There's time even now.   185

CLIT. Mind you don't; you mustn't, father.

CH. Why?

CLIT. Because it's still not clear what he's going to do with himself. He's only just arrived, and he's apprehensive about everything - his father's temper, how his girl-friend's feelings stand towards him. He's crazy about her, and it's because of her that all this   190
fuss came about, and his disappearance.

CH. Yes, I know.

CLIT. Now he's sent his slave into town to fetch her, and I've sent our Syrus along as well.

CH. What's he got to say for himself?

CLIT. What's he got to say? Just that he's miserable.

CH. Miserable? Who's it possible to think *less* miserable? What's left among the so-called blessings in a man's life that he doesn't have? He's got his parents, a prosperous country, friends, family, relations and money; these are possessions which   195
exactly match the mind of the man who's got them - good for the one who knows how to handle them, but bad for the one who doesn't use them properly.

CLIT. Yes, but that old man of his was always troublesome, and there's nothing I'm more afraid of now than that in his fury he may do something to him that's more than he deserves, father.

CH. Menedemus? *(Aside.)* I'll bite my tongue, because it's useful to his father for this boy of his to stand in awe of him.

59

CLIT. quid tute tecum?

CH.   dicam; utut erat, mansum tamen oportuit.   200
    fortasse aliquanto iniquior erat praeter eius lubidinem;
    pateretur; nam quem ferret si parentem non ferret suom?
    huncine erat aequom ex illius more an illum ex huius vivere?
    et quod illum insimulat durum, id non est; nam parentum iniuriae
    unius modi sunt ferme, paullo qui est homo tolerabilis;   205
    scortari crebro nolunt, nolunt crebro convivarier,
    praebent exigue sumptum; atque haec sunt tamen ad virtutem omnia.
    verum ubi animus semel se cupiditate devinxit mala,
    necesse est, Clitipho, consilia consequi consimilia. hoc
    scitum est, periclum ex aliis facere tibi quod ex usu siet.   210

CLIT. ita credo.

CH.   ego ibo hinc intro, ut videam nobis cenae quid siet.
    tu, ut tempus est diei, vide sis nequo hinc abeas longius.

ACTVS II

II I   CLITIPHO

CLIT. quam iniqui sunt patres in omnes adulescentis iudices!
    qui aequom esse censent nos a pueris ilico nasci senes,
    neque illarum adfinis esse rerum quas fert adulescentia.   215
    ex sua lubidine moderantur nunc quae est, non quae olim fuit.
    mihi si umquam filius erit, ne ille facili me utetur patre;
    nam et cognoscendi et ignoscendi dabitur peccati locus.
    non ut meus, qui mihi per alium ostendit suam sententiam.

---

201   aliquanto DPCF : aliquando E : aliquantum A.
210   facere AD^1PCFE^1 : face $D^2E^2L^2\eta^2$, Kauer-Lindsay.
211   nobis cenae quid siet PCF : cenae quid nobis siet DE (quod D^1E) : nobis quid cenae
          siet Iov. : nobis quid incensiet A : nobis quid in cena siet Kauer-Lindsay.
214   a pueris A : iam a pueris Σ.
217   mihi AD^1FE^1, Eugr. : mihin D^2PCE^2, Kauer-Lindsay.
218   peccati A : peccatis Σ, schol. Bemb.

CLIT. What's that you're muttering?   200

CH. I'll tell you. However things stood, he should still have
stayed. Perhaps his father was a bit harsher than the boy would
have liked, but he could have put up with it; I mean, who should
he put up with, if not his own father? Was it right for the son
to live according to his father's standards, or the father
according to his son's? And, as for his pretence that his
father's a hard man, that's not so, because the so-called
'injustices' of parents are usually of one sort, if the father's   205
a reasonably tolerant man. They don't want their sons to visit
prostitutes a lot, they don't want them to live it up at dinner
parties a lot, they supply them with an allowance in pretty short
measure - and yet this is all with a view to forming a good
character. But when a person's mind has once shackled itself
with unhealthy desires, it's inevitable, Clitipho, that it will
pursue schemes which are similarly unhealthy. The clever course   210
is this, to test from the cases of others what may be of profit
to you.

CLIT. So I imagine.

CH. I'm going inside to see what we've got for supper. As for you,
seeing what time it is, please make sure you don't go anywhere
too far away. *(He goes into his house.)*

ACT TWO

II 1

CLIT. What unfair judges fathers are of all the young! They think it
right that we should spring to life as old men straight from
boyhood, and not get involved in those activities which are   215
natural to being young. They control us according to their own
desires - the ones they have now, that is, not the ones they once
had! If ever I have a son, he'll certainly find in me an
easy-going father, because I'll give myself scope for finding and
forgiving his wrong-doing - not like *my* father, who shows me what
he thinks himself by using someone else as an example. Damn it!   220

61

perii! is mi, ubi adbibit plus paullo, sua quae narrat facinora!   220
nunc ait: "periclum ex aliis facito tibi quod ex usu siet."
astutus! ne ille haud scit quam mihi nunc surdo narret fabulam.
magis nunc me amicae dicta stimulant: "da mihi" atque "adfer mihi";
quoi quod respondeam nil habeo; neque me quisquam est miserior.
nam hic Clinia, etsi is quoque suarum rerum satagit, attamen   225
habet bene et pudice eductam, ignaram artis meretriciae.
mea est potens, procax, magnifica, sumptuosa, nobilis;
tum quod dem "recte" est; nam nil esse mihi religio est dicere.
hoc ego mali non pridem inveni, neque etiamdum scit pater.

II ii   **CLINIA   CLITIPHO**

CLIN. si mihi secundae res de amore meo essent, iamdudum scio   230
venissent; sed vereor ne mulier me absente hic corrupta sit.
concurrunt multae opiniones quae mihi animum exaugeant:
occasio, locus, aetas, mater quoius sub imperio est mala,
quoi nil iam praeter pretium dulce est.

CLIT.   Clinia!

CLIN.   ei misero mihi!

CLIT. etiam caves ne videat forte hic te a patre aliquis exiens?   235

CLIN. faciam; sed nescioquid profecto mi animus praesagit mali.

CLIT. pergin istuc prius diiudicare quam scis quid veri siet?

CLIN. si nil mali esset, iam hic adessent.

CLIT.   iam aderunt.

CLIN.   quando istuc erit?

---

228   quod dem A, Gel. 4.9.11 : quod dem ei Iov., Σ, Sacerdos 461.
235   hic Σ : hinc A.
237   scis APC^{1}F^1 : scias DC^{2}F^{2}E.
238   adessent D^{1}pη^{2}ε : adesset AD^{2}PCFE.
       aderunt A : aderint D^{1}p : aderit D^{2}PCFE.

62

When he's had a drop too much, what escapades of his own he tells
me! Now he's saying: "Test from the cases of others what may be
of profit to you." Smart fellow! He's certainly got no idea how
deaf I am when he spins that yarn to me! At the moment it's the
words of my mistress - her "give me" and "bring me" - that
excite me more; I haven't a word to say to her in reply, and
there's no one more wretched than I am. My friend Clinia here,   225
even though he's got his hands full with his own problems, has at
least got himself a girl who's been well and modestly brought up
and knows nothing of the professional girl-friend's role. Mine's
grand and grasping, full of airs and graces, extravagant, and
high and mighty. And as for what I'm to give her, my answer's
"Oh, yes ... certainly", because I shrink from admitting that I
haven't got a thing. This is a spot of bother I've only recently
got myself into - my father doesn't know about it yet.

(CLINIA comes out of Chremes' house.)

II 2

CLIN. If things were going well for me in my love-affair, they'd have   230
come here long ago, I know; I'm afraid that while I've been away
the woman's been corrupted. Many a thought comes rushing in to
increase my fears: the opportunity, the situation, her youth,
that evil mother of hers whose thumb she's under - a woman who
finds nothing attractive but money.

CLIT. Clinia!

CLIN. Oh I feel so wretched!

CLIT. Is this what you call being careful not to be seen round here by   235
anyone coming out of your father's house?

CLIN. I'll be careful; but my mind really is filled with forebodings
of disaster.

CLIT. Are you persisting in deciding the matter before you know the
truth?

CLIN. If there wasn't any trouble, they'd be here already.

CLIT. They'll be here any minute.

CLIN. When will that be?

CLIT. non cogitas hinc longule esse? et nosti mores mulierum;
       dum moliuntur, dum conantur, annus est.

CLIN.   o Clitipho,   240
       timeo.

CLIT.   respira; eccum Dromonem cum Syro una; adsunt tibi.

II iii   SYRVS   DROMO   CLINIA   CLITIPHO

SY.   ain tu?
DR.   sic est.
SY.   verum interea, dum sermones caedimus,
      illae sunt relictae.
CLIT.   mulier tibi adest. audin, Clinia?
CLIN. ego vero audio nunc demum et video et valeo, Clitipho.
SY.   minime mirum; adeo inpeditae sunt. ancillarum gregem   245
      ducunt secum.
CLIN.   perii! unde illi sunt ancillae?
CLIT.   men rogas?
SY.   non oportuit relictas; portant quid rerum!
CLIN.   ei mihi!
SY.   aurum, vestem; et vesperascit, et non noverunt viam.
      factum a nobis stulte est. abi dum tu, Dromo, illis obviam;
      propera. quid stas?
CLIN.   vae misero mihi, quanta de spe decidi!   250
CLIT. quid istuc? quae res te sollicitat autem?
CLIN.   rogitas quid siet?
      viden tu? ancillas, aurum, vestem, quam ego cum una ancillula
      hic reliqui, unde esse censes?
CLIT.   vah! nunc demum intellego.
SY.   di boni, quid turbae est! aedes nostrae vix capient, scio.

_____

245-6   SY. minime ... secum ADP[1]CFE : DR. minime ... secum P[2], Kauer-Lindsay.
  250   propera A(?)D[1] : propere D[2]PCFE.

64

CLIT.   Don't you recall that it's quite a way away? And you know how
        women carry on - while they're getting things on the move, while   240
        they're trying to get going, a year's gone by.
CLIN.   Oh, Clitipho, I'm frightened.
CLIT.   You can breathe again; here comes Dromo, and Syrus too. They're
        here.

(SYRUS *and* DROMO *enter from the audience's right, conversing. They
do not notice the others.*)

II 3

SY.   Really?
DR.   Yes.
SY.   (*looking over his shoulder*)   But while we've been chatting away,
        the women have been left behind.
CLIT.   Your woman's here. Do you hear that, Clinia?
CLIN.   Yes indeed, now I do hear it at long last, and I see and I'm
        quite restored, Clitipho.
SY.   It's not at all surprising;   they're so weighed down with   245
        baggage; and they're bringing a whole gaggle of maids with them.
CLIN.   That's me done for! Where's she got maids from?
CLIT.   Don't ask me.
SY.   We shouldn't have left them behind. What stuff they're carrying!
CLIN.   Oh, poor me!
SY.   That gold, those clothes! And evening's coming on and they don't
        know the way. We've acted stupidly. Go and meet them, Dromo.
        Get a move on! Why are you hanging about?   (*Dromo goes off in*   250
        the same direction as he came.)
CLIN.   Oh, how miserable I am! Such high hopes, and now they've all
        been dashed.
CLIT.   What is it? What's worrying you?
CLIN.   You're asking me what it is? Don't you see? The maids, the
        gold, the clothes - where do you think she's got them from when I
        left her here with just a single servant girl?
CLIT.   Oh, now at last I understand.
SY.   Good god, what a crowd! Our house will hardly have room for them

65

	quid comedent! quid ebibent! quid sene erit nostro miserius?	255
	sed video eccos quos volebam.	

CLIN.   o Iuppiter, ubinam est fides?
dum ego propter te errans patria careo demens, tu interea loci
conlocupletasti, Antiphila, te, et me in his deseruisti malis,
propter quam in summa infamia sum et meo patri minus obsequens;
quoius nunc pudet me et miseret, qui harum mores cantabat mihi,   260
monuisse frustra neque eum potuisse umquam ab hac me expellere.
quod tamen nunc faciam; tum, quom gratum mi esse potuit, nolui.
nemo est miserior me.

SY.   hic de nostris verbis errat videlicet
quae hic sumus locuti. Clinia, aliter tuom amorem atque est accipis;
nam et vita est eadem et animus te erga idem ac fuit,   265
quantum ex ipsa re coniecturam fecimus.

CLIN. quid est, obsecro? nam mihi nunc nil rerum omnium est
quod malim quam me hoc falso suspicarier.

SY. hoc primum, ut ne quid huius rerum ignores; anus,
quae est dicta mater esse ei antehac, non fuit;   270
ea obiit mortem. hoc ipsa in itinere alterae
dum narrat forte audivi.

CLIT.   quaenam est altera?

SY. mane; hoc quod coepi primum enarrem, Clitipho;
post istuc veniam.

CLIT.   propera.

SY.   iam primum omnium,
ubi ventum ad aedis est, Dromo pultat fores;   275
anus quaedam prodit; haec ubi aperuit ostium,
continuo hic se coniecit intro, ego consequor;
anus foribus obdit pessulum, ad lanam redit.
hic sciri potuit aut nusquam alibi, Clinia,
quo studio vitam suam te absente exegerit,   280

---

258   Antiphila te Σ : te Antiphila A, Kauer-Lindsay.
259   minus obsequens Σ, Don. **Ph.** 408 : minus sum obsequens A.
266   fecimus A : cepimus DPCFE.
279   hic AE : hinc DPCF.

66

all, I'm sure. What a lot they'll eat! And drink! What more 255
unhappy creature will there be than our old master? *(He notices
Clinia and Clitipho for the first time.)* But here they are; I
can see them, just the people I wanted.

CLIN. Oh, Jupiter, what on earth's happened to loyalty? While I've
been away from home on your account, wandering about like a thing
possessed, you've been making yourself rich, Antiphila, and
abandoning me in the midst of all my troubles. And it's because
of you that I'm in real disgrace and very disobedient to my
father. I'm ashamed to see him now, and I'm sorry that, when he 260
used to go on at me about the ways of this sort of woman, his
warnings went unheeded and he could never get me away from her.
Still, I'll do it now - I refused when it could have won me back
his favour. There's nobody more wretched than I am.

SY. *(aside)* He's wrong about the conversation we were having here,
that's obvious. *(To Clinia.)* Clinia, you're interpreting your
love-affair quite differently from what it is; her way of life 265
and her feelings for you áre just the same as ever, as far as we
could tell from what we saw.

CLIN. What's that you're saying, please? At the moment there's nothing
in the world I'd like more than to know my suspicions are
unfounded.

SY. First, so you'll know all about her circumstances, there's this:
the old girl, who up till now was said to be her mother, wasn't; 270
and she's died. I heard this by chance while your girl was
telling the other one on our way here.

CLIT. Who's the other one?

SY. Wait; let me finish the story I've started first, Clitipho -
I'll come to that bit later.

CLIT. Get on with it, then.

SY. First of all, when we got to the house, Dromo banged on the door. 275
An old woman came out and, when she opened the door, he
immediately pushed his way inside and I followed. The old woman
put the bolt on the door and went back to her spinning. It's
here, if anywhere, Clinia, we could get to know the way she's 280
been living her life while you've been away (when we dropped in

67

```
                ubi de inproviso est interventum mulieri.
                nam ea res dedit tum existumandi copiam
                cotidianae vitae consuetudinem,
                quae quoiusque ingenium ut sit declarat maxume.
                texentem telam studiose ipsam offendimus,                    285
                mediocriter vestitam veste lugubri
                (eius anuis causa, opinor, quae erat mortua)
                sine auro;  tum ornatam ita uti quae ornantur sibi,
             †nulla mala re esse expolitam muliebri;
                capillus passus prolixus circum caput                        290
                reiectus neglegenter;  pax.
CLIN.                                    Syre mi, obsecro,
                ne me in laetitiam frustra conicias.
SY.                                                   anus
                subtemen nebat.  praeterea una ancillula
                erat;  ea texebat una, pannis obsita,
                neglecta, inmunda illuvie.
CLIT.                                    si haec sunt, Clinia,                295
                vera, ita uti credo, quis te est fortunatior?
                scin hanc quam dicit sordidatam et sordidam?
                magnum hoc quoque signum est dominam esse extra noxiam,
                quom eius tam negleguntur internuntii.
                nam disciplina est isdem munerarier                          300
                ancillas primum ad dominas qui adfectant viam.
CLIN.           perge, obsecro te, et cave ne falsam gratiam
                studeas inire.  quid ait ubi me nominas?
SY.             ubi dicimus redisse te et rogare uti
                veniret ad te, mulier telam desinit                          305
                continuo et lacrimis opplet os totum sibi,
                ut facile scires desiderio id fieri.
```

---

289   esse expolitam **codd.** : os expolitam Dziatzko : os expolitum Havet.
290   passus Σ (sparsus p²) : pexus A, Kauer-Lindsay.
297   scin hanc A : scin tu hanc Σ.
305   desinit A, Arusian. 464 : deserit Iov., Σ, Eugr.
307   fieri **edd. plerique** : fieri tuo **codd.**, Eugr., Marouzeau.

68

on the woman unexpectedly, I mean), because that situation gave
us a chance of judging the usual style of her day-to-day life -
that's what shows best the state of every person's character. We   285
found the lady herself busily weaving at her loom, soberly got up
in mourning clothes (because of that old woman who'd died, I
suppose) without any jewelry; dressed just like women who dress
for their own company, not finished off with any horrid female
stuff; her hair was spread out, flowing round her head and   290
carelessly thrown back; that's all there is to it.

CLIN. Syrus, my boy, please, don't plunge me into happiness for
nothing.

SY. The old woman was spinning wool for the loom. Besides her there
was just a single servant girl; she was weaving along with her,
all covered in rags, unkempt and grubby with grime.   295

CLIT. Clinia, if this is true, as I trust it is, then who's a luckier
chap than you? Do you understand about this girl he mentions
being shabby and scruffy? This is another sign that the mistress
hasn't come to any harm, when her go-betweens are so poorly
looked after. It's the regular practice for people trying to get   300
to the mistress to give presents to the servant-girls first.

CLIN. Go on, please, and watch out you're not over-eager to win empty
favour with me. What did she say when you mentioned my name?

SY. When we said you'd returned and were asking her to come to you,   305
she immediately stopped her weaving and tears poured all down her
face, so you could easily tell she was behaving like that because
she missed you so.

69

CLIN. prae gaudio, ita me di ament, ubi sim nescio;
       ita timui.
CLIT.   at ego nil esse scibam, Clinia.
       agedum vicissim, Syre, dic quae illa est altera.   31·
SY.   adducimus tuam Bacchidem.
CLIT.   hem! quid? Bacchidem?
       eho sceleste, quo illam ducis?
SY.   quo ego illam? ad nos scilicet.
CLIT. ad patrem?
SY.   ad eum ipsum.
CLIT.   o hominis inpudentem audaciam!
SY.   heus!
       non fit sine periclo facinus magnum nec memorabile.
CLIT. hǫc vide; in mea vita tu tibi laudem is quaesitum, scelus?   31⸱
       ubi si paullulum modo quid te fugerit, ego perierim.
       quid illo facias?
SY.   at enim ...
CLIT.   quid "enim"?
SY.   si sinas, dicam.
CLIN.   sine.
CLIT. sino.
SY.   ita res est haec nunc quasi quom ...
CLIT.   quas, malum, ambages mihi
       narrare occipit?
CLIN.   Syre, verum hic dicit; mitte, ad rem redi.
SY.   enimvero reticere nequeo. multimodis iniurius,   32·
       Clitipho, es, neque ferri potis es.
CLIN.   audiundum hercle est; tace.
SY.   vis amare, vis potiri, vis quod des illi effici;
       tuom esse in potiundo periclum non vis; haud stulte sapis,
       siquidem id sapere est velle te id quod non potest contingere.

---

313   patrem A : patremne Iov., Σ.
314   nec A, Non. p.309M : et D²GPCFE : ac Eugr.
321   Clitipho es AD¹G : Clitipho est D²PCFE.
       potis es **edd.** : potis est Σ : potes A.
       CLIN. **om.** A.
                                        70

CLIN. Heaven help me, I don't know where I am for joy. I was so afraid.

CLIT. I knew there was nothing to worry about, Clinia. Come on, now   310
it's my turn, Syrus; tell us who that other woman is.

SY. We're bringing your Bacchis along.

CLIT. Eh? What? Bacchis? You villain, where are you taking her?

SY. Where am I taking her? To our house, of course.

CLIT. To my father?

SY. Yes, to your father in person.

CLIT. Oh, the brazen effrontery of the fellow!

SY. But listen; no mighty or memorable deed is ever done without some risk.

CLIT. Look here; are you setting out to win glory for yourself by   315
gambling with my life, you scoundrel? It's a situation where, if
any tiny little point escapes you, I'm done for. *(To Clinia.)*
What would you do with him?

SY. But indeed ...

CLIT. "Indeed" what?

SY. If you let me, I'll tell you.

CLIN. Let him.

CLIT. Very well.

SY. At present this affair is ... just like ... when ...

CLIT. Damn it, what's this long-winded yarn he's starting to spin me?

CLIN. Syrus, what your master says is right. Drop it, and come to the
point.

SY. Yes indeed; I can't keep quiet. You're being unfair on many   320
points, Clitipho, and you're quite impossible.

CLIN. *(to Clitipho, before he can react)* We must hear him out; do keep
quiet.

SY. You want to love her, you want to have her, you want money to be
got to give to her; but, in having her, you don't want any risk
to yourself. The wisdom you show in this is far from stupid -
if, that is, it's wisdom for you to want what can't happen.

71

aut haec cum illis sunt habenda, aut illa cum his mittenda sunt.   325
harum duarum condicionum nunc utram malis vide,
etsi consilium quod cepi rectum esse et tutum scio.
nam apud patrem tua amica tecum sine metu ut sit copia est.
tum quod illi argentum es pollicitus, eadem hac inveniam via,
quod ut efficerem orando surdas iam auris reddideras mihi.   330
quid aliud tibi vis?

CLIT.   siquidem hoc fit.
SY.   siquidem? experiundo scies.
CLIT. age, age, cedo istuc tuom consilium; quid id est?
SY.   adsimulabimus
tuam amicam huius esse amicam.
CLIT.   pulchre! quid faciet sua?
an ea quoque dicetur huius, si una haec dedecori est parum?
SY. immo ad tuam matrem abducetur.
CLIT.   quid eo?
SY.   longum est, Clitipho,   335
si tibi narrem quam ob rem id faciam; vera causa est.
CLIT.   fabulae!
nil satis firmi video quam ob rem accipere hunc mi expediat metum.
SY. mane; habeo aliud, si istuc metuis, quod ambo confiteamini
sine periclo esse.
CLIT.   huius modi obsecro aliquid reperi.
SY.   maxume.
ibo obviam, hinc dicam ut revortantur domum.
CLIT.   hem!   340
quid dixti?

325   mittenda A : amittenda Σ.
327   etsi consilium A : etsi hoc consilium Σ.
331   tibi vis A : vis tibi Σ.
333   esse amicam **codd.** : amicam **om. edd. plerique.**
      pulchre quid A(?) : pulchre cedo quid Iov. : cedo quid D^{2}PCFE : quid D^{1}G.
      hic **post** quid **codd.** : **om. edd. plerique.**
      faciet Iov., Σ : faciat A(?), Kauer-Lindsay.
336   vera causa est **Syro continuant** Iov., Σ : **Cliniae trib.** A, Kauer-Lindsay.
339-40 SY. maxume. ibo ... Σ, **edd. plerique** : CLIN. maxume. SY. ibo ... A, Kauer-Lindsay.

Either you must have the risks along with your desires, or you 325
must say goodbye to your desires along with the risks. Think now
which of these two choices you prefer - though I'm convinced the
plan I've embarked on is a right one, and a safe one too. You've
got the chance for your girl to be with you in your father's
house without any worries. And as for your having promised her
money, I'll find that in the same way - you'd already deafened my 330
ears with begging me to get it. What else do you want?

CLIT. If indeed this does happen ...
SY.   "If indeed"? You'll find out by experience.
CLIT. Come on, come on, tell us this plan of yours. What is it?
SY.   We'll pretend your girl belongs to Clinia here.
CLIT. Brilliant! And what will he do with his own? Will she be called
       his too, as if this one of mine wasn't enough of a disgrace for
       him?
SY.   No, she'll be taken to your mother. 335
CLIT. Why there?
SY.   It's a long story, Clitipho, for me to tell you why I'm doing it.
       There's a very good reason.
CLIT. Rubbish! I don't see any really sound reason why it would pay me
       to take this worry on.
SY.   Wait; I've got another plan if you're afraid of this one - one
       you'd both admit is free from any risk.
CLIT. Yes, please find us something of that sort.
SY.   Certainly. I'll go and meet them and tell them to go back home. 340
CLIT. What? What did you say?

SY.   ademptum tibi iam faxo omnem metum,
        in aurem utramvis otiose ut dormias.
CLIT.   quid ago nunc?
CLIN.   tune? quod boni ...
CLIT.   Syre, dic modo
        verum.
SY.   age modo; hodie sero ac nequiquam voles.
CLIN.   ... datur, fruare dum licet; nam nescias ...   345
CLIT.   Syre, inquam!
SY.   perge porro; tamen istuc ago.
CLIN.   ... eius sit potestas posthac an numquam tibi.
CLIT.   verum hercle istuc est. Syre, Syre, inquam! heus! heus! Syre!
SY.   concaluit. quid vis?
CLIT.   redi! redi!
SY.   adsum; dic quid est.
        iam hoc quoque negabis tibi placere.
CLIT.   immo, Syre,   350
        et me et meum amorem et famam permitto tibi.
        tu es iudex; nequid accusandus sis vide.
SY.   ridiculum est istuc me admonere, Clitipho,
        quasi istic minor mea res agatur quam tua.
        hic siquid nobis forte advorsi evenerit,   355
        tibi erunt parata verba, huic homini verbera.
        quapropter haec res ne utiquam neglectu est mihi.
        sed istunc exora ut suam esse adsimulet.
CLIN.   scilicet
        facturum me esse; in eum iam res rediit locum
        ut sit necessus.
CLIT.   merito te amo, Clinia.   360
CLIN.   verum illa nequid titubet.
SY.   perdocta est probe.
CLIT.   at hoc demiror qui tam facile potueris
        persuadere illi, quae solet quos spernere!

---

355   evenerit Σ : venerit A.
357   neglectu est edd. plerique : neglectui est DGPCFE : neglectum est A.
360   necessus A : necesse Σ, Eugr.   74

SY.	I'll have made sure all your worry's been removed, so you can sleep easily on either ear.
CLIT.	*(to Clinia)* What am I to do now?
CLIN.	You? When a good chance ...
CLIT.	Syrus, just tell me the truth.
SY.	Come on, now; later today you'll want it - too late and all in vain.
CLIN.	... is offered, enjoy it while you can, because you'll never know ...
CLIT.	Syrus, I tell you!
SY.	You just go on in your own way, but this is what I'm doing. *(He moves off towards the audience's right.)*
CLIN.	... whether you'll have the opportunity later or not.
CLIT.	My goodness, that's true. Syrus, Syrus, I say! Hey! Hey! Syrus! *(Syrus stops.)*
SY.	*(aside)* He's warming to it. *(To Clitipho.)* What do you want?
CLIT.	Come back! Come back!
SY.	*(coming back)* Here I am; tell me what's the matter. You'll soon be saying that this doesn't please you either.
CLIT.	No, no, Syrus, I entrust myself, my love-affair and my reputation to you. You're the judge; just make sure you're not in court for anything yourself.
SY.	It's ridiculous for you to warn me of that, Clitipho, as if my fortunes were less involved in this than yours. If anything untoward happens to befall us over this, it'll be a scolding lined up for you, but a flogging for me; that's why I'll not be at all neglectful in this business. Now prevail on your friend here to pretend the girl is his.
CLIN.	You can be sure I'll do it; the situation's reached the point now where it's essential.
CLIT.	How right I am to have you for a friend, Clinia.
CLIN.	Make sure she doesn't slip up over anything.
SY.	She's been well schooled.
CLIT.	But I'm amazed how you were able to persuade her so easily, considering what people she usually turns down.

345

350

355

360

SY.   in tempore ad eam veni, quod rerum omnium est
       primum. nam quendam misere offendi ibi militem   365
       eius noctem orantem; haec arte tractabat virum,
       ut illius animum cupidum inopia incenderet
       eademque ut esset apud te hoc quam gratissimum.
       sed heus tu! vide sis nequid inprudens ruas.
       patrem novisti ad has res quam sit perspicax;   370
       ego te autem novi quam esse soleas inpotens.
       inversa verba, eversas cervices tuas,
       gemitus, screatus, tussis, risus abstine.
CLIT. laudabis.
SY.   vide sis.
CLIT.   tutemet mirabere.
SY.   sed quam cito sunt consecutae mulieres!   375
CLIT. ubi sunt? quor retines?
SY.   iam nunc haec non est tua.
CLIT. scio, apud patrem; at nunc interim ...
SY.   nihilo magis.
CLIT. sine.
SY.   non sinam, inquam.
CLIT.   quaeso, paullisper.
SY.   veto.
CLIT. saltem salutem ...
SY.   abeas si sapias.
CLIT.   eo.
       quid istic?
SY.   manebit.
CLIT.   hominem felicem!
SY.   ambula!   380

---

365   quendam misere A, cf. schol Bemb. : misere quendam p¹ : miserum quendam DGPCFE,
          Eugr.
368   hoc om. D¹PC¹F¹ : ob hoc D²C²F²E.
       gratissimum Ap : gratissima DGPCFE.
379   salutem A : salutare Iov., Σ.
380   hominem edd. plerique : o hominem codd.

SY.   I went to her at the right time, the most important point of all.
        I found a soldier there, desperately begging for a night with   365
        her; she was handling the man with her usual skill, to inflame
        his desire by his failure to get what he wanted, and at the same
        time to see that her action would please you as much as possible.
        But look here, please make sure you don't get careless and come
        unstuck. You know how observant your father is about such things   370
        - and I know how headstrong you can often be. None of those
        double-entendres, those over-the-shoulder glances of yours,
        sighing, clearing your throat, coughs and giggles.

CLIT.   You'll give me full marks.

SY.   Please make sure then.

CLIT.   Even you will be astonished.

SY.   (looking off stage to the audience's right) How quickly the ladies   375
        have caught up!

CLIT.   Where are they?   (He makes as if to go off to the approaching
        women, but is held back by Syrus.) Why are you stopping me?

SY.   She isn't yours now.

CLIT.   I know that, when she's in my fathers's house. But now, for the
        time being ...

SY.   She's not a bit more yours now.

CLIT.   Oh, let me!

SY.   I won't, I tell you.

CLIT.   Please, just for a little while.

SY.   No, I forbid it.

CLIT.   At least let me say hullo.

SY.   You'd be off if you'd got any sense.

CLIT.   (sulkily) I'm going. What will my friend here do?   380

SY.   He'll be staying.

CLIT.   The lucky chap.

SY.   On your way.

(Clitipho goes reluctantly into Chremes' house. Dromo leads BACCHIS
and ANTIPHILA on from the audience's right, and they are followed
by a number of maids struggling with a large amount of luggage.
Clinia and Syrus remain unnoticed, listening to their conversation.)

77

BA. edepol te, mea Antiphila, laudo et fortunatam iudico,
id quom studuisti isti formae ut mores consimiles forent;
minimeque, ita me di ament, miror si te sibi quisque expetit.
nam mihi quale ingenium haberes fuit indicio oratio,
et, quom egomet nunc mecum in animo vitam tuam considero   385
omniumque adeo vostrarum volgus quae ab se segregant,
et vos esse istius modi et nos non esse haud mirabile est.
nam expedit bonas esse vobis; nos, quibuscum est res, non sinunt;
quippe forma inpulsi nostra nos amatores colunt;
haec ubi imminuta est, illi suom animum alio conferunt.   390
nisi si prospectum interea aliquid est, desertae vivimus.
vobis cum uno semel ubi aetatem agere decretum est viro,
quoius mos maxume est consimilis vostrum, hi se ad vos adplicant.
hoc beneficio utrique ab utrisque vero devincimini,
ut numquam ulla amori vostro incidere possit calamitas.   395

AN. nescio alias; mequidem semper scio fecisse sedulo
ut ex illius commodo meum compararem commodum.

CLIN.   ah,
ergo, mea Antiphila, tu nunc sola reducem me in patriam facis;
nam dum abs te absum, omnes mihi labores fuere quos cepi leves,
praeter quam tui carendum quod erat.

SY.   credo.

CLIN.   Syre, vix suffero;   400
hocin me miserum non licere meo modo ingenium frui!

SY. immo ut patrem tuom vidi esse habitum, diu etiam duras dabit.

BA. quisnam hic adulescens est qui intuitur nos?

AN.   ah, retine me, obsecro!

BA. amabo, quid tibi est?

AN.   disperii! perii misera!

---

390   imminuta A : immutata Iov., D[1]GPCF, Kauer-Lindsay : mutata D[2]E.
392   semel A : simul Σ.
393   hi **om**. A.
401   ingenium A : ingenio Σ, Eugr.

BA. My goodness, Antiphila my dear, I do congratulate you, and I count you really lucky, because you've taken pains to see that your character matches your beauty. Heaven knows, I'm not at all surprised that every man wants you for himself, because your conversation made quite clear to me the sort of character you've got. When I reflect on your life, and on the life of all of you   385
who keep the common herd at arm's length, it's not surprising that you're of that sort while people like me aren't. It pays you to be good; the people we do business with don't let us. Our lovers cultivate us because they're egged on by our beauty, and when that's faded they transfer their attentions elsewhere;   390
unless we've shown some foresight in between times, we live a lonely life. But once you've decided to spend your days with one man whose character is most closely like your own, they devote themselves to you. Through this blessing you're both bound together by one another, so no disaster can ever befall your   395
love.

AN. I don't know about other women; I do know that I've always carefully contrived to arrange my interests to suit his.

CLIN. So, Antiphila my love, it's you alone who now bring me back to my country; while I was away from you, all the sufferings I endured were easy ones to bear, except having to be without you.   400

SY. I can believe that.

CLIN. Syrus, I can hardly bear it. To think, poor wretch, that I can't enjoy this gem of a girl as I would like.

SY. Far from it - from what I've seen of your father's mood, he'll give you a hard time of it for quite a while to come.

BA. *(noticing Clinia for the first time)*   Who's this young man who's staring at us?

AN. Oh, hold me up, please!

BA. What's the matter with you? Tell me, please.

AN. I feel faint ... I feel so weak ... oh, dear!

BA.   quid stupes,
      Antiphila?
AN.   videon Cliniam an non?
BA.   quem vides?   405
CLIN. salve, anime mi!
AN.   o mi Clinia, salve!
CLIN.   ut vales?
AN.   salvom venisse gaudeo.
CLIN.   teneone te,
      Antiphila, maxume animo exoptatam meo?
SY.   ite intro; nam vos iamdudum exspectat senex.

ACTVS III

III i   CHREMES MENEDEMVS

CH.   luciscit hoc iam. cesso pultare ostium   410
       vicini, primum e me ut sciat sibi filium
       redisse? etsi adulescentem hoc nolle intellego.
       verum quom videam miserum hunc tam excruciarier
       eius abitu, celem tam insperatum gaudium,
       quom illi pericli nil ex indicio siet?   415
       haud faciam; nam quod potero adiutabo senem.
       item ut filium meum amico atque aequali suo
       video inservire et socium esse in negotiis,
       nos quoque senes est aequom senibus obsequi.
ME.   aut ego profecto ingenio egregio ad miserias   420
       natus sum, aut illud falsum est quod volgo audio
       dici, diem adimere aegritudinem hominibus;
       nam mihi quidem cotidie augescit magis
       de filio aegritudo, et quanto diutius
       abest, magis cupio tanto et magis desidero.   425

─────────────
406   o mi expectate Clinia D²PCFE.
408   exoptatam p, gl. II : exoptata ADGF² : expectata PCF¹E : exspectatam Kauer-Lindsay.
411   e A : ex Iov., Σ.
415   pericli nihil PCFE : nihil pericli ADG.
417   item AD¹ : ita D²GPCFE.

BA.   Why are you so dazed, Antiphila?   405

AN.   Is it Clinia I see, or not?

BA.   Who can you see?

CLIN.   *(moving across to Antiphila)*   Hullo, my love.

AN.   Clinia my darling, hullo.

CLIN.   Are you all right?

AN.   Overjoyed that you're back safe and sound.

CLIN.   Am I really holding you, Antiphila, you who I've longed for in my heart of hearts?

SY.   Go indoors; my master's been waiting for you for quite a while.

(He ushers them all into Chremes' house, and the stage is left empty. The action resumes immediately, but time is presumed to have passed, and it is the next morning. Chremes comes out of his house.)

ACT THREE

III 1

CH.   Daybreak already. Why don't I knock at my neighbour's door, so I   410
can be the first to tell him that his son's returned - even if I
realize the young chap doesn't want me to? Yet when I see
Menedemus here in such a sorry state and so tormented by the
boy's going away, should I conceal so unexpected a pleasure when   415
there's no risk to the lad from my telling his father? I won't;
I'll help the old man as much as I can. In much the same way as
I see my son rallying round a friend of his own age, and sharing
his problems, it's right that old men like me, too, should do a
good turn for other old men.

(Menedemus comes out of his house; he does not at first notice Chremes.)

ME.   Either I've been born with a really outstanding talent for being   420
miserable, or else what I commonly hear said - that time takes
away men's sorrow - is quite untrue. As far as I'm concerned, my
grief about my son increases more every day, and the longer he's   425
away, the more I want him and miss him.

CH.   sed ipsum foras egressum video; ibo adloquar.
        Menedeme, salve; nuntium adporto tibi
        quoius maxume te fieri participem cupis.
ME.   num quid nam de gnato meo audisti, Chreme?
CH.   valet atque vivit.
ME.   ubinam est, quaeso?
CH.   apud me domi.   430
ME.   meus gnatus?
CH.   sic est.
ME.   venit?
CH.   certe.
ME.   Clinia
        meus venit?
CH.   dixi.
ME.   eamus; duc me ad eum, obsecro.
CH.   non volt te scire se redisse etiam et tuom
        conspectum fugitat; propter peccatum hoc timet,
        ne tua duritia antiqua illa etiam adaucta sit.   435
ME.   non tu illi dixti ut essem?
CH.   non.
ME.   quam ob rem, Chreme?
CH.   quia pessume istuc in te atque in illum consulis,
        si te tam leni et victo esse animo ostenderis.
ME.   non possum; satis iam, satis pater durus fui.
CH.   ah,
        vehemens in utramque partem, Menedeme, es nimis,   440
        aut largitate nimia aut parsimonia.
        in eandem fraudem ex hac re atque ex illa incides.
        primum olim potius quam paterere filium
        commetare ad mulierculam, quae paullulo
        tum erat contenta quoique erant grata omnia,   445

---

436   illi A : ei Iov., Σ, Eugr.
437   atque in illum **codd.** : in **om.** Kauer-Lindsay.
438   ostenderis Σ : ostenderes A.
444   commetare schol. Bemb., Bentley : commeare **codd.**

CH.   It's the very man himself I see - he's just come outside; I'll
go and speak to him. Good morning, Menedemus. I've got some news
for you, news you want to share in more than anything.

ME.   You haven't heard anything about my son, have you, Chremes?

CH.   He's alive and well.   430

ME.   Please, where is he?

CH.   At home at my house.

ME.   My son?

CH.   Yes, he is.

ME.   He's arrived?

CH.   Yes, indeed.

ME.   My dear boy Clinia's arrived?

CH.   That's what I said.

ME.   Let's go; take me to him, please.

CH.   He doesn't want you to know he's got back yet, and he's keeping
out of your sight. It's because of what he did wrong that he's
afraid like this - afraid that that earlier harshness of yours   435
may have increased still more.

ME.   Didn't you tell him what my feelings are?

CH.   No.

ME.   Why, Chremes?

CH.   Because you're acting in your own worst interests and in his if
you show that you're in so weak and subdued a state of mind about
him.

ME.   I can't do it; I've already been harsh enough, harsh enough as a
father.

CH.   Oh, Menedemus, you're too extreme in each direction with your   440
excessive generosity or your excessive tight-fistedness; you'll
fall into the same trap from the one as from the other. First, a
while ago, rather than let your son keep visiting a young woman
who at the time was content with very little and who found   445

83

proterruisti hinc; ea coacta ingratiis
postilla coepit victum volgo quaerere.
nunc quom sine magno intertrimento non potest
haberi, quidvis dare cupis. nam ut tu scias
quam ea nunc instructa pulchre ad perniciem siet,   45()
primum iam ancillas secum adduxit plus decem,
oneratas veste atque auro; satrapes si siet
amator, numquam sufferre eius sumptus queat,
nedum tu possis.

ME.   estne ea intus?

CH.   sit rogas?

sensi. nam unam ei cenam atque eius comitibus   45!
dedi; quod si iterum mihi sit danda, actum siet.
nam ut alia omittam, pytissando modo mihi
quid vini absumsit, "sic hoc," dicens; "asperum,
pater, hoc est; aliud lenius sodes vide."
relevi dolia omnia, omnis serias;   46(
omnis sollicitos habui; atque haec una nox.
quid te futurum censes quem adsidue exedent?
sic me di amabunt ut me tuarum miseritum est,
Menedeme, fortunarum.

ME.   faciat quidlubet;
sumat, consumat, perdat; decretum est pati,   465
dum illum modo habeam mecum.

CH.   si certum est tibi
sic facere, illud permagni referre arbitror
ut ne scientem sentiat te id sibi dare.

ME.   quid faciam?

CH.   quidvis potius quam quod cogitas;
per alium quemvis ut des, falli te sinas   470
techinis per servolum; etsi subsensi id quoque,
illos ibi esse, id agere inter se clanculum.

---

471   techinis gl. II, Ritschl : technis **codd.** (thegnis D[1]).
       servolum Iov., Σ : servom A.

everything acceptable, you frightened him away from here; under compulsion and against her will, she later began to look for a living among the public at large. Now, when nobody can keep her except at ruinous cost, you're eager to give him anything he wants. You need to know how splendidly she's been taught how to 450 ruin a man; first, she's brought with her more than ten maidservants laden with dresses and gold trinkets; if her lover was a sheik he'd never be able to stand her expenses - much less could you.

ME. Is she inside?

CH. You're asking me if she's in there? I've *felt* it. I've given 455 just one supper to her and her crew, and if I had to give it a second time, that would be it. Not to mention everything else, what a lot of my wine she's wasted, just by tasting; "This is so-so," she says; "This is rough, father; please see if you've got another one that's smoother." I opened all my jars and all 460 my bottles, I had everyone busily on their toes - and this was just one night. What do you think will become of you, now you're the one they're going to eat out of house and home all the time? Heaven knows, I do feel sorry for your finances, Menedemus.

ME. Let him do whatever he likes; let him take, spend and squander; 465 I've made up my mind to put up with it, just as long as I have that boy of mine with me.

CH. If you're determined to act that way, I think it's most important he shouldn't realize you're giving it to him consciously.

ME. What should I do?

CH. Anything rather than what you're contemplating; arrange that you 470 give the money through someone else, arrange to let yourself be taken in by his slave-boy's tricks - and that's something I've got wind of too, that they're on to it and are secretly planning

85

Syrus cum illo vostro consusurrant, conferunt
consilia ad adulescentes; et tibi perdere
talentum hoc pacto satius est quam illo minam.   475
non nunc pecunia agitur sed illud quo modo
minimo periclo id demus adulescentulo.
nam si semel tuom animum ille intellexerit,
prius proditurum te tuam vitam et prius
pecuniam omnem quam abs te amittas filium, hui   480
quantam fenestram ad nequitiem patefeceris,
tibi autem porro ut non sit suave vivere!
nam deteriores omnes sumus licentia.
quod quoique quomque inciderit in mentem, volet,
neque id putabit pravom an rectum sit; petet.   485
tu rem perire et ipsum non poteris pati.
dare denegaris; ibit ad illud ilico
qui maxume apud te se valere sentiet;
abiturum se abs te esse ilico minitabitur.
ME. videre vera atque ita uti res est dicere.   490
CH. somnum hercle ego hac nocte oculis non vidi meis,
dum id quaero, tibi qui filium restituerem.
ME. cedo dextram; porro te idem oro ut facias, Chreme.
CH. paratus sum.
ME.   scin quid nunc facere te volo?
CH. dic.
ME.   quod sensisti illos me incipere fallere,   495
id ut maturent facere; cupio illi dare
quod volt, cupio ipsum iam videre.

---

473   consusurrant ADP[1]CF[1] : consusurrat Iov., GP[2]F[2]E.
481   nequitiem A : nequitiam Iov., Σ.
484-5 **secl.** Bentley.
486   ipsum AG, Eugr. : illum DPCFE.
488   qui Σ : quo A.
489   minitabitur DGCFE[2] : minabitur APE[1].
490   vera A, schol. Bemb. : verum Iov., Σ.
493   idem oro A : oro idem Σ.
496   ut ADPCFE : uti G, Kauer-Lindsay.

the business among themselves. Syrus and that chap of yours are
whispering together, and taking their plans to our young lads;
it's better for you to lose a whole talent this way than a mina   475
that. It's not a matter of the money now, but of how we can give
it to the boy with the least risk. If once he realizes your
feelings - that you'll sacrifice your life and your entire   480
fortune before you'll send your son away - well, what an
opportunity you'll have opened up for scandalous behaviour, and
the result will be you'll have no more pleasure in living! We're
all of us worse when there's no restraint. A man will want
whatever comes into his head, and he won't consider if it's wrong   485
or right - he'll go for it. You won't be able to endure the ruin
of your property and of your son; you'll refuse to give him what
he wants, and he'll go straight to the point where he realizes
he's got most hold on you - he'll immediately threaten to leave.

ME. You seem to be telling the truth and describing the situation   490
just as it is.

CH. Believe me, I didn't get a wink of sleep last night while I was
puzzling out how to restore your son to you.

ME. Give me your hand; I beg you, Chremes, to go on doing just that.

CH. I'm ready to.

ME. Do you know what I want you to do now?

CH. Tell me.   495

ME. Because you've realized they're setting out to trick me, arrange
for them to hurry up and do so. I really want to give him what
he wants; I really want to see him now in person.

CH.   operam dabo.
      paullum negoti mi obstat; Simus et Crito
      vicini nostri hic ambigunt de finibus;
      me cepere arbitrum; ibo ac dicam, ut dixeram   500
      operam daturum me, hodie non posse is dare.
      continuo hic adero.
ME.   ita quaeso. di vostram fidem,
      ita conparatam esse hominum naturam omnium,
      aliena ut melius videant et diiudicent
      quam sua! an eo fit quia in re nostra aut gaudio   505
      sumus praepediti nimio aut aegritudine?
      hic mihi nunc quanto plus sapit quam egomet mihi!
CH.   dissolvi me, otiosus operam ut tibi darem.
      Syrus est prendendus atque adhortandus mihi.
      a me nescioquis exit; concede hinc domum,   510
      ne nos inter nos congruere sentiant.

III ii   SYRVS   CHREMES

SY.   hac illac circumcursa; inveniundum est tamen
      argentum, intendenda in senem est fallacia.
CH.   num me fefellit hosce id struere? videlicet
      ill' Cliniai servos tardiusculust;   515
      idcirco huic nostro tradita est provincia.
SY.   quis hic loquitur? perii. numnam haec audivit?
CH.   Syre!
SY.   hem!

498-508 **post** 497 Bentley : 497, 509-11, 498-508, 512ff. **codd.**
   498   paulum A : paululum G : paulum hoc DPCFE.
   499   hic Iov., Σ, Eugr. : hinc A.
   501   iis A : eis D^1 : his D^{2}GPCFE.
   509   prendendus **edd. plerique** : prehendendus schol. Bemb., Marouzeau : adprehendendus Σ:
           prehendus A.
   511   congruere **codd.**, schol. Bemb., Arusian. 463 : congruisse Tyrell : congruere illi
           Dziatzko.
   514   id struere PCFE, Eugr. : instruere AD^1 : id instruere G.
   515   Cliniai Bentley : Cliniae **codd.**, Sacerdos 445.

H. I'll give the matter my attention. There's just one little bit of business in my way. Our neighbours Simus and Crito are in dispute about some boundaries hereabouts; they've chosen me to arbitrate; since I told them I'd attend to the matter, I'll go and tell them I can't do so for them today. I'll be back here right away. 500

E. Yes, please do. *(Chremes hurries off to the audience's right.)* Good heavens, to think that human nature's so arranged that everyone can see and decide about other people's problems better than their own! Does that come about because in our own affairs 505 we're hampered by excessive joy or grief? How much more sense my friend here's showing in my interests now than I am in my own. *(Chremes comes hurrying back.)*

H. I've got myself out of it, so I can give my attention to you at my leisure. I must get hold of Syrus and give him a bit of encouragement. Someone's coming out of my house; go back indoors, 510 so they won't realize there's an understanding between us.

(Menedemus goes into his house. Almost immediately, Syrus comes out of Chremes' house; he is talking to himself, and at first does not notice Chremes.)

II 2

Y. Run here, run there; the money's got to be found, and a trap laid for the old man.

H. So it didn't escape me, did it, that this lot are hatching their plot? Evidently that slave of Clinia's is a bit on the slow 515 side, and because of that the mission's been transferred to our man here.

Y. *(looking round)* Who's that talking here? *(Seeing Chremes.)* I've had it now. He hasn't heard what I was saying, has he?

H. Syrus!

Y. *(with an exaggerated pretence of being startled)* Eh?

89

CH.   quid tu istic?

SY.   recte equidem; sed te miror, Chreme,
tam mane, qui heri tantum biberis.

CH.   nil nimis.

SY.   "nil", narras? visa vero est, quod dici solet,   520
aquilae senectus.

CH.   heia!

SY.   mulier commoda et
faceta haec meretrix.

CH.   sane.

SY.   idem visa est tibi?
et quidem hercle forma luculenta.

CH.   sic satis.

SY.   ita non ut olim, sed, uti nunc, sane bona.
minimeque miror Clinia hanc si deperit.   525
sed habet patrem quendam avidum, miserum atque aridum
vicinum hunc; nostin? at quasi is non ditiis
abundet, gnatus eius profugit inopia.
scis esse factum ut dico?

CH.   quid ego ni sciam?
hominem pistrino dignum!

SY.   quem?

CH.   istunc servolum   530
dico adulescentis ...

SY.   Syre, tibi timui male!

CH.   ... qui passus est id fieri.

SY.   quid faceret?

---

518   sed te miror A : te demiror DGP[1]CFE, Eugr. : sed te demiror P[2].
520   vero est APCF : est vero DG : vero in te est E.
522   SY. om. Σ.
        tibi AD[1]G[1](?) : mihi D[2]G[2]PCFE.
523   SY. et quidem Σ.
527   at quasi is **edd. plerique** : at quasi si is D[2] : atquit si is A : atquid si is P[1]C[1]
        : atqui si is Iov., GF, Eugr. : aut qui si is E.
529   ni sciam Paumier : nesciam **codd.**, Eugr.

CH.	What are you up to?
SY.	Oh, nothing much; but I'm surprised that you're about so early in the morning, Chremes, seeing you drank so much last night.
CH.	Nothing in excess.
SY.	"Nothing" you say? It certainly seemed like your 'eagle's years', as the saying goes.

520

CH.	Huh!
SY.	This mistress of his is a pleasant and polished woman.
CH.	To be sure.
SY.	She seemed the same to you too? And, heavens, she's got a splendid figure.
CH.	Nice enough.
SY.	Not like they were in the old days, but, for nowadays, pretty good. I'm not in the least surprised if Clinia's besotted with her. But he's got a greedy father, our wretched, mean neighbour here - do you know him? Even so, as if he wasn't rolling in money, his son ran away, he was so poor. Are you aware it's happened as I say?

525

CH.	Why shouldn't I be? The fellow deserves a spell in the mill!
SY.	Who?
CH.	That young slave of Clinia's, I mean ...
SY.	*(aside)* Syrus, I was terribly afraid for you!
CH.	... who let it happen.
SY.	What was he to do?

530

CH.   rogas?
        aliquid reperiret, fingeret fallacias
        unde esset adulescenti amicae quod daret,
        atque hunc difficilem invitum servaret senem.   53!
SY.   garris.
CH.   haec facta ab illo oportebant, Syre.
SY.   eho, quaeso, laudas qui eros fallunt?
CH.   in loco
        ego vero laudo.
SY.   recte sane.
CH.   quippe qui
        magnarum saepe id remedium aegritudinum est.
        iam huic mansisset unicus gnatus domi.   54(
SY.   iocone an serio ille haec dicat nescio,
        nisi mihi quidem addit animum quo lubeat magis.
CH.   et nunc quid exspectat, Syre? an dum hic denuo
        abeat, quom tolerare illius sumptus non queat?
        nonne ad senem aliquam fabricam fingit?
SY.   stolidus est.   54
CH.   at te adiutare oportet adulescentuli
        causa.
SY.   facile equidem facere possum, si iubes;
        etenim quo pacto id fieri soleat calleo.
CH.   tanto hercle melior.
SY.   non est mentiri meum.
CH.   fac ergo.
SY.   at heus tu, facito dum eadem haec memineris,   55
        siquid huius simile forte aliquando evenerit,
        ut sunt humana, tuos ut faciat filius.
CH.   non usus veniet, spero.

---

536   oportebant Σ: oportebat A.
541   ille haec v, Bentley : illa haec Eugr. : illaec ADGPCFE.
543   hic A : hinc Σ.

92

| CH. | You're asking me that? He should have hit on something, devised some trick or other by which the young man would have something to give his lady-love, and saved this troublesome old man in spite of himself. | 535 |

CH. You're asking me that? He should have hit on something, devised some trick or other by which the young man would have something to give his lady-love, and saved this troublesome old man in   535 spite of himself.

SY. You're not being serious.

CH. That's what he should have done, Syrus.

SY. What! Tell me, do you approve of slaves who deceive their masters?

CH. In the right situation, yes, I do.

SY. And quite right, too.

CH. Because, you see, that's often the cure for grievous ills; in   540 this instance this man's only son would have stayed at home.

SY. *(aside)* I don't know whether he's talking in jest or in earnest - but it puts me in the frame of mind to have a bit more fun.

CH. What's he waiting for now, Syrus? Waiting till the boy goes away again, because he can't support her expenses? Isn't he devising   545 some ploy to use against the old man?

SY. He's pretty stupid.

CH. Then you ought to give him a helping hand, for the young man's sake.

SY. I can easily do so if you tell me to; the fact is I know quite a bit about how that sort of thing's usually done.

CH. So much the better man for the job, my goodness.

SY. It's not my way to tell lies.

CH. Get on with it, then.   550

SY. But, listen, make sure you remember these words of yours if it turns out one day - seeing what human nature is - that your own son does something similar.

CH. The need won't arise, I hope.

93

SY.   spero hercle ego quoque,
        neque eo nunc dico quo quicquam illum senserim;
        sed siquid, nequid. quae sit eius aetas vides,   55!
        et ne ego te, si usus veniat, magnifice, Chreme,
        tractare possim.
CH.   de istoc, quom usus venerit,
        videbimus quid opus sit; nunc istuc age.
SY.   numquam commodius umquam erum audivi loqui,
        nec quom male facere crederem mi impunius   56▪
        licere. quisnam a nobis egreditur foras?

III iii   CHREMES CLITIPHO SYRVS

CH.   quid istuc, quaeso? qui istic mos est, Clitipho? itane fieri
                                                               [oportet?
CLIT.   quid ego feci?
CH.   vidin ego te modo manum in sinum huic meretrici
        inserere?
SY.   acta haec res est; perii.
CLIT.   mene?
CH.   hisce oculis; ne nega.
        facis adeo indigne iniuriam illi, qui non abstineas manum.   56▪
        nam istaec quidem contumelia est,
        hominem amicum recipere ad te atque eius amicam subigitare.
        vel here in vino quam inmodestus fuisti ...
SY.   factum.
CH.   ... quam molestus!
        ut equidem, ita me di ament, metui quid futurum denique esset!
        novi ego amantis; animum advortunt graviter quae non censeas.   5▪
CLIT.   at mihi fides apud hunc est nil me istius facturum, pater.

554   quo A : quod Σ, Eugr.
562   qui Iov., DG : quid AF^{2}E^1 : quis PCF^{1}E^2, Eugr.
568   here A : heri Iov.,Σ, Eugr.
570   amantis; animum Paumier, Umpfenbach : amantium animum; **codd.**, Kauer-Lindsay.

SY.   Of course, I hope so too, and I'm not saying it now because I've
      realized he's up to something; but if he does, then don't. You   555
      see how young he is. And I could certainly manage you superbly,
      Chremes, if the need arose.

CH.   As to that, we'll see what has to be done when the need does
      arise. For now, you see to it. *(He goes into his house.)*

SY.   I've never ever heard the master talking more agreeably, and   560
      there's never been a time when I felt I was being allowed to do a
      spot of mischief more safely. Whoever's coming out of our house?

(Chremes comes out of his house again, dragging Clitipho with him.)

III 3

CH.   What's all this, then? What sort of behaviour's this, Clitipho?
      Is this the way you ought to carry on?

CLIT. What have I done?

CH.   Did I see you just now slipping your hand inside that woman's
      dress?

SY.   *(aside)* It's all over; I'm done for.

CLIT. Me?

CH.   Yes, you - with my own eyes; don't deny it. You're wronging   565
      your friend quite disgracefully in not keeping your hands off.
      It really is an insult, to take a friend into your house and
      interfere with his mistress. For instance, how lewd you were
      yesterday when you were drunk ...

SY.   *(aside)* That's true.

CH.   ... and how obnoxious! Heaven knows, I was afraid of what would
      happen in the end! I know lovers; they take offence at what you   570
      wouldn't think they would.

CLIT. But my friend trusts me not to do any of that, father.

95

CH.	esto; at certe concedas aliquo ab ore eorum aliquantisper.
	multa fert lubido; ea facere prohibet tua praesentia.
	ego de me facio coniecturam; nemo est meorum amicorum hodie
	apud quem expromere omnia mea occulta, Clitipho, audeam. 57!
	apud alium prohibet dignitas; apud alium ipsius facti pudet,
	ne ineptus, ne protervos videar; quod illum facere credito.
	sed nostrum est intellegere utquomque atque ubiquomque opus sit
	[obsequi.
SY.	quid istic narrat?
CLIT.	perii!
SY.	Clitipho, haec ego praecipio tibi?
	hominis frugi et temperantis functu's officium?
CLIT.	tace, sodes! 58(
SY.	recte sane.
CLIT.	Syre, pudet me.
SY.	credo; neque id iniuria; quin
	mihi molestum est.
CLIT.	perdis hercle.
SY.	verum dico quod videtur.
CLIT.	nonne accedam ad illos?
CH.	eho, quaeso, una accedundi via est?
SY.	actum est; hic prius se indicarit quam ego argentum effecero.
	Chreme, vin tu homini stulto mi auscultare?
CH.	quid faciam?
SY.	iube hunc 58!
	abire hinc aliquo.
CLIT.	quo ego hinc abeam?
SY.	quo lubet. da illis locum;
	abi deambulatum.
CLIT.	deambulatum? quo?

---

572 at D²FE, Eugr. : ad APC : ac D¹G.
581 CLIT. A : CH. Σ.
582 perdis A : pergin Σ.
583 nonne Iov., DPCFE : non A.

CH.	Granted, but at least you might go off somewhere out of their sight for a bit. Many things come naturally to lovers; your presence stops them from indulging in them. This is something I assume from my own case; today there's not one of my friends before whom I'd dare reveal all my secrets, Clitipho. In front of one my position prevents me; in front of another I'm ashamed of the actual deed, for fear of seeming silly or indecent; you must realize that that friend of yours does just the same. It's our place to understand when and where we must humour him.	575
SY.	*(to Clitipho, as he comes across to join them)* What's he saying?	
CLIT.	*(realizing that Syrus has overheard the conversation)* Damn it!	
SY.	Clitipho, is this how I've been telling you to behave? Was this the part for an honest and decent man to play?	580
CLIT.	Shut up, won't you?	
SY.	Oh, very nice!	
CLIT.	Syrus, I'm sorry.	
SY.	I suppose you are - and quite right too; in fact, it's really annoying for me.	
CLIT.	Heavens, you'll be the death of me!	
SY.	I'm only telling you what seems to me to be the truth.	
CLIT.	Can't I go near them?	
CH.	Oh, I ask you, is there only one way of going near people?	
SY.	*(aside)* That's done it; Clitipho'll have given himself away before I've got the money. *(To Chremes.)* Chremes, are you willing to listen to me, stupid though I am?	585
CH.	What should I do?	
SY.	Tell this son of yours to go off somewhere.	
CLIT.	Where to?	
SY.	Where you like. Give them a bit of breathing space; go for a walk.	
CLIT.	For a walk? Where to?	

SY.   vah! quasi desit locus!
       abi sane istac, istorsum, quovis.
CH.   recte dicit; censeo.
CLIT.   di te eradicent, Syre, qui me hinc extrudis!
SY.   at
       tu pol tibi istas posthac comprimito manus!   590
       censen vero? quid illum porro credas facturum, Chreme,
       nisi eum, quantum tibi opis di dant, servas, castigas, mones?
CH.   ego istuc curabo.
SY.   atqui nunc, ere, tibi istic adservandus est.
CH.   fiet.
SY.   si sapias; nam mihi iam minus minusque obtemperat.
CH.   quid tu? ecquid de illo quod dudum tecum egi egisti, Syre, aut   595
       repperisti tibi quod placeat an non?
SY.   de fallacia
       dicis? est; inveni nuper quandam.
CH.   frugi es. cedo, quid est?
SY.   dicam, verum ut aliud ex alio incidit.
CH.   quidnam, Syre?
SY.   pessuma haec est meretrix.
CH.   ita videtur.
SY.   immo si scias!
       vah! vide quod inceptet facinus. fuit quaedam anus Corinthia   600
       hic; huic drachumarum haec argenti mille dederat mutuom.
CH.   quid tum?
SY.   ea mortua est; reliquit filiam adulescentulam.
       ea relicta huic arraboni est pro illo argento.

589-90 Syre, qui me hinc extrudis. SY. at | tu pol ... Craig : Syre, qui me hinc
            extrudis. | SY. at tu pol ... A.
   590   pol A : om. Σ.
   591   credas A : credis Σ, Eugr.
   593   nova scaena F.
   595   egi del. Iov.
   596   an non Guyet, edd. : an nondum etiam codd.
   597   nuper quandam A : quandam nuper Σ.
   600   vah A : hoc D^2G^2PCFE.
   601   hic om. A.
   602   ea om. A.

                              98

SY.	Huh! As if there was a shortage of places to go! Just go away; this way, that way, anywhere.	
CH.	He's quite right in what he says; I think so too.	
CLIT.	Blast you, Syrus, for shoving me out of here! *(He goes off to the audience's left.)*	

SY.	*(calling after him)* And keep those hands of yours under control	590
	in future. *(To Chremes.)* Is that what you really think? What do you suppose he'll do in future, Chremes, if you don't watch him, reprimand him and admonish him with all the power heaven gives you?	
CH.	I'll be taking care of that.	
SY.	But you must keep an eye on him *now*, sir.	
CH.	It'll be done.	
SY.	Yes, if you're wise, because he's less and less obedient to me these days.	

CH.	And what have you been up to? Have you done anything about that	595
	business I discussed with you a little while ago, Syrus? Have you hit on anything which might appeal to you, or not?	
SY.	About the trick, you mean? Yes, there is something; I thought of one just now.	
CH.	You're an excellent fellow. Tell me, what is it?	
SY.	I'll tell you, but in the right order, point by point.	
CH.	What on earth do you mean, Syrus?	
SY.	This mistress of his is a very bad lot.	
CH.	She seems so.	

SY.	If only you did but know! Just you consider what an outrageous	600
	plan she's embarking on. There was an old woman from Corinth living round here, and Bacchis had given her a thousand drachmas in silver on loan.	
CH.	What then?	
SY.	The old woman died and left a young daughter; and *she* was left with Bacchis as security for the money.	

CH.   intellego.
SY.   hanc secum huc adduxit, ea quae est nunc apud uxorem tuam.
CH.   quid tum?
SY.   Cliniam orat sibi uti nunc det; illam illi tamen   605
       post daturum; mille nummum poscit.
CH.   et poscit quidem?
SY.   hui!
       dubium id est? ego sic putavi.
CH.   quid nunc facere cogitas?
SY.   egon? ad Menedemum ibo; dicam hanc esse captam ex Caria
       ditem et nobilem; si redimat, magnum inesse in ea lucrum.
CH.   erras.
SY.   quid ita?
CH.   pro Menedemo nunc tibi ego respondeo: 610
       "non emo"; quid ages?
SY.   optata loquere.
CH.   qui?
SY.   non est opus.
CH.   non opus est?
SY.   non hercle vero.
CH.   qui istuc miror.
SY.   iam scies.
CH.   mane, mane, quid est quod tam a nobis graviter crepuerunt fores?

---

605   uti nunc AD^{1}G^{1}E^2 : uti id nunc D^{2}G^{2}PCFE^1.
606   daturum D^{2}GP^{2}F^{2}E : daturam AD^{1}P^{1}CF^1.
607   ego sic putavi **Syro continuat** A : **Chremeti trib.** Σ.
610   nunc tibi ego A : nunc ego tibi DG : ego nunc tibi CF: ego tibi P : nunc tibi E.
611   ages D^{1}G^1 : agis AD^{2}G^{2}P^{1}CF^{1}E : ais P^{2}F^2.
       non est opus **Syro trib.** A : **Chremeti continuant** Iov., Σ.
612   SY. non ... CH. non ... SY. qui ... CH. iam ... Σ.
613   **Chremeti trib.** G, Kauer-Lindsay : **Syro** ADPCFE.

CH.	I see.
SY.	It's this girl that Bacchis has brought here with her - the one who's now inside with your wife.
CH.	And?

605

SY.	Bacchis is asking Clinia to give her the money now, and says she'll then give him the girl; she's demanding the thousand drachmas.
CH.	Demanding, is she?
SY.	Huh! Is there any doubt about it? That's what *I* thought she was doing.
CH.	What are you considering doing now?
SY.	Me? I'll go to Menedemus and say she's been abducted from Caria and is rich and nobly born - and that, if he were to buy her, there's a handsome profit to be made from her.
CH.	You're wrong there.

610

SY.	Why so?
CH.	I'm giving you the answer now as if I was Menedemus: "I'm not buying her." Now what will you do?
SY.	You're telling me just what I want to hear.
CH.	How's that?
SY.	There's no need for him to.
CH.	No need?
SY.	Good heavens no, really.
CH.	I wonder how that can be.
SY.	You'll know very shortly.
CH.	Wait, wait a minute; why such noisy creaking from our door?

(SOSTRATA, *Chremes' wife, and an elderly* NURSE *come out of Chremes' house. They are both in a state of some excitement, and at first fail to notice the presence of Chremes and Syrus.*)

101

ACTVS IV

IV i   SOSTRATA CHREMES NVTRIX SYRVS

SO.   nisi me animus fallit, hic profecto est anulus quem ego suspicor,
      is quicum exposita est gnata.
CH.   quid volt sibi, Syre, haec oratio?   61?
SO.   quid est? isne tibi videtur?
NV.   dixi equidem, ubi mi ostendisti, ilico
      eum esse.
SO.   at ut satis contemplata modo sis, mea nutrix.
NV.   satis.
SO.   abi nunciam intro atque illa si iam laverit mihi nuntia.
      hic ego virum interea opperibor.
SY.   te volt; videas quid velit.
      nescioquid tristis est; non temere est; timeo quid sit.
CH.   quid siet? 62(
      ne ista hercle magno iam conatu magnas nugas dixerit.
SO.   ehem, mi vir!
CH.   ehem, mea uxor!
SO.   te ipsum quaero.
CH.   loquere quid velis.
SO.   primum hoc te oro, nequid credas me advorsum edictum tuom
      facere esse ausam.
CH.   vin me istuc tibi, etsi incredibile est, credere?
      credo.
SY.   nescioquid peccati portat haec purgatio.   62?
SO.   meministin me gravidam et mihi te maxumo opere edicere,
      si puellam parerem, nolle tolli?
CH.   scio quid feceris;
      sustulisti.

---

624   vin A : vis Σ.
626   me Bentley : me esse **codd.**, Eugr., Kauer-Lindsay.
      edicere Iov. : dicere AD^1 : interminatum D^{2}G^{2}PCFE : interminatum dicere G^1(?).

IV 1

SO.   Unless my mind's playing tricks on me, this is definitely the
       ring I think it is, the one my daughter was exposed with.   615
CH.   What do these words of hers mean, Syrus?
SO.   What's the truth of the matter? Does it seem to you to be it?
NU.   Yes, when you showed it to me, I told you straightaway it was the
       one.
SO.   But make sure you've examined it closely enough, nurse dear.
NU.   I have, quite closely enough.
SO.   Go indoors at once, and tell me if she's finished her bath by
       now.   Meanwhile, I'll wait here for my husband. *(The nurse
       returns into Chremes' house.)*
SY.   It's you she's after; see what she wants. She's a bit upset,   620
       and there must be some reason.   I'm worried what it's all about.
CH.   What it's all about? Heavens, I tell you, very soon with a
       mammoth show of effort she'll come out with a mammoth piece of
       nonsense.
SO.   *(noticing Chremes for the first time)*   Goodness, my dear husband!
CH.   *(mockingly imitating her)*   Goodness, my dear wife!
SO.   You're just the person I'm looking for.
CH.   Tell me what it is you want.
SO.   First, I beg you not to think that I've dared do anything
       contrary to your instructions.
CH.   You want me to believe that of you, even if it's unbelievable?
       All right, I do.   625
SY.   *(aside)* This defensive talk implies she's done something wrong.
SO.   Do you remember that I was pregnant and that you gave me the
       strictest orders that, if I had a girl, she wasn't to be accepted
       into our family?
CH.   I know what you did; you accepted it.

SY.   sic est factum; domina ego, erus damno auctus est.
SO.   minime; sed erat hic Corinthia anus haud inpura; ei dedi
       exponendam.
CH.   o Iuppiter! tantam esse in animo inscitiam!   630
SO.   perii; quid ego feci?
CH.   rogitas?
SO.   si peccavi, mi Chreme,
       insciens feci.
CH.   id equidem ego, si tu neges, certo scio,
       te inscientem atque inprudentem dicere ac facere omnia.
       tot peccata in hac re ostendis. nam iam primum, si meum
       imperium exsequi voluisses, interemptam oportuit,   635
       non simulare mortem verbis, re ipsa spem vitae dare.
       at id omitto; misericordia, animus maternus; sino.
       quam bene vero abs te prospectum est quod voluisti cogita!
       nempe anui illi prodita abs te filia est planissume,
       per te vel uti quaestum faceret vel uti veniret palam.   640
       credo, id cogitasti: "quidvis satis est dum vivat modo."
       quid cum illis agas qui neque ius neque bonum atque aequom sciunt?
       melius peius, prosit obsit, nil vident nisi quod lubet.
SO.   mi Chreme, peccavi, fateor; vincor. nunc hoc te obsecro,
       quanto tuos est animus natu gravior, ignoscentior,   645
       ut meae stultitiae in iustitia tua sit aliquid praesidi.
CH.   scilicet equidem istuc factum ignoscam; verum, Sostrata,
       male docet te mea facilitas multa. sed istuc quidquid est
       qua hoc occeptum est causa loquere.

628   SY. sic est factum; domina ... Σ : SO. sic est factum. SY. domina ... A.
631   rogitas A : at rogitas Σ.
632   equidem A : quidem DGPCFE, Eugr.
       si A : etsi Σ, Eugr.
638   quod Bothe : quid **codd.**
644   hoc te APCE : te hoc D²G : hoc **om.** D¹F.
646   in **om.** D²GPCFE.

SY.   *(aside)* That's what happened; so I've got the bonus of another mistress, and my master's got the bonus of a thumping loss.

SO.   Certainly not, but there was an old lady from Corinth living round here, quite a respectable person; I gave the child to her to be exposed.   630

CH.   Good god! To think there could be so much stupidity in a person's mind!

SO.   Oh dear, what have I done?

CH.   You ask me that?

SO.   If I did anything wrong, Chremes, I did it unwittingly.

CH.   Of this I'm perfectly certain, even if you should deny it - that you say and do *everything* unwittingly and unknowingly. You   635
display so many faults in what you did. To begin with, if you'd really been willing to carry out my instructions, the child should have been killed, and you shouldn't have pretended, by what you said, that it was dead, while actually giving it some chance of life. But I let that pass; there was your sense of pity, your feeling as a mother; I accept that. But just think how well you made provision for your plan! Why, your daughter was totally abandoned to that old woman, so that, as far as you were   640
concerned, she could earn a living on the streets or be put up for public sale. You thought like this, I suppose: "Anything's good enough, provided she just stays alive." What dealings can one have with people who have no idea of what's right or good or fair? Better or worse, advantage or disadvantage, they see nothing but what they like to see.

SO.   Chremes my dear, I've done wrong, I admit; you've convinced me. I beg you now - in as much as your mind is more sensible because   645
of your years, and more prone to forgive - that my foolishness may find some refuge in your sense of fairness.

CH.   I suppose I'll forgive what you've done; but my easy-going nature's a bad teacher for you, Sostrata, over many things. Still, out with it, whatever it is that prompted this whole business.

105

SO.   ut stultae et misere omnes sumus

religiosae, quom exponendam do illi, de digito anulum   6⁵

detraho et eum dico ut una cum puella exponeret,

si moreretur, ne expers partis esset de nostris bonis.

CH. istuc recte; conservasti te atque illam.

SO.   is hic est anulus.

CH. unde habes?

SO.   quam Bacchis secum adduxit adulescentulam ...

SY.   hem!

CH. quid illa narrat?

SO.   ... ea lavatum dum it, servandum mihi dedit.   65⁵

animum non advorti primum; sed postquam aspexi, ilico

cognovi, ad te exsilui.

CH.   quid nunc suspicare aut invenis

de illa?

SO.   nescio, nisi ex ipsa quaeras unde hunc habuerit,

si potis est reperiri.

SY.   interii; plus spei video quam volo.

nostra est, si ita est.

CH.   vivitne illa quoi tu dederas?

SO.   nescio.   66⁰

CH. quid renuntiavit olim?

SO.   fecisse id quod iusseram.

CH. nomen mulieris cedo quid sit, ut quaeratur.

SO.   Philterae.

SY. ipsa est. mirum ni illa salva est et ego perii.

CH.   Sostrata,

sequere me intro hac.

SO.   ut praeter spem evenit! quam timui male

ne nunc animo ita esses duro ut olim in tollendo, Chreme! 66⁵

---

655   quid illa narrat? **Syro continuant** D²GF¹.

      illa A : ea Σ.

656   primum AE : primo DGPCF.

661   CH. quid renuntiavit olim? SO. fecisse id ... Iov., D¹ : CH. quid renuntiavit
      fecisse? SO. id ... AD²GPCFE.

665   in tollendo A : in tollenda Iov., D²GPCFE : intellegenda D¹.

SO. Seeing how silly and wretchedly superstitious all we mothers are,   650
when I gave her to the old woman to be exposed, I took a ring
from my finger and told her to abandon it with the child, so that
if she died she shouldn't be without some share in our
possessions.

CH. *(sarcastically)* Well done! You salved your conscience and you
saved the child!

SO. *(producing a ring and showing it to Chremes)* This is that ring.

CH. Where have you got it from?

SO. The young woman Bacchis brought with her ...

SY. *(aside)* What?

CH. What's she got to say?   655

SO. ... gave it to me to look after while she went for a bath. I
didn't take any notice of it at first, but when I looked at it I
recognised it straightaway and rushed outside to you.

CH. What are your suspicions now, or what have you found out about
the girl?

SO. I don't know, except that you could ask her where she got it, if
we can find that out.

SY. *(aside)* That's done it! I see rather more grounds for hope in
this than I like. If it's the case, she's one of us.   660

CH. Is the woman you gave her to still alive?

SO. I don't know.

CH. What did she tell you at the time?

SO. That she'd done what I told her to.

CH. Tell me what the woman's name is, so we can make some enquiries.

SO. Philtera.

SY. *(aside)* That's the one. It's a miracle if the girl's not saved
and I'm not done for!

CH. Follow me indoors, Sostrata.

SO. How much better this has turned out than I expected! How
terribly afraid I was that you'd be as hard-hearted now, Chremes,   665
as you were long ago over accepting the child!

CH.   non licet hominem esse saepe ita ut volt, si res non sinit.
        nunc ita tempus est mi ut cupiam filiam; olim nil minus.

IV ii   SYRVS

SY.   nisi me animus fallit multum, haud multum a me aberit infortunium;
        ita hac re in angustum oppido nunc meae coguntur copiae,
        nisi aliquid video ne esse amicam hanc gnati resciscat senex.   67
        nam quod de argento sperem aut posse postulem me fallere,
        nil est; triumpho si licet me latere tecto abscedere.
        crucior bolum tantum mi ereptum tam desubito e faucibus.
        quid agam? aut quid comminiscar? ratio de integro ineunda est mihi.
        nil tam difficile est quin quaerendo investigari possiet.   67
        quid si hoc nunc sic incipiam? nilst. quid si sic? tantundem
                                                [egero.

        at sic opinor. non potest. immo optume! euge, habeo optumam!
        retraham hercle, opinor, ad me idem illud fugitivom argentum tamen.

IV iii   CLINIA SYRVS

CLIN. nulla mihi res posthac potest iam intervenire tanta
        quae mi aegritudinem adferat; tanta haec laetitia oborta est.   68
        dedo patri me nunciam, ut frugalior sim quam volt.
SY.   nil me fefellit; cognita est, quantum audio huius verba.
        istuc tibi ex sententia tua obtigisse laetor.
CLIN. o mi Syre, audisti, obsecro?

---

666   si res Σ: si ita res A.
669   hac re AD¹PC¹ : hercle D²GC²FE.
         angustum Σ, Eugr. : angusto A.
673   tantum mihi **codd.** : mihi tantum Arusian. 468.
         desubito Arusian. 468 : desubio A : subito Σ.
676   nilst Kauer-Lindsay : nihil est **codd.**
         quid si sic **codd.** : si **om.** Umpfenbach.
678   opinor ad me idem illud PCFE : illuc opinor ad me D¹G : opinor idem ad me ego
         hodie A : opinor ad me idem ego illuc hodie Kauer-Lindsay, Marouzeau, **qui iamb**
         dim. catal. et iamb. sen. ex hoc versu faciunt.
679   **nulla nova scaena** E.   108

CH. Often a man can't be as he likes, if circumstances don't let him. Now's the sort of time I'd like a daughter; previously there was nothing I wanted less.

(Sostrata follows Chremes into Chremes' house.)

IV 2

SY. Unless my mind's playing tricks on me a lot, a lot of trouble won't be very far away. Because of this my resources are pushed into a very tight corner now - unless, that is, I can see some   670 way of stopping the old man tumbling to the fact that this woman is his son's girl-friend. As for my hopes about the money or my expectation that I'd be able to trick him, that's come to nothing; it'll be a triumph if I can get away from here with my flanks protected. It's agony for me that such a dainty titbit's been snatched so abruptly from my lips. What can I do? What can I dream up? I must think out a plan all over again. Nothing's   675 so tough it can't be tracked down by a bit of investigation. What if I start off this way now? ... That's no good. What if this way? ... I'll achieve just as much there. This way, I think. ... Impossible. ... No, excellent! Hooray, I've got a splendid scheme! By god, I really think I'll catch that runaway money after all!

(Clinia comes out of Chremes' house in a state of high excitement.)

IV 3

CLIN. From now on nothing can happen to me that's serious enough to   680 cause me any anxiety - that's how great this joy is that's burst upon me! I surrender myself to my father's wishes at once, so that I'll be better behaved than he wants me to.

SY. *(aside)* I've not been deceived in anything; the girl's been recognised, from what I hear him saying. *(To Clinia.)* I'm so pleased that this has turned out to your liking.

CLIN. Oh Syrus, dear Syrus, have you heard then?

SY.   quidni, qui usque una adfuerim?

CLIN. quoi aeque audisti commode quicquam evenisse?

SY.   nulli.   685

CLIN. atque ita me di ament ut ego nunc non tam meapte causa
laetor quam illius; quam ego scio esse honore quovis dignam.

SY. ita credo. sed nunc, Clinia, age, da te mihi vicissim;
nam amici quoque res est videnda in tuto ut conlocetur,
nequid de amica nunc senex.

CLIN.   o Iuppiter!

SY.   quiesce.   690

CLIN. Antiphila mea nubet mihi.

SY.   sicin mi interloquere?

CLIN. quid faciam? Syre mi, gaudeo; fer me.

SY.   fero hercle vero.

CLIN. deorum vitam apti sumus.

SY.   frustra operam, opinor, sumo.

CLIN. loquere; audio.

SY.   at iam hoc non ages.

CLIN.   agam.

SY.   videndum est, inquam,
amici quoque res, Clinia, tui in tuto ut conlocetur.   695
nam si nunc a nobis abis et Bacchidem hic relinquis,
senex resciscet ilico esse amicam hanc Clitiphonis;
si abduxeris, celabitur, itidem ut celata adhuc est.

CLIN. at enim istoc nil est magis, Syre, meis nuptiis advorsum.
nam quo ore appellabo patrem? tenes quid dicam?

SY.   quidni?   700

CLIN. quid dicam? quam causam adferam?

SY.   qui nolo mentiare;
aperte ita ut res sese habet narrato.

---

689   in tuto Iov., Σ : in tutum A, Kauer-Lindsay (cf. 695).

693   operam opinor D²PCFE : operam opinor hanc AD¹G : operam opino hanc Kauer-Lindsay.

694   ages D¹GPCFE : agis A.

697   senex A : noster Σ.

701   quid Don. **Eu.** 212 : quid D²PC¹F² : quin AD¹GC²F¹E, Eugr.
       mentiare D¹GPCFE, Don. **Eu.** 212, Eugr. : mentiaris AD².

SY.	Naturally; I was here with them all through.
CLIN.	Have you ever heard of anyone having anything happen to him so agreeably? 685
SY.	Nobody.
CLIN.	Heaven knows, I'm not so much delighted for my own sake now as for hers, because I know she deserves any token of esteem you can think of.
SY.	I don't doubt it. But come on, it's your turn now, Clinia; make your services available to me. We must see to it that your friend's affairs are put on a sure footing too, so that old 690 Chremes doesn't find out anything about his mistress.
CLIN.	Oh, god in heaven!
SY.	Do calm down.
CLIN.	My Antiphila's going to marry me.
SY.	Are you going to keep interrupting me like this?
CLIN.	What can I do? My dear Syrus, I'm overjoyed; you must put up with me.
SY.	I certainly *am* putting up with you.
CLIN.	We've won a life like the life of the gods!
SY.	I think I'm wasting my time.
CLIN.	Carry on; I'm listening.
SY.	But in a minute you won't be paying attention.
CLIN.	I will be.
SY.	I tell you we must see to it, Clinia, that the affairs of that 695 friend of yours are put on a sure footing too. If you move out of our house now, leaving Bacchis behind here, our old man will immediately tumble to the fact that she's Clitipho's mistress; but if you take her with you, your friend's position will be kept a secret, just as it's been kept a secret up to now.
CLIN.	But, Syrus, there's nothing that's more detrimental to my getting married than that. How shall I have the face to speak to my 700 father? Have you got anything I can say to him?
SY.	Of course I have.
CLIN.	What can I say? What reason can I put forward?
SY.	Oh, I don't want you to tell lies. Tell him quite openly, exactly as things stand.

111

CLIN.	quid ais?
SY.	iubeo;

      illam te amare et velle uxorem, hanc esse Clitiphonis.

CLIN. bonam atque iustam rem oppido imperas et factu facilem.

      et scilicet iam me hoc voles patrem exorare ut celet   705

      senem vostrum?

SY.   immo ut recta via rem narret ordine omnem.

CLIN.   hem!

      satis sanus es et sobrius? tuquidem illum plane perdis.

      nam qui ille poterit esse in tuto, dic mihi?

SY.   huic equidem consilio palmam do; hic me magnifice ecfero,

      qui vim tantam in me et potestatem habeam tantae astutiae   710

      vera dicendo ut eos ambos fallam; ut, quom narret senex

      voster nostro esse istam amicam gnati, non credat tamen.

CLIN. at enim spem istoc pacto rursum nuptiarum omnem eripis;

      nam dum amicam hanc meam esse credet, non committet filiam.

      tu fors quid me fiat parvi pendis, dum illi consulas.   715

SY. quid, malum, me aetatem censes velle id adsimularier?

      unus est dies dum argentum eripio; pax; nil amplius.

CLIN. tantum sat habes? quid tum, quaeso, si hoc pater resciverit?

SY. quid si redeo ad illos qui aiunt: "quid si nunc caelum ruat?"

CLIN. metuo quid agam.

SY.   metuis? quasi non ea potestas sit tua   720

      quo velis in tempore ut te exsolvas, rem facias palam!

CLIN. age, age, transducatur Bacchis.

SY.   optume ipsa exit foras.

---

707   satis A : satin Iov., Σ.

      et A : aut DGPCF[1]   an F[2]E.

      perdis A : prodis Σ.

712   esse istam A : istam esse Σ, Kauer-Lindsay.

713   rursum A : rursus Σ.

714   credet Σ : credat A.

715   fors Guyet : fortasse **codd.**

716   aetatem AD[1]P[1]C[1] : tandem P[2]C[2]FE : aetatem tandem D[2] : **om.** G.

CLIN. What!

SY. That's what I'm telling you to do; say you're in love with Antiphila and want to get married to her, and that Bacchis belongs to Clitipho.

CLIN. That's a perfectly fair and just instruction, and one that's easy to carry out. And I suppose you'll now be wanting me to beg my father to keep it a secret from your old man?   705

SY. On the contrary, I want you to ask him to tell the whole ⁻story straight out, from start to finish.

CLIN. What? Are you quite sane and sober? You're completely ruining Clitipho. How will he be able to be "on a sure footing" then, answer me that?

SY. This is my prize-winning plan, and I'm terribly proud of it - I who've got so much power inside me, and the capacity for so much   710 cunning, that I can deceive both of them just by telling the truth; result - when your old fellow tells ours that Bacchis is Clitipho's mistress, he simply won't believe it.

CLIN. But that way you're again removing all hope of my getting married. As long as Chremes thinks Bacchis is *my* mistress, he won't entrust his daughter to me. Perhaps while you're looking   715 to Clitipho's interests you're putting little value on what becomes of me.

SY. Damn it, why are you imagining that I want this pretence to be kept up for ever? It's just a matter of a single day while I extract the money; that's all, nothing more.

CLIN. Do you think that's long enough? Tell me, what if my father finds out?

SY. What if I refer to people who keep saying: "What if the sky falls in?"

CLIN. I'm afraid of what I'm to do.   720

SY. Afraid? As if you haven't got the opportunity to extricate yourself any time you like, and reveal the truth!

CLIN. All right, all right; Bacchis can be brought across to our house.

SY. She's coming outside herself now - what a piece of luck!

(Bacchis comes out of Chremes' house, accompanied by her maid, PHRYGIA.)

113

BA.   satis pol proterve me Syri promissa huc induxerunt,
         decem minas quas mihi dare pollicitust. quod si is nunc me
         deceperit, saepe obsecrans me ut veniam frustra veniet;   725
         aut quom venturam dixero et constituero, quom is certe
         renuntiarit, Clitipho quom in spe pendebit animi,
         decipiam ac non veniam, Syrus mihi tergo poenas pendet.
CLIN. satis scite promittit tibi.
SY.   atqui tu hanc iocari credis?
         faciet nisi caveo.
BA.   dormiunt; ego pol istos commovebo.   730
         mea Phrygia, audisti modo iste homo quam villam demonstravit
         Charini?
PH.   audivi.
BA.   proxumam esse huic fundo ad dextram?
PH.   memini.
BA.   curriculo percurre; apud eum miles Dionysia agitat.
SY.   quid inceptat?
BA.   dic me hic oppido esse invitam atque adservari,
         verum aliquo pacto verba me his daturam esse et venturam.   735
SY.   perii hercle. Bacchis, mane, mane! quo mittis istam, quaeso?
         iube maneat.
BA.   i!
SY.   quin est paratum argentum.
BA.   quin ego maneo.
SY.   atqui iam dabitur.
BA.   ut lubet. num ego insto?

---

723   induxerunt AP[1]CF : adduxerunt DGP[2]E.
724   quod si is Iov., Σ: quod ni A : quod si Kauer-Lindsay.
725   **post** veniam **dist.** Kauer-Lindsay.
727   renuntiarit Σ : renuntiabit A.
       in **om.** Σ.
731   audisti A : audistin Σ.
736   istam ADG : istanc PCFE, Kauer-Lindsay.
737   ego maneo A : ego hic maneo Σ.

114

BA.	Syrus has been pretty impudent in enticing me here with his promises - the ten minae he promised to give me. If he's misled me now, he'll have many a fruitless journey in future when he begs me to come. Or else, when I say I'll come and have made the arrangements, when he's definitely brought back the message and when Clitipho's on tenterhooks with expectation, I'll frustrate him and not turn up, and Syrus will give me the satisfaction of being punished with a flogging.
CLIN.	*(to Syrus)* That's a really neat little promise she's making you!
SY.	You think she's joking? She'll do it if I don't watch out.
BA.	*(quietly, aside to Phrygia)* They're only half-awake. I'll put a bit of life into them. *(Aloud, so Clinia and Syrus can hear.)* Phrygia my dear, did you hear which house that fellow pointed out recently as Charinus's?
PH.	Yes, I did.
BA.	Did he say it was the one next to this farm over to the right?
PH.	That's what I recall.
BA.	Run over there quickly. That's where my soldier's celebrating the Dionysia.
SY.	What's she up to?
BA.	Tell him I'm here completely against my will and being watched, but that somehow or other I'll give this crowd the slip and come to him.
SY.	Oh god, that's me done for! Wait, Bacchis, wait. Where are you sending this girl of yours, please? Tell her to wait.
BA.	*(to Phrygia)* Off you go! *(Phrygia starts to move off to the audience's left.)*
SY.	But the money's ready.
BA.	Then I'll wait. *(Phrygia stops and returns.)*
SY.	You'll be given it now.
BA.	Just as you like. *(Sweetly.)* I'm not pressing you, am I?

725

730

735

SY.	at scin quid sodes?
BA.	quid?
SY.	transeundum est nunc tibi ad Menedemum et tua pompa eo transducenda est.
BA.	quam rem agis, scelus?
SY.	egon? argentum cudo 740 quod tibi dem.
BA.	dignam me putas quam inludas?
SY.	non est temere.
BA.	etiamne tecum hic res mihi est?
SY.	minime; tuom tibi reddo.
BA.	eatur.
SY.	sequere hac. heus, Dromo!
DR.	quis me volt?
SY.	Syrus.
DR.	quid est rei?
SY.	ancillas omnis Bacchidis transduce huc ad vos propere.
DR.	quam ob rem?
SY.	ne quaeras; ecferant quae secum huc attulerunt. 745 sperabit sumptum sibi senex levatum esse harunc abitu; ne ille haud scit hoc paullum lucri quantum ei damnum adportet. tu nescis id quod scis, Dromo, si sapies.
DR.	mutum dices.

---

738   at **om**. A.
739   transeundum est ... ad Menedemum A : transeundum ... ad Menedemum est Σ. nunc A : **om**. PCFE : huc nunc D¹G.
745   ecferant A : et ferant Σ.
747   damnum AE : damni DGPCF.

SY.	But do you know what I'd like you to do now, please?
BA.	What?
SY.	You must move over to Menedemus' house at once, and your party must be taken across there too.

740

BA.	What are you up to, you scoundrel?
SY.	Me? I'm coining the money to give you.
BA.	Do you think I'm a worthy subject for your tricks?
SY.	The move isn't without its purpose.
BA.	Then have I any more business to discuss with you here?
SY.	No, not at all; I'm just giving you back what's yours.
BA.	Let's go then.
SY.	Follow me over here. *(He crosses to Menedemus' house and knocks.)* Hey Dromo!
DR.	*(calling from inside the house)* Who is it wants me?
SY.	Syrus.
DR.	*(appearing at the door)* What's the matter?
SY.	Bring all Bacchis's maids across here to your house, and be quick about it.
DR.	Why?

745

SY.	Don't ask questions. *(As Dromo crosses into Chremes' house, Syrus shouts after him.)* And make sure they bring out what they brought with them. *(While Syrus continues talking, Dromo re-emerges from Chremes' house, followed by Bacchis' maids with the luggage.)* Our old man will be hoping his expenses have been reduced now these women have gone, but he's certainly got no idea what a great loss this little gain will bring him. If you're wise, Dromo, you'll know nothing of what you've seen.
DR.	You'll say I've been struck dumb!

(Dromo ushers Bacchis, Phrygia and all Bacchis' other maids into Menedemus' house, and Clinia follows them inside. Almost immediately, Chremes comes out of his house.)

117

CH.	ita me di amabunt ut nunc Menedemi vicem
	miseret me tantum devenisse ad eum mali. 750
	illancin mulierem alere cum illa familia!
	etsi scio, hosce aliquot dies non sentiet,
	ita magno desiderio fuit ei filius.
	verum ubi videbit tantos sibi sumptus domi
	cotidianos fieri nec fieri modum, 755
	optabit rursum ut abeat a se filius.
	Syrum optume eccum.
SY.	cesso hunc adoriri?
CH.	Syre!
SY.	hem!
CH.	quid est?
SY.	te mihi ipsum iamdudum optabam dari.
CH.	videre egisse iam nescioquid cum sene.
SY.	de illo quod dudum? dictum factum reddidi. 760
CH.	bonan fide?
SY.	bona hercle.
CH.	non possum pati
	quin tibi caput demulceam; accede huc, Syre;
	faciam boni tibi aliquid pro istac re ac lubens.
SY.	at si scias quam scite in mentem venerit!
CH.	vah! gloriare evenisse ex sententia? 765
SY.	non hercle vero; verum dico.
CH.	dic quid est.
SY.	tui Clitiphonis esse amicam hanc Bacchidem
	Menedemo dixit Clinia, et ea gratia
	secum adduxisse ne tu id persentisceres.
CH.	probe.
SY.	dic sodes.
CH.	nimium, inquam.

---

760   SY. **om.** D[1]G : SY. dictum ... G.
        dictum factum Dziatzko, Kauer-Lindsay (cf. 904) : dictum ac factum **codd.**

CH.	Heaven knows, I'm sorry on Menedemus' account that such a load of	750
	trouble's fallen on him. Just think of maintaining that woman	
	and her gang! Still, I know he won't notice it for the next few	
	days, so great was his longing for his son. But when he sees	
	such enormous expenses being incurred in his house day in day	755
	out, with no limit set, he'll want his son to go away again.	
	Here's Syrus - how convenient.	
SY.	(aside) Why don't I tackle him now?	
CH.	Syrus!	
SY.	(feigning surprise and delight) Ah!	
CH.	What's up?	
SY.	You're just the person I've been wanting to cross my path for	
	quite a while.	
CH.	It looks as if you've already done some sort of deal with old	
	Menedemus.	
SY.	About that problem we were discussing a little while ago? It's a	760
	case of 'no sooner said than done' with me.	
CH.	Honestly?	
SY.	Honestly.	
CH.	I can't stop myself giving you a pat on the head; come over	
	here, Syrus. In return for this I'll do you a good turn, and be	
	glad to do so.	
SY.	If only you knew how ingeniously the idea came into my mind.	
CH.	Huh! Are you bragging that it turned out as you wanted?	765
SY.	Good god, no; just telling the truth.	
CH.	Tell me, what's your idea?	
SY.	Clinia's told Menedemus that this woman Bacchis is your	
	Clitipho's mistress, and that the reason he's brought her with	
	him to his place is to stop you realizing it.	
CH.	Well done!	770
SY.	Pardon?	
CH.	Extremely well done, I say.	

119

SY.   immo si scias.   770

    sed porro ausculta quod superest fallaciae;

    sese ipse dicit tuam vidisse filiam;

    eius sibi conplacitam formam, postquam aspexerit;

    hanc cupere uxorem.

CH.   modone quae inventa est?

SY.   eam;

    et quidem iubebit posci.

CH.   quam ob rem istuc, Syre?   775

    nam prorsum nil intellego.

SY.   vah! tardus es.

CH.   fortasse.

SY.   argentum dabitur ei ad nuptias,

    aurum atque vestem qui ... tenesne?

CH.   comparet?

SY.   id ipsum.

CH.   at ego illi neque do neque despondeo.

SY.   non? quam ob rem?

CH.   quam ob rem? me rogas? homini ...?

SY.   ut lubet.   780

    non ego dicebam in perpetuom ut illam illi dares,

    verum ut simulares.

CH.   non mea est simulatio;

    ita tu istaec tua misceto ne me admisceas.

    egon, quoi daturus non sum, ut ei despondeam?

SY.   credebam.

CH.   minime.

SY.   scite poterat fieri;   785

    et ego hoc, quia dudum tu tanto opere suaseras,

    eo coepi.

770   si scias A : sic satis Σ.

772   dicit A : dicet Σ.

776   prorsum A : prorsus Σ.

781   dicebam in perpetuum A ; dicebam perpetuo DG : perpetuo dicebam PCFE.

784   sum AD^2 : sim D^{1}GPCFE.

786   suaseras A : iusseras Σ, Kauer-Lindsay.

SY.   *(aside)*   If only you did but know!   *(To Chremes.)*   But just
listen to the rest of my trick.   Clinia's saying that he's seen
your daughter, that he took a fancy to her good looks as soon as
he caught sight of her, and that he wants to have her as his
wife.

CH.   My daughter who's just been found, you mean?

SY.   Yes, her.   And he's going to tell his father to ask for her hand   775
in marriage.

CH.   Why's he doing that, Syrus?   I really don't understand any of
this.

SY.   Oh, you *are* slow!

CH.   Perhaps so.

SY.   For the wedding he'll be given money, for jewelry and clothes ...
do you get it?

CH.   To be bought, you mean?

SY.   Exactly.

CH.   But I'm not giving her to him, and not betrothing her.

SY.   No?   Why?   780

CH.   Why?   You're asking me that?   To a fellow who ...?

SY.   As you wish.   I wasn't telling you to hand your daughter to him
permanently, only to pretend to.

CH.   Pretending isn't my way.   You mix your recipe in such a way that
I'm not an ingredient.   Am I to betroth her to a man I don't
intend to give her away to?

SY.   I thought you might.   785

CH.   Certainly not.

SY.   It could have been managed so cleverly.   And the only reason I
started it is because you'd been urging me to so earnestly a
little while ago.

121

CH.	credo.
SY.	ceterum equidem istuc, Chreme,
	aequi bonique facio.
CH.	atqui quam maxume
	volo te dare operam ut fiat, verum alia via.
SY.	fiat; quaeratur aliquid. sed illud quod tibi
	dixi de argento quod ista debet Bacchidi,
	id nunc reddendum est illi; neque tu scilicet
	illuc confugies; "quid mea? num mihi datum est?
	num iussi? num illa oppignerare filiam
	meam me invito potuit?" verum illuc, Chreme,
	dicunt: "ius summum saepe summa est malitia."
CH.	haud faciam.
SY.	immo aliis si licet, tibi non licet;
	†omnes te in lauta et bene acta parte putant.
CH.	quin egomet iam ad eam deferam.
SY.	immo filium
	iube potius.
CH.	quam ob rem?
SY.	quia enim in eum suspicio est
	translata amoris.
CH.	quid tum?
SY.	quia videbitur
	magis veri simile id esse, quom hic illi dabit;
	et simul conficiam facilius ego quod volo.
	ipse adeo adest; abi, ecfer argentum.
CH.	ecfero.

Line numbers in right margin: 790, 795, 800

---

788   quam A : cum D^1GP^1 : tum D^2CFE.

793   illuc A : eo nunc Σ.

796   summa est malitia AG, Eugr. : est summa malitia D^1 : summa malitia est D^2PCFE.

798   et bene acta parte putant **codd.**, Eugr. : et bene parata re putant Thierfelder : esse et bene aucta re putant Bentley : **versum del.** Guyet.

CH.	I've no doubt.
SY.	However, I regard your stand as fair and right, Chremes.
CH.	I do want you to devote all possible attention to getting it done, but in some other way.
SY.	Very well, we must look for some other solution. But what I told you about the money that old woman owes Bacchis - it's got to be paid to her now, and I'm sure you won't take refuge in this sort of argument: "What's it to do with me? The money wasn't given to me, was it? Did I give the instructions? She couldn't offer my daughter as security without my consent, could she?" It's quite true what people say, Chremes: "Strictest law is often greatest mischief."
CH.	I won't do that.
SY.	No; if others can, you can't. Everyone believes you're prosperous and well-to-do.
CH.	Well, I'll take it to her now.
SY.	Oh, no! Better tell your son to.
CH.	Why?
SY.	Because the suspicion of being her lover has been transferred to him.
CH.	And?
SY.	Because it will appear more natural when *he* gives it to her; and at the same time I'll achieve the result I want more easily. *(He looks off stage to the audience's left.)* Here's the man himself. *(To Chremes.)* Off you go; bring out the money.
CH.	Very well.

790

795

800

(Chremes goes into his house, and at the same moment Clitipho walks on from the audience's left.)

CLIT. nulla est tam facilis res quin difficilis siet,   805

quam invitus facias. vel me haec deambulatio,

quam non laboriosa, ad languorem dedit.

nec quicquam magis nunc metuo quam ne denuo

miser aliquo extrudar hinc, ne accedam ad Bacchidem.

ut te quidem omnes di deae quantum est, Syre,   810

cum istoc invento cumque incepto perduint!

huius modi mihi res semper comminiscere

ubi me excarnufices.

SY.   is tu hinc quo dignus es?

quam paene tua me perdidit protervitas!

CLIT. vellem hercle factum; ita meritu's.

SY.   meritus? quo modo?   815

ne me istuc ex te prius audisse gaudeo

quam argentum haberes quod daturus iam fui.

CLIT. quid igitur dicam tibi vis? abiisti; mihi

amicam adduxti quam non licitum est tangere.

SY. iam non sum iratus. sed scin ubi sit nunc tibi   820

tua Bacchis?

CLIT.   apud nos.

SY.   non.

CLIT.   ubi ergo?

SY.   apud Cliniam.

CLIT. perii.

SY.   bono animo es; iam argentum ad eam deferes

quod ei pollicitu's.

---

808   magis nunc AD^{2}G : nunc magis PCFE : nunc **om.** D^1.

810   deae Bentley : deaeque **codd.**

812   mihi res semper A : semper mihi res DG : res semper PCFE.

813   is tu C^{1}λ : ii tu P^{1}F^1 : i tu P^{2}F^{2}E : in tu D^2 : is A : in D^1 : ii G.

818   abiisti Kauer-Lindsay : abisti **codd.**

819   licitum est **edd.** : licitum sit A : liceat Σ.

823   pollicitus AC^1 : es pollicitus DGP^{2}C^{2}FE.

124

CLIT.   Nothing's so easy that it isn't difficult when you do it against   805
       your will. For instance, this walk of mine wasn't at all hard,
       but it's exhausted me. There's nothing I'm more afraid of now
       than being pushed off again somewhere else, poor fool, to stop me
       getting to Bacchis. May all the powers in heaven damn you,   810
       Syrus, with that plan and scheme of yours! You're for ever
       inventing tricks of this sort to torture me.

SY.   You can go to hell - where it's right and proper you should be!
       How near your brazenness came to ruining me!

CLIT.   I wish it *had* ruined you, by god; you deserved it.   815

SY.   Deserved it? How? I'm certainly glad I heard you say that
       before you'd got hold of the money I was just going to give you.

CLIT.   So what do you want me to say? You went off, you brought me my
       mistress, and I'm not allowed to touch her.

SY.   I'm not angry with you now. But do you know where your Bacchis   820
       is at this moment?

CLIT.   In our house.

SY.   She's not.

CLIT.   Where then?

SY.   At Clinia's.

CLIT.   That's me finished.

SY.   Cheer up; you'll soon be taking her the money you promised her.

CLIT.	garris. unde?	
SY.	a tuo patre.	
CLIT.	ludis fortasse me?	
SY.	ipsa re experibere.	
CLIT.	ne ego homo sum fortunatus. deamo te, Syre.	82
SY.	sed pater egreditur. cave quicquam admiratus sis	
	qua causa id fiat; obsecundato in loco;	
	quod imperabit facito; loquitor paucula.	

IV vii   CHREMES CLITIPHO SYRVS

CH.	ubi Clitipho hic est?	
SY.	"eccum me" inque.	
CLIT.	eccum hic tibi.	
CH.	quid rei esset dixti huic?	
SY.	dixi pleraque omnia.	83
CH.	cape hoc argentum ac defer.	
SY.	i! quid stas, lapis?	
	quin accipis?	
CLIT.	cedo sane.	
SY.	sequere hac me ocius.	
	tu hic nos dum eximus interea opperibere;	
	nam nil est illic quod moremur diutius.	
CH.	minas quidem iam decem habet a me filia,	83
	quas hortamentis esse nunc duco datas;	
	hasce ornamentis consequentur alterae;	
	porro haec talenta dotis adposcunt duo.	
	quam multa iniusta ac prava fiunt moribus!	

---

825   homo sum fortunatus DG : sum homo fortunatus A, Kauer-Lindsay : fortunatus homo s
      PCF : homo fortunatus sum E.

829   **nulla nova scaena** D.
      hic D^1G^1 : hinc A : nunc D^2G^2PCFE.

832   hac me A : me hac Eugr. : me hac nunc PC^2F : hac nunc C^1E : hac D^1.

836   hortamentis $C^1p^2\lambda$, Eugr., gl. II : ornamentis APF^1E^1 : pro ornamentis D^1G : pro
      alimentis F^2E^2.

838   adposcunt A : adposcent Σ.

CLIT. You're talking rubbish. Where shall I get it?

SY. From your father.

CLIT. You're making fun of me, I presume?

SY. You'll find that out when it happens.

CLIT. Then I really am a lucky fellow! Syrus, I really am fond of you.   825

SY. Your father's coming out. Make sure you don't show any surprise
at why this is happening. Go along with him when occasion
demands, do what he tells you, and don't say too much.

(Chremes comes out of his house again, carrying a bag of money.)

IV 7

CH. Where's Clitipho?

SY. *(nudging him, and whispering)* Say "Here I am".

CLIT. Here I am.

CH. Have you told him what this is all about?   830

SY. I've told him just about everything.

CH. Take this money and deliver it.

SY. *(as Clitipho hesitates)* Go on! What are you standing about for,
you blockhead? Why don't you take it?

CLIT. Give it to me then. *(Chremes hands him the bag.)*

SY. *(to Clitipho)* Follow me over here quickly. *(To Chremes.)* You
can wait for us here till we come out again - there's no reason
for us to hang about in there for very long. *(He follows Clitipho
into Menedemus' house.)*

CH. My daughter's already got ten minae from me, which I regard as   835
payment for her food and lodging; another ten can be added to
that for her wardrobe, and these amounts entail another couple of
talents for a dowry. How many unjust and misguided things are
done in deference to convention! Now I've got to put business   840

mihi nunc relictis rebus inveniundus est

aliquis, labore inventa mea quoi dem bona.

IV viii

MENEDEMVS   CHREMES

ME. multo omnium nunc me fortunatissimum

factum puto esse quom te, gnate, intellego

resipisse.

CH.   ut errat!

ME.   te ipsum quaerebam, Chreme;

serva, quod in te est, filium, me ac familiam.   845

CH. cedo, quid vis faciam?

ME.   invenisti hodie filiam.

CH. quid tum?

ME.   hanc uxorem sibi dari volt Clinia.

CH. quaeso, quid tu hominis es?

ME.   quid est?

CH.   iamne oblitus es

inter nos quid sit dictum de fallacia,

ut ea via abs te argentum auferretur?

ME.   scio.   850

CH. ea res nunc agitur ipsa.

ME.   quid narras, Chreme?

immo haec quidem quae apud me est Clitiphonis est

amica.

---

842 nunc me A : me nunc D²PCFE : nunc D¹G.
843 cum te gnate A : gnate cum te Σ.
845 me ac A : et me et Σ.
846 cedo Σ: dic A.
847 uxorem sibi Σ : sibi uxorem A.
848 tu om. Σ.
     hominis es **codd.** : homini's Kauer-Lindsay.
     quid est Ap : quid DGPCFE.
851 narras A : dixti DGPCE : dixtin F¹.
     Chreme erravi res acta est quanta de spe decidi DGE (res om. G) : Chreme erravi c
        res acta est quanta de spe decidi **in margine** PCF (sic res F : cecidi P) : 851a
        erravi? acta est res? quanta de spe decidi! Kauer-Lindsay (cf. 250).

aside and find some young man on whom to bestow the wealth I've worked so hard to win.

(Menedemus comes out of his house, talking back to Clinia inside as he does so.)

IV 8

ME. I consider I've become much the luckiest man in the world, now that I've realized you've come to your senses, my boy.

CH. *(aside)* How wrong he is!

ME. Just the man I was looking for, Chremes. As far as in you lies, prove yourself the saviour of my son, myself and all my household.   845

CH. Tell me, what do you want me to do?

ME. You've found a daughter today.

CH. What of that?

ME. Clinia wants her to be given to him as his wife.

CH. I ask you, what sort of a man are you?

ME. What's that?

CH. Have you already forgotten the conversation we had together about the trick - for money to be got out of you that way?   850

ME. I remember.

CH. It's that very process that's now in hand.

ME. What's that you're saying, Chremes? No, no, that woman in my house is Clitipho's mistress.

129

CH.   ita aiunt; et tu credis omnia.

et illum aiunt velle uxorem, ut, quom desponderim,

des qui aurum ac vestem atque alia quae opus sunt comparet.   85

ME. id est profecto; id amicae dabitur.

CH.   scilicet

daturum.

ME.   ah! frustra sum igitur gavisus miser.

quidvis tamen iam malo quam hunc amittere.

quid nunc renuntiem abs te responsum, Chreme,

ne sentiat me sensisse atque aegre ferat?   86

CH. aegre? nimium illi, Menedeme, indulges.

ME.   sine;

inceptum est; perfice hoc mi perpetuo, Chreme.

CH. dic convenisse, egisse te de nuptiis.

ME. dicam. quid deinde?

CH.   me facturum esse omnia,

generum placere; postremo etiam, si voles,

desponsam quoque esse dicito.

ME.   em, istuc volueram.

CH. tanto ocius te ut poscat et tu, id quod cupis,

quam ocissime ut des.

ME.   cupio.

CH.   ne tu propediem,

ut istam rem video, istius obsaturabere.

sed haec utut sunt, cautim et paulatim dabis,   87

si sapies.

ME. faciam.

---

853 CH. ita aiunt. et tu ... A : ita aiunt **Menedemo continuant** Iov., Σ, Kauer-Linds

853-4 ME. omnia. CH. et illum ... Iov., $D^2P^2C^2F^2E$.

854 desponderim Σ: desponderis A, Kauer-Lindsay.

857 ah **edd. plerirque** : vah **codd.**

   sum igitur A : igitur sum Sa, Σ.

858 **om.** A.

869 istam APCFE : istanc DG, Kauer-Lindsay.

870 haec ut ut p : haec uti A : haec ut G : haec ita ut E : haec ut ista ut F^1 : hae
   ista ut DF^2 : ut ut istaec C : ut uti istaec P, Kauer-Lindsay.

CH.	That's what they tell you, and you believe every word of it! And they're also saying that Clinia wants to get married so that, when I've betrothed my daughter to him, you'll give him money for him to buy jewelry and clothes and other necessaries.	855
ME.	That's it of course! And he'll give it to his mistress!	
CH.	Of course he will.	
ME.	Oh, dear me, so my rejoicing was all for nothing. Still, at this stage I prefer anything to losing him. What response am I to take back from you now, Chremes, so he won't realize that I've caught on and get annoyed?	860
CH.	Get annoyed? You're much too lenient with him, Menedemus.	
ME.	Let me be. I've started on my course; help me carry it through to the end, Chremes.	
CH.	Tell him you've met me and had a discussion about the wedding.	
ME.	I will. And what then?	
CH.	That I'll make all the arrangements, that my prospective son-in-law is quite acceptable, and finally, if you want to, say that she's engaged to him as well.	865
ME.	Ah! That's what I wanted you to say.	
CH.	So he can make his demands of you that much quicker, and so you can give him what he asks for as quickly as possible - which is just what you want to do.	
ME.	Yes, I do.	
CH.	As I see the situation, before very long you'll have had your fill of it. But, however things stand, you'll give him the money carefully and by instalments if you're wise.	870
ME.	I will.	

CH.   abi intro; vide quid postulet.
       ego domi ero, siquid me voles.
ME.   sane volo;
       nam te scientem faciam quidquid egero.

                         ACTVS V

V i   MENEDEMVS CHREMES

ME.   ego me non tam astutum neque ita perspicacem esse id scio;
       sed hic adiutor meus et monitor et praemonstrator Chremes   875
       hoc mihi praestat. in me quidvis harum rerum convenit
       quae sunt dicta in stulto: caudex, stipes, asinus, plumbeus;
       in illum nil potest; exsuperat eius stultitia haec omnia.
CH.   ohe, iam desine deos, uxor, gratulando obtundere
       tuam esse inventam gnatam, nisi illos ex tuo ingenio iudicas   880
       ut nil credas intellegere, nisi idem dictum est centiens.
       sed interim quid illic iamdudum gnatus cessat cum Syro?
ME.   quos ais homines, Chreme, cessare?
CH.   ehem, Menedeme, advenis?
       dic mihi, Cliniae quae dixi nuntiastin?
ME.   omnia.
CH.   quid ait?
ME.   gaudere adeo coepit, quasi qui cupiunt nuptias.   885
CH.   hahahae!
ME.   quid risisti?
CH.   servi venere in mentem Syri
       calliditates.
ME.   itane?
CH.   voltus quoque hominum fingit scelus.

---

874   ita AD²PCF : tam D¹G : om. E.
877   stulto A : stultum Sa,Σ, Don. Eu. 6.
878   exsuperat A, Sa : nam exsuperat Iov., Σ.

                         132

CH.   Go indoors, and see what he's asking for; I'll be at home if you
      want me for anything.
ME.   I certainly do want you, because I'll be keeping you informed of
      whatever I do.

*(Menedemus and Chremes go into their respective houses, and the stage
is left empty. The action resumes almost immediately with the
re-emergence of Menedemus from his house, by which time a short
period is supposed to have elapsed.)*

ACT FIVE

V 1

ME.   I know I'm not all that clever and observant, but this helper,   875
      counsellor and guide of mine Chremes leaves me way behind in
      this. Any one of the terms which are abusive names for a fool
      suit me - chump, dolt, ass, leaden-wit - but none of them can be
      said of him; his stupidity outdoes them all.

(Chremes enters from his house, talking back to Sostrata inside.)

CH.   Oh, wife, do stop belabouring the gods with thanks that your   880
      daughter's been found - unless you judge them by the standards of
      your own intellect, so you believe they don't understand anything
      unless the same point's been repeated a hundred times over! But
      why's my son hanging about over there with Syrus all this time?
ME.   Who do you say's hanging about, Chremes?
CH.   Oh, Menedemus, back again? Tell me, did you tell Clinia what I
      said?
ME.   All of it.
CH.   What does he say?   885
ME.   He began to be really pleased, just like people who genuinely
      want to get married.
CH.   Ha! Ha! Ha!
ME.   What are you laughing at?
CH.   I was reminded of my slave Syrus' crafty tricks.
ME.   And so?
CH.   The scoundrel counterfeits people's expressions as well!

133

ME.   gnatus quod se adsimulat laetum, id dicis?
CH.   id.
ME.   idem istuc mihi
       venit in mentem.
CH.   veterator!
ME.   magis, si magis noris, putes
       ita rem esse.
CH.   ain tu?
ME.   quin tu ausculta.
CH.   mane; hoc prius scire expeto,   890
       quid perdideris. nam ubi desponsam nuntiasti filio,
       continuo iniecisse verba tibi Dromonem scilicet,
       sponsae vestem aurum atque ancillas opus esse, argentum ut dares.
ME.   non.
CH.   quid? non?
ME.   non, inquam.
CH.   neque ipse gnatus?
ME.   nil prorsum, Chreme;
       magis unum etiam instare ut hodie conficiantur nuptiae.   895
CH.   mira narras. quid Syrus meus? ne is quidem quicquam?
ME.   nihil.
CH.   quam ob rem, nescio.
ME.   equidem miror, qui alia tam plane scias.
       sed ille tuom quoque Syrus idem mire finxit filium,
       ut ne paullulum quidem subolat esse amicam hanc Cliniae.
CH.   quid agit?
ME.   mitto iam osculari atque amplexari; id nil puto.   900
CH.   quid est quod amplius simuletur?
ME.   vah!
CH.   quid est?

---

894   prorsum A : prorsus Σ.
895   conficiantur A : conficerentur Σ.
897   nescio. ME. equidem ... Guyet, Bentley : ME. nescio. equidem ... **codd**.
899   subolat AP^{1}CF^1 : suboleat DGP^{2}F^{2}E.
900   agit A : ais Σ.

ME.	You mean, because my son's pretending to be glad?
CH.	Just that.
ME.	The same point crossed my mind.
CH.	He's an old hand at it!
ME.	You'd think it was even more the case, if you knew more.

890

CH.	Really?
ME.	Just listen.
CH.	Wait a moment. First I'm eager to know how much you're out of pocket. When you announced that Antiphila was engaged to your son, I suppose Dromo immediately put in a word about the need for clothes, jewels and maids for the future bride, so that you'd give them some money.
ME.	No, he didn't.
CH.	What? He didn't?
ME.	I'm telling you, he didn't.
CH.	And your son didn't either?
ME.	He didn't ask for anything at all, Chremes. He pressed even harder for just one thing - that the wedding formalities should be completed today.

895

CH.	Amazing! And what of my slave Syrus? Didn't even he say anything?
ME.	Nothing.
CH.	I've no idea why that was.
ME.	I'm surprised at that, when you're the type to know other things so clearly. But that same Syrus did a remarkable job on your son, so there's not even the slightest whiff of a suspicion that Bacchis is Clinia's mistress.
CH.	What's he up to?

900

ME.	I'm not saying anything now about kissing and cuddling - I think that's of no significance.
CH.	What further show of pretence could there be?
ME.	Huh!
CH.	What do you mean by that?

135

ME.	audi modo.	

ME.
           audi modo.
est mihi ultimis conclave in aedibus quoddam retro;
huc est intro latus lectus, vestimentis stratus est.

CH. quid postquam hoc est factum?

ME.   dictum factum huc abiit Clitipho.

CH. solus?

ME.   solus.

CH.   timeo.

ME.   Bacchis consecuta est ilico.   90

CH. sola?

ME.   sola.

CH.   perii!

ME.   ubi abiere intro, operuere ostium.

CH.   hem!
Clinia haec fieri videbat?

ME.   quidni? mecum una simul.

CH. fili est amica Bacchis; Menedeme, occidi!

ME. quam ob rem?

CH.   decem dierum vix mi est familia.

ME. quid? istuc times quod ille operam amico dat suo? 91

CH. immo quod amicae.

ME.   si dat.

CH.   an dubium id tibi est?
quemquamne animo tam comi esse aut leni putas
qui se vidente amicam patiatur suam ...?

ME.   ah,
quidni? quo verba facilius dentur mihi.

CH. derides merito. mihi nunc ego suscenseo; 91
quot res dedere ubi possem persentiscere,
ni essem lapis! quae vidi! vae misero mihi!
at ne illud haud inultum, si vivo, ferent.
nam iam ...

---

902 ultimis conclave in aedibus D^{1}G : in ultimis conclave aedibus AD^{2}PCFE.

904 dictum factum A : dictum ac factum Σ.

912 quemquamne AD^{1}p^2 : quemquam GP^{1}CFE.

      comi **edd.** : communi **codd.**

      aut A : et Σ.

ME.	Just you listen. Right at the back of my house I've got a back room. They took a bed in there and made it up.
CH.	What happened after they'd done that?
ME.	In less time than it takes to say so, Clitipho nipped off inside.
CH.	By himself?
ME.	By himself.
CH.	I'm getting alarmed.
ME.	Bacchis followed him straightaway.
CH.	By herself?
ME.	By herself.
CH.	Damnation!
ME.	When they went inside, they closed the door.
CH.	What? And was Clinia watching this happen?
ME.	Of course. He was there right next to me.
CH.	Then Bacchis is my son's mistress! Menedemus, I'm done for!
ME.	Why?
CH.	My property's barely enough to last ten days.
ME.	What? Are you worried because he's helping out a friend?
CH.	No, but because it's a *girl*-friend.
ME.	If he really is.
CH.	Can there be any doubt about it? Do you think anyone's so obliging or easy-going as to let his mistress, under his very eyes ...?
ME.	Oh, why not? It's so that I can be hoodwinked more easily.
CH.	It serves me right that you're making fun of me. It's myself I'm angry with now. How many clues they gave me which meant I could have twigged it if I wasn't such a blockhead! What things I saw! Oh, what a pitiful creature I am! But, as sure as I'm alive, they'll not get away with this scot-free. Now I'll ...

905

910

915

137

ME.   non tu te cohibes? non te respicis?
non tibi ego exempli satis sum?
CH.   prae iracundia,   920
Menedeme, non sum apud me.
ME.   tene istuc loqui!
nonne id flagitium est te aliis consilium dare,
foris sapere, tibi non posse te auxiliarier?
CH.   quid faciam?
ME.   id quod me fecisse aiebas parum.
fac te patrem esse sentiat; fac ut audeat   925
tibi credere omnia, abs te petere et poscere,
nequam aliam quaerat copiam ac te deserat.
CH.   immo abeat multo malo quovis gentium
quam hic per flagitium ad inopiam redigat patrem.
nam si illi pergo suppeditare sumptibus,   930
Menedeme, mihi illaec vere ad rastros res redit.
ME.   quot incommoditates in hac re capies, nisi caves!
difficilem te esse ostendes et ignosces tamen
post, et id ingratum.
CH.   ah, nescis quam doleam!
ME.   ut lubet.
quid hoc quod rogo, ut illa nubat nostro? nisi quid est 935
quod magis vis.
CH.   immo et gener et adfines placent.
ME.   quid dotis dicam te dixisse filio?
quid obticuisti?
CH.   dotis?
ME.   ita dico.
CH.   ah!

---

924   parum Iov., Σ : paulum A.
925   esse sentiat APCF : esse ut sentiat D¹GE, Eugr.
       audeat Iov., Σ : audeant A.
932   incommoditates A : incommoda tibi D²GPCFE¹ : incommodia tibi D¹E².
       in **codd.**, Kauer-Lindsay : **om. edd. plerique.**
       capies Σ : accipies A.
936   magis vis A : mavis PC : malis DGFE.

ME. Can't you restrain yourself? Or show some consideration for yourself? Aren't I sufficient warning to you?   920

CH. I'm beside myself with fury, Menedemus.

ME. Fancy you saying that! Don't you think it's a disgrace that you advise other people and show good sense to outsiders, but can't be any help to yourself?

CH. What am I to do?

ME. What you kept telling me I did too little of. Make sure he   925
realizes *you're* his father, make sure he's got the courage to trust *you* with all his secrets, and to make his requests and demands of *you*, so he won't go looking for any other source of supply and desert you.

CH. No! I'd much rather him go off anywhere in the world than stay here and reduce his father to poverty by his scandalous behaviour. If I go on supplying him with his expenses,   930
Menedemus, it's really and truly a life with the hoe for me.

ME. What a load of misfortune you'll be bringing on yourself over this if you don't watch out! You'll show him you're obdurate, yet later you'll forgive him, and it won't be appreciated.

CH. Oh, you don't know how upset I am!

ME. As you wish, then. Now what about my request that Antiphila   935
should marry my son - unless, that is, there's anything you'd like better?

CH. No, no, I'm delighted with my future son-in-law and his family.

ME. What dowry shall I say you've settled on for my boy? *(After a pause.)* Why the silence?

CH. *(abstractedly)* Dowry?

ME. That's what I mean.

CH. *(still deep in thought)* Ah!

ME.   Chreme,
      nequid vereare, si minus; nil nos dos movet.
CH.   duo talenta pro re nostra ego esse decrevi satis;   940
      sed ita dictu opus est, si me vis salvom esse et rem et filium,
      me mea omnia bona doti dixisse illi.
ME.   quam rem agis?
CH.   id mirari te simulato et illum hoc rogitato simul,
      quam ob rem id faciam.
ME.   quin ego vero quam ob rem id facias nescio.
CH.   egone? ut eius animum, qui nunc luxuria et lascivia   945
      diffluit, retundam, redigam, ut quo se vortat nesciat.
ME.   quid agis?
CH.   mitte; sine me in hac re gerere mihi morem.
ME.   sino.
      itane vis?
CH.   ita.
ME.   fiat.
CH.   ac iam uxorem ut accersat paret.
      hic ita ut liberos est aequom dictis confutabitur.
      sed Syrum quidem ego ne, si vivo, adeo exornatum dabo,   950
      adeo depexum, ut dum vivat meminerit semper mei,
      qui sibi me pro deridiculo ac delectamento putat.
      non, ita me di ament, auderet facere haec viduae mulieri
      quae in me fecit.

V ii   CLITIPHO MENEDEMVS CHREMES SYRVS

CLIT.   itane tandem, quaeso, Menedeme, ut pater
      tam in brevi spatio omnem de me eiecerit animum patris?   955

---

939   si minus ACF : si est minus E : si minus est DG : si quid minus P.
943   illum hoc A : illum Σ.
946   redigam A : et redigam Σ.
947   sine A : ac sine Σ.
948   ac A : age Σ.
950   Syrum quidem A : Syrum. ME. quid eum? CH. Σ, Don. Ad. 400, Kauer-Lindsay.
954   **nulla nova scaena** D.
      quaeso A : quaeso est Σ.   140

ME.	Chremes, don't be afraid if it's rather small; the matter of the dowry doesn't bother us at all.
CH.	*(with sudden decisiveness)* I've decided two talents is enough, considering my circumstances; but if you want to ensure the salvation of myself, my property and my son, you must say that I've fixed on my entire fortune as the amount of dowry for him.
ME.	What are you up to?
CH.	Pretend you're amazed, and at the same time ask my son why I'm doing it.
ME.	But I really *don't* know why you're doing it.
CH.	Why I'm doing it? To take the edge off his high spirit and bring it back on to the straight and narrow, because just now it's weakened with good living and unruly behaviour - so he won't know which way to turn.
ME.	What are you up to?
CH.	Never you mind; let me please myself over this.
ME.	Very well. Is that how you want it?
CH.	Yes.
ME.	Then so be it.
CH.	Now get Clinia to prepare to fetch his wife. *(Menedemus goes into his house.)* This son of mine will be put in his place by a telling off - just the right thing to do to one's children. But as for Syrus, as sure as I'm alive, for thinking I'm an object of his ridicule and his plaything, I'll make him such a pretty sight, such a punchbag, that he'll always remember me as long as he lives. Heavens, he wouldn't dare do to a poor widow woman what he's done to me!

(Menedemus comes out of his house, accompanied by Clitipho and Syrus.)

V 2

CLIT.	Please, is it really the case, Menedemus, that my father's thrown off all fatherly feeling for me so quickly? For what

Line numbers: 940, 945, 950, 955

```
          quodnam ob facinus?  quid ego tantum sceleris admisi miser?
          volgo faciunt.
ME.                  scio tibi esse hoc gravius multo ac durius,
          quoi fit;  verum ego haud minus aegre patior, id qui nescio
          nec rationem capio, nisi quod tibi bene ex animo volo.
CLIT.  hic patrem astare aibas?
ME.                  eccum.
CH.                          quid me incusas, Clitipho?                    96
          quidquid ego huius feci, tibi prospexi et stultitiae tuae.
          ubi te vidi animo esse omisso et suavia in praesentia
          quae essent prima habere neque consulere in longitudinem,
          cepi rationem ut neque egeres neque ut haec posses perdere.
          ubi, quoi decuit primo, tibi non licuit per te mihi dare,       96
          abii ad proxumum tibi qui erat;  ei commisi et credidi.
          ibi tuae stultitiae semper erit praesidium, Clitipho,
          victus, vestitus, quo in tectum te receptes.
CLIT.                                        ei mihi!
CH.    satius est quam te ipso herede haec possidere Bacchidem.
SY.    disperii!  scelestus quantas turbas concivi insciens!              97
CLIT.  emori cupio.
CH.                prius, quaeso, disce quid sit vivere.
          ubi scies, si displicebit vita, tum istoc utitor.
SY.    ere, licetne?
CH.                loquere.
SY.                          at tuto?
CH.                                  loquere.
```

---

956   facinus D²PCFE : factum AG, Eugr. : **om.** D¹.

958   qui DGPCF² : quod AF¹E¹.

960   astare PCFE : stare DG : esse A.

      aibas **edd. plerique** : aiebas **codd.**

966   **om.** G.

      proxumum ... erat; ei D¹ : proxumos ... erant; eis D²GPCFE : proxumum ... erat;

      A (et Iov.).

967   ibi PCFE : ubi A(?)D¹G.

      erit Iov., Σ: id A.

968   receptes PCFE : recipies A : recipias D¹G.

offence? Oh dear, what great crime have I committed? People are
doing it all the time.

ME. I know this is much more serious and difficult for you, because
it's you it's happening tò; but I'm no less put out by it. I
know nothing about it and can't make any sense of it - but I wish
you well with all my heart.

CLIT. You told me my father was waiting out here?   960

ME. There he is. *(Menedemus goes back into his house.)*

CH. Why are you criticizing me, Clitipho? In whatever I've done in
this, I've been making provision for you and your stupid
behaviour. When I saw you were so remiss, attaching prime
importance to current pleasures and not planning for the long
term, I thought up a plan to stop you living in want and to
prevent you being able to squander what we've got. When, because   965
of your behaviour, I couldn't give my property to you - the first
person I should have given it to - I had recourse to the relative
who was closest to you, and consigned and entrusted it to him.
In him you'll always have a sure defence against your own
stupidity, and food and clothing and somewhere you can go for a
roof over your head.

CLIT. Oh, dear!

CH. It's preferable to Bacchis getting hold of it if you were my heir
yourself.

SY. *(aside)* What a mess I'm in! What enormous trouble I've stirred   970
up by my dirty tricks, without even realizing it!

CLIT. I wish I could drop dead.

CH. Please learn first what it is to live. Then, when you know that,
if life displeases you, you can take the other course.

SY. Master, may I ...?

CH. Yes, have your say.

SY. Without any risk?

CH. Have your say.

SY.   quae ista est pravitas

quaeve amentia est, quod peccavi ego, id obesse huic?

CH.   ilicet.

ne te admisce; nemo accusat, Syre, te; nec tu aram tibi   975

nec precatorem pararis.

SY.   quid agis?

CH.   nil suscenseo

neque tibi nec tibi; nec vos est aequom quod facio mihi.

SY.   abiit? vah! rogasse vellem ...

CLIT.   quid?

SY.   ... und' mihi peterem cibum;

ita nos alienavit. tibi iam esse ad sororem intellego.

CLIT. adeon rem rediisse ut periclum etiam a fame mihi sit, Syre!   980

SY.   modo liceat vivere, est spes ...

CLIT.   quae?

SY.   ... nos esurituros satis.

CLIT. inrides in re tanta neque me consilio quicquam adiuvas?

SY.   immo et ibi nunc sum et usque id egi dudum dum loquitur pater;

et quantum ego intellegere possum ...

CLIT.   quid?

SY.   non aberit longius.

CLIT. quid id ergo?

SY.   sic est; non esse horum te arbitror.

CLIT.   quid istuc, Syre?   985

satin sanus es?

SY.   ego dicam quod mi in mentem est; tu diiudica.

---

976   pararis Σ, Don. **Ph.** 140 : parabis A.
977   neque A : nec Iov., Σ.
       nec tibi AP[1]C[1]F[1] : nec huic DGP[2]C[2]F[2]E.
978   **nova scaena** Kauer-Lindsay.
979   alienavit ACF[1] : abalienavit PF[2]E : abalienabit DG.
980   **nova scaena** DG.
       rediisse **edd.** : redisse **codd.**
       a fame P[1]CF : fame ADGP[2]E.
986   in mentem est D[1]PCFE[1] : in mente est AD[2]GE[2].

144

SY.   Why are you being so perverse and foolish as to make the wrong
       I've committed a stick to beat Clitipho with?
CH.   You run along; don't get yourself mixed up in this. Nobody's   975
       accusing *you*, Syrus; no need for you to line up a place of
       sanctuary or someone to plead for you.
SY.   What are you doing?
CH.   I'm not annoyed with you, nor with you, Clitipho; so it's not
       right for *you* to get annoyed at what *I'm* doing. *(He disappears
       into his house.)*
SY.   Has he gone? Bother! I'd like to have asked him ...
CLIT. What?
SY.   ... where I could get my rations from - he's renounced us so
       completely. But I gather there's still food for you at your
       sister's.
CLIT. To think that things have got to such a state that I'm in danger   980
       of starving, Syrus!
SY.   Provided we can just survive, there's a hope ...
CLIT. What of?
SY.   ... of us going to be pretty hungry.
CLIT. Are you cracking jokes about something as important as this,
       instead of giving me some helpful advice?
SY.   No, no, I'm on to something at this very moment, and I was giving
       it my attention for quite a time while your father was talking.
       As far as I can understand it ...
CLIT. What?
SY.   It won't be long before it comes to me.
CLIT. What is it, then?   985
SY.   It's just this: I don't think you're their son.
CLIT. What's that, Syrus? Are you sure you're in your right mind?
SY.   I'll tell you what's occurred to me, and you decide. As long as

145

<pre>
          dum istis fuisti solus, dum nulla alia delectatio
          quae propior esset, te indulgebant, tibi dabant; nunc filia
          postquam est inventa vera, inventa est causa qui te expellerent.
CLIT.   est veri simile.
SY.   an tu ob peccatum hoc esse illum iratum putas?   990
CLIT.   non arbitror.
SY.   nunc aliud specta; matres omnes filiis
          in peccato adiutrices, auxilio in paterna iniuria
          solent esse; id non fit.
CLIT.   verum dicis. quid ergo nunc faciam, Syre?
SY.   suspicionem istanc ex illis quaere, rem profer palam.
          si non est verum, ad misericordiam ambos adduces cito,   99!
          aut scibis quoius sis.
CLIT.   recte suades; faciam.
SY.   sat recte hoc mihi
          in mentem venit; nam quam maxume huic vana haec suspicio
          erit, tam facillume patris pacem in leges conficiet suas.
          etiam haud scio anne uxorem ducat; ac Syro nil gratiae!
          quid hoc autem? senex exit foras; ego fugio. adhuc quod factum
                                                      [est,   100(
          miror non continuo adripi iusse. ad Menedemum hunc pergam;
          eum mihi precatorem paro; seni nostro fide nil habeo.
</pre>

_____

989   postquam est inventa vera inventa est AD¹G : postquam vera inventa est inventa es
      PC : postquam vera inventa est D²FE.
      qui A : qua Iov., Σ.
996   quoius sis **codd.** : quoius (quoiu's **dubitanter**) Kauer-Lindsay.
997   nam quam maxume huic vana haec suspicio Geppert : namque adulescens maxime huic
      vana(?) haec suspicio A : namque adulescens quam in minima spe situs Σ, Eugr.
      namque adulescens quam maxime (mini)ma spe situs Iov. : nam quam maxume huic
      visa haec suspicio | erit vera, quamque adulescens maxume quam in minima spe
      situs Kauer-Lindsay, **qui duos versus 997, 997a faciunt.**
1000 autem A : autem est Σ.
1001 non continuo adripi iusse Kauer-Lindsay : continuo hunc adripuisse A : non iusse
      me adripi Iov. : non iussisse ilico arripi me Σ.
      ad Menedemum hunc A : ad Menedemum hinc Iov., D¹G : ad Menedemum hinc nunc D² :
      hinc nunc ad Menedemum PCFE.
1002 seni nostro **codd.**, Eugr. : seni **om.** Bothe : nostro **om.** Kauer.
      fide D²L¹ηε : fidei AD¹GPCF, Eugr. : fidem E.

you were the only child they had, and they hadn't got any other source of happiness which was closer to their hearts, they kept pampering you and giving you things; but now, after they've found a daughter who's really theirs, they've found a reason for turning you out.

CLIT. That's quite likely.   990

SY. Do you really think your father's furious just because of this bit of naughtiness?

CLIT. No, I don't.

SY. And there's another point to consider; all mothers are inclined to champion their sons when they've done wrong and to help them when their fathers are treating them too harshly; that's not happening.

CLIT. It's true what you say. So what must I do now, Syrus?

SY. Find out from them about your suspicions, and bring the matter out into the open. If it's not true, you'll quickly move the   995 pair of them to pity you - or you'll know whose son you are.

CLIT. Sound advice; I'll do that. *(He goes into Chremes' house.)*

SY. A good idea that came into my head, that was; the fact is the more unfounded these suspicions of his are, the more easily he'll make peace with his father on his own terms. He may even find a bride for all I know - and there'll be no thanks for Syrus! What's that noise? The old fellow's coming outside; I'm getting   1000 out of here. In view of what's happened so far, I'm surprised he hasn't ordered me to be carted off for punishment straightaway. I'll go to our neighbour Menedemus, and get him lined up to intervene on my behalf; I've got no faith in our old man.

(As Syrus goes into Menedemus' house, Sostrata and Chremes come out of Chremes' house.)

147

SO.   profecto nisi caves tu homo, aliquid gnato conficies mali;
        idque adeo miror, quo modo
        tam ineptum quicquam tibi venire in mentem, mi vir, potuerit.   1005

CH.   oh, pergin mulier esse? nullamne ego rem umquam in vita mea
        volui quin tu in ea re mi fueris advorsatrix, Sostrata!
        at si rogem iam quid est quod peccem aut quam ob rem hoc faciam,
                                                          [nescias;
        in qua re nunc tam confidenter restas, stulta.

SO.   ego nescio?

CH.   immo scis, potius quam quidem redeat ad integrum eadem oratio.

SO.   oh!   1010
        iniquos es qui me tacere de re tanta postules.

CH.   non postulo iam; loquere; nihilo minus ego hoc faciam tamen.

SO.   facies?

CH.   verum.

SO.   non vides quantum mali ex ea re excites?
        subditum se suspicatur.

CH.   "subditum", ain tu?

SO.   sic erit,
        mi vir.

CH.   confitere?

SO.   au te obsecro, istuc inimicis siet.   1015
        egon confitear meum non esse filium, qui sit meus?

CH.   quid? metuis ne non, quom velis, convincas esse illum tuom?

SO.   quod filia est inventa?

CH.   non; sed, quo magis credundum siet,

1008   hoc A : id Σ.
        faciam Iov., Σ, Eugr. : facias A, Kauer-Lindsay.
1014   sic erit Guyet : certe sic erit A : certe inquam DPCFE : certe G.
1015   te obsecro edd. plerirque : obsecro te codd.
1018   SO. quod filia est inventa? CH. non ... Σ: cum (quod Iov.) filia est inventa? SO
        non ... A.
1018-9 secl. Fleckeisen.

148

SO.	Really, if you're not careful, you'll do our son some harm. I'm truly amazed, my dear, how anything so stupid could have entered your head.	1005
CH.	Oh, still persisting in being the woman you are? There's nothing in my entire life I've ever wanted, Sostrata, without your opposing me over it. But if I asked you what it is I'm doing wrong, or why I'm behaving like this, you wouldn't know the answer; and yet you're holding out against me over this business, you silly woman, and with so much assurance, too.	
SO.	I don't know, did you say?	
CH.	No, no, you *do* know - anything rather than having the same arguments starting up all over again.	1010
SO.	Goodness, you're unfair, expecting me to keep quiet over something so important.	
CH.	I'm not expecting that any more; have your say, but I'll do it just the same.	
SO.	You'll do it?	
CH.	Certainly I will.	
SO.	Don't you see how much trouble you're stirring up as a result of all this? Our son suspects he's not really ours.	
CH.	"Not ours," you say?	
SO.	That's what the end result will be, my dear.	1015
CH.	Do you admit it, then?	
SO.	Oh, please, leave that sort of thing to our enemies. Am I to admit that he's not my son when he is?	
CH.	What? Are you afraid you can't prove him yours whenever you want to?	
SO.	Because I've discovered my daughter, you mean?	
CH.	No, but for a far more credible reason, because he's so like you	

149

id quod est consimilis moribus.

convinces facile ex te natum; nam tui similis est probe.   1020

nam illi nil viti est relictum quin siet itidem tibi;

tum praeterea talem nisi tu nulla pareret filium.

sed ipse egreditur; quam severus! rem quom videas, censeas.

V iv   CLITIPHO SOSTRATA CHREMES

CLIT.   si umquam ullum fuit tempus, mater, quom ego voluptati tibi

fuerim, dictus filius tuos vostra voluntate, obsecro   1025

eius ut memineris atque inopis nunc te miserescat mei,

quod peto aut volo, parentis meos ut conmonstres mihi.

SO.   obsecro, mi gnate, ne istuc in animum inducas tuom

alienum esse te.

CLIT.   sum.

SO.   miseram me! hoccin quaesisti, obsecro?

ita mihi atque huic sis superstes ut ex me atque ex hoc natus es;   1030

et cave posthac, si me amas, umquam istuc verbum ex te audiam.

CH.   at ego, si me metuis, mores cave in te esse istos sentiam.

CLIT. quos?

CH.   si scire vis, ego dicam: gerro, iners, fraus, helluo,

ganeo's, damnosus; crede, et nostrum te esse credito.

CLIT. non sunt haec parentis dicta.

CH.   non, si ex capite sis meo   1035

natus, item ut aiunt Minervam esse ex Iove, ea causa magis

patiar, Clitipho, flagitiis tuis me infamem fieri.

1019   est consimilis ADGPC : consimilis F¹ : consimilis est F²E : consimilest
          Kauer-Lindsay.

1020   **secl.** Umpfenbach.

          similis est **codd.** : similest Kauer-Lindsay.

1021   quin siet itidem Umpfenbach : quin sit et idem A : quin itidem sit Σ.

1024   **nulla nova scaena** D.

1025   vostra A : tua Σ.

1027   volo Σ : quod volo A, Kauer-Lindsay : quod volo aut peto Prisc. in G.L. 2.355.

          parentis F¹, Prisc. in **G.L.** 2.355 ; parentes ADGPCF²E, Kauer-Lindsay.

1034   ganeos A : ganeo Σ.

in character. You'll easily prove he's your offspring; he's   1020
thoroughly like you. There's not a single fault left over for
him that's not found in exactly the same way in you; besides,
nobody but you would give birth to such a son. *(The door of
Chremes' house opens, and Clitipho comes out.)*   He's coming
outside - how serious he looks. You'd think him so too, if you
knew the facts!

V 4

CLIT. If ever there was a time, mother, when I brought you joy and,   1025
       with the consent of you both, was called your son, I implore you
       to remember it, to have pity on me now in my helplessness, and to
       show me who my parents are; that's what I'm looking for, or at
       least what I want.

SO.   My dear boy, I beg you not to get into your head the idea that
       you're someone else's child.

CLIT. But I am.

SO.   Oh, dear me! I ask you, can you really have asked a question
       like that? As surely as I pray you'll outlive your father and   1030
       me, you *are* my son and his. From now on, if you love me, make
       sure I never hear words like that from you again.

CH.   And, if you've any respect for me, make sure I don't see
       behaviour like that in you again.

CLIT. What behaviour?

CH.   If you really want to know, I'll tell you: you're useless, idle,
       dishonest, gluttonous, debauched and spendthrift. Believe that,
       and you can believe you're our son.

CLIT. Those aren't a true father's words.   1035

CH.   If you'd been born out of my head, as they say Minerva was from
       Jupiter's, I couldn't for that reason find it any easier to
       endure getting an infamous reputation through your disgraceful
       conduct, Clitipho.

SO.   di istaec prohibeant!

CH.   deos nescio; ego, quod potero, sedulo.
       quaeris id quod habes, parentes; quod abest non quaeris, patri
       quo modo obsequare et ut serves quod labore invenerit.   1040
       non mihi per fallacias adducere ante oculos ... pudet
       dicere hac praesente verbum turpe; at te id nullo modo
       facere puduit.

CLIT.   eheu! quam nunc totus displiceo mihi!
       quam pudet! neque quod principium incipiam ad placandum scio.

V v   MENEDEMVS CHREMES SOSTRATA CLITIPHO

ME.   enimvero Chremes nimis graviter cruciat adulescentulum   104
       nimisque inhumane; exeo ergo ut pacem conciliem. optume
       ipsos video.

CH.   ehem, Menedeme, quor non accersi iubes
       filiam, et quod dotis dixi firmas?

SO.   mi vir, te obsecro
       ne facias.

CLIT.   pater, obsecro mi ignoscas.

ME.   da veniam, Chreme;
       sine te exorem.

CH.   egon mea bona ut dem Bacchidi dono sciens?   1050
       non faciam.

ME.   at id nos non sinemus.

CLIT.   si me vivom vis, pater,
       ignosce.

SO.   age, Chreme mi.

~1040   invenerit Iov., Σ, Don. Eu. 210 : inveneris A.
1042   te id AG : te DPCFE.
1043   facere puduit A : facere piguit DG : piguit facere PCF²E : piguit dicere F¹.
        nunc AG : ego nunc DPCFE.
1044   incipiam ad placandum APFE : incapiam ad placandum C : ad placandum inveniam D¹G
1049   obsecro mihi A : obsecro ut mihi Σ.
1050   exorem DC²F²Evηε : exorent APC¹F¹ : exoret Iov.
1051   id om. PCF¹.

152

SO. Heaven forbid!

CH. I don't know about heaven; *I'll*, "forbid" it vigorously, as far
as I can. You're looking for what you've got - parents; you're
not looking for what you haven't got - knowledge of how to óbey   1040
your father and to preserve what he's managed to acquire by his
labours. You didn't baulk at using tricks and bringing indoors
before my very eyes a ... - I'm ashamed to mention the disgusting
word when your mother's here. But you weren't at all ashamed to
do it.

CLIT. *(aside)* Oh dear! How heartily sick of myself I am now, and how
ashamed! And I've no idea what start to make on placating him.

*(Menedemus comes out of his house; at first, as he talks to himself, he
does not notice the others.)*

V 5

ME. Chremes is definitely tormenting the young lad too harshly and   1045
too cruelly, so I'm on my way outside now to bring about some
peace between them. Ah, I see they're both here - excellent!

CH. Oh, Menedemus, why aren't you giving the orders for my daughter
to be fetched, and securing the dowry I fixed on?

SO. My dear, I beg you not to do this.

CLIT. Father, I beg you to forgive me.

ME. Pardon him, Chremes; let me prevail on you.   1050

CH. So I can deliberately hand over my property to Bacchis as a free
gift? No, I won't.

ME. But we won't let that happen.

CLIT. If you want me to go on living, father, then forgive me.

SO. Come along, Chremes, my dear.

153

ME.   age, quaeso, ne tam offirma te, Chreme.
CH.   quid istic? video non licere ut coeperam hoc pertendere.
ME.   facis ut te decet.
CH.   ea lege hoc adeo faciam, si facit
        quod ego hunc aequom censeo.
CLIT.   pater, omnia faciam; impera.   1055
CH.   uxorem ut ducas.
CLIT.   pater!
CH.   nil audio.
SO.   ad me recipio;
        faciet.
CH.   nil etiam audio ipsum.
CLIT.   perii!
SO.   an dubitas, Clitipho?
CH.   immo utrum volt.
SO.   faciet omnia.
ME.   haec dum incipias, gravia sunt,
        dumque ignores; ubi cognoris, facilia.
CLIT.   faciam, pater.
SO.   gnate mi, ego pol tibi dabo illam lepidam, quam tu facile ames,   1060
        filiam Phanocratae nostri.
CLIT.   rufamne illam virginem,
        caesiam, sparso ore, adunco naso? non possum, pater.
CH.   heia! ut elegans est! credas animum ibi esse.
SO.   aliam dabo.
CLIT.   immo, quandoquidem ducenda est, egomet habeo propemodum
        quam volo.
CH.   nunc laudo, gnate.

1053   quid istic D^{1}PCF : quid istuc AD^{2}E.
1056   SO. ad me ... A : ME. ad me ... Σ.
1057   CLIT. perii! SO. an ... Σ : SO. perii! an ... A.
1058   SO. faciet omnia. ME. haec ... AF^1 : ME. faciet omnia. SO. haec ... DPCF^{2}E.
1064   immo A : quid istic Σ.
1065   CH. A : SO. Σ.

ME.   Yes, come on, please; don't be so hard-hearted, Chremes.

CH.   Very well. I can see I'm not being allowed to persist in this as I'd begun.

ME.   Now you're acting as you should.

CH.   I'll do it on this one condition - that he does what I consider   1055 right for him to do.

CLIT. I'll do anything, father; just tell me.

CH.   I'm telling you to choose a wife.

CLIT. Father!

CH.   I hear no word of acceptance.

SO.   I'll take it upon myself; he'll do it.

CH.   Still no word from *him*.

CLIT. *(aside)* Oh, damnation!

SO.   Are you hesitant about it, Clitipho?

CH.   He can choose whichever course he wants to.

SO.   He'll do it all.

ME.   *(to Clitipho)* When you start on something like this and you're unfamiliar with it, it's difficult; but when you've got used to it, it's easy.

CLIT. *(resignedly)* I'll do it, father.

SO.   My dear boy, I'll get you a bride you'll find it easy to love,   1060 that sweet thing, our friend Phanocrates' daughter.

CLIT. That red-headed girl with grey eyes, spotty face and hook nose? I can't marry her, father.

CH.   Huh! How particular he is! You'd think his heart was really in the business.

SO.   I'll get you another girl.

CLIT. No, since I have to take a wife, I've got someone I like well   1065 enough.

CH.   Now I *am* pleased with you, my son.

CLIT.   Archonidi huius filiam.
SO.   perplacet.
CLIT.   pater, hoc nunc restat.
CH.   quid?
CLIT.   Syro ignoscas volo
        quae mea causa fecit.
CH.   fiat.
ω   vos valete et plaudite.

1066   perplacet Σ: satis placet A.

CLIT. The daughter of Archonides, our neighbour.

SO. She's very suitable.

CLIT. Father, there's one thing left.

CH. What's that?

CLIT. I want you to forgive Syrus for what he did because of me.

CH. Very well.

CANTOR Farewell, and give us your applause.

(Chremes, Sostrata and Clitipho go into Chremes' house. Menedemus watches them go, and then goes into his own house.)

COMMENTARY

Notes in square brackets and/or with Latin *lemmata* are intended primarily for readers using the Latin text.

PRODUCTION NOTICE

For the *didascaliae* "production notices" in general, see Introduction p. 8.

1   **Megalensian Games:**   Part of the festival held annually at Rome in April in honour of the goddess Cybele, *magna mater* "great mother" of Asia Minor.   The name is taken from the feminine of the Greek word for "great", *megalē.*

2   **curule aediles:**   The magistrates responsible for the games; see Introduction p. 7.

3   **produced by Lucius Ambivius Turpio:**   So A; the Σ MSS add another producer, Lucius Atilius Praenestinus "of Praeneste", whose name also appears in the production notices of *Eu., Ph.* and *Ad.*, and in Don.'s version of the production notice of *An.*   Since it is unlikely that a company of actors would have more than one leader to act as producer, Atilius' name probably crept in as producer of a revival. Ambivius himself was a famous actor (Cic. *Sen.* 48), coupled with the almost legendary Roscius by Tacitus (*Dial.* 20.3).
    music composed by ...:   Little is known of the music for Ter.'s plays; it was played on *tibiae* "pipes", and accompanied the whole play except those longish sections written in the metre known as iambic senarii.   Its importance is demonstrated by its mention in all the production notices, and it must have made a great contribution to the entertainment.   Flaccus, slave of Claudius, was composer for all Ter.'s plays.

4   **first on unequal pipes ...:**   This is Ter.'s only play where the music is not played on the same set of pipes throughout — unless "first ... then" refers to the original production and a revival.

5   [**Menandru:**   A retains the transliteration of the Greek gen. of Men.'s name, Μενάνδρου; the Σ MSS substitute the gen. of the Latin form, *Menandri.*]
    composed third: See Introduction p. 10.
    Manius Iuventius and Tiberius Sempronius: Consuls in 163 B.C.   A does not include the second name, but adds that of Gnaeus Cornelius (Lentulus), consul in 146 B.C.   In the production notice of *Eu.*, the Σ MSS include the name of Gaius Mummius, the other consul of 146. These facts are weighty evidence for a 'Terence revival' in that year.

159

SUMMARY

Ter's plays are prefaced by twelve—line *periochae* "summaries", written in iambic senarii in the second century A.D. by Gaius Sulpicius Apollinaris of Carthage, tutor of the emperor Pertinax and the writer Aulus Gellius. Even when additional proper names are introduced in translation to assist clarity (4, 9), this one, like them all, is a poor synopsis of the plot. The writer imitates the diction and prosody of Ter.'s day.

3   [**animique:** Probably a locative case; cf. 727n.]
4   [**reversust:** = *reversus est*; cf. 82n. The subject is Clinia.]
     [**clam patrem:** As a preposition, *clam* regularly takes the acc. in early Latin (cf. 98n., 118), and Sulpicius imitates this; but most MSS alter the acc. to the later abl.]

CHARACTERS

No such list appears in any MS, but it is customary to insert one in modern editions, compiled from information given in the scene—headings (see Introduction p. 24). Ter. habitually altered the proper names he found in his originals, though the ones he substituted were Greek, not Latin. He seems to have had a liking for certain names. Chremes is also a *senex* "old man" in *An.* and *Ph.* and an *adulescens* "young man" in *Eu.*, and slaves called Syrus and Dromo appear in *Ad.* and *An.* respectively; a *meretrix* "courtesan" called Bacchis and a *matrona* "married woman"/"widow" called Sostrata also appear in both *Hec.* and *Ad.*

The nurse is only named in A where, in the scene heading before 614, she is called Canthara; this is also the name of the midwife's assistant in *An.* and the nurse in *Ad.* Bacchis' *grex ancillarum* "retinue of maids" appears twice in a non—speaking role.

Syrus means "Syrian (man)" and, like Phrygia "Phrygian (woman)", indicates the place of the slave's origin; cf. Geta "member of the tribe of the Getae (in Thrace)", the name of slaves in *Ph.* and *Ad.*, Lesbia "woman of Lesbos", the name of the midwife in *An.*, and Syra "Syrian (woman)" in *Hec.*

PROLOGUE

1—2 **has given an old man like me a role ...:** It is clearly implied here that a younger actor usually delivered the prologue; but it is spoken here, for reasons given at 11ff., by someone older, presumably the *dux gregis* "leader of the company", L. Ambivius Turpio himself (see production notice). This happens again in the second prologue to *Hec.* (10ff.), and on both occasions the speaker has a difficult job to do which requires particular presence and powers of oratory. Here, the audience must be persuaded to hear a play by an author who was under attack, and whose last play (*Hec.* at its first performance) had failed.

3 I shall explain that point first, then give ...: In 11−15 and 16ff. respectively. But before doing either, the speaker gives, almost in parentheses as the recapitulation of 10 shows, the essential facts concerning the origin of the play (4−9). These can appear nowhere else, since if inserted in the prologue they would interrupt the argument, and if put at the end they would spoil the effect of the speaker's plea. Once these essentials have been dealt with, the plan set out here is faithfully carried out; there is thus no need to transpose large sections of the prologue, as did some earlier editors in attempts to avoid a seeming inconsistency.

[**quod veni eloquar:** Usually explained as being, in full, (*id propter*) *quod veni eloquar.*]

4 a fresh Greek comedy from a fresh Greek source: "a play never before represented in Latin, from a Greek original of which no adaptation had before been made" (Shuckburgh 64). The words translated "fresh" (*integra, integram*) literally mean "untouched" (cf. *Ad.* 10), and there is disagreement about whether they should be interpreted here as "new, fresh, untreated" or as "whole, entire, unadulterated". The former interpretation involves no conflict with 6 (where see note), whereas the latter does because it seems to contradict Ter.'s statement there that he has altered the play in his adaptation. However, that the former is correct is confirmed by the recapitulation in 7: *novam esse ostendi* "I've shown that it's new". See further Brothers 97−9.

[**integra ... integram:** Such repetition is one form of that play on words which occurs much more frequently in the rhetorical language of Ter.'s prologues than in the plays themselves; cf. *exemplum ... exemplo* 20, and compare juxtaposition of contrasted words, such as *iniquom ... aequom* 27.]

5 Heautontimorumenon: For Ter.'s retention of the Greek title, see Introduction pp. 10−11. [*Heauton−* or *Hauton−* (Greek ἑαυτόν or αὑτόν) are equally acceptable linguistically for "himself" in "The man who torments himself". However, because metrically −ŭs Hĕaūt− gives a badly divided anapaest in the third foot, some editors prefer *Hauton−*, to give an iambus −ŭs Haūt−. But an iambus −ŭs Hĕaūt− by synizesis is satisfactory; see Marouzeau II 97.]

6 from being a single plot ..." *simplici* "single", the reading of Iov. and the Σ MSS, is correct. A's *duplici* "double" must be rejected because (i) it is more likely that a copyist would write *duplici* for *simplici* in A under the influence of a preceding *duplex* than that one would write *simplici* for *duplici* in Σ without any such preceding influence; and (ii) *simplici* is perfectly acceptable metrically, whereas it is very doubtful if the first syllable of *duplici* can be scanned long,

as it would have to be to occur at this position in the line.   See
Brothers 100−2.

Ter. clearly here admits to altering his original to a significant extent;
but this is not inconsistent with what he says in 4 (where see note),
and there is therefore no reason to suspect that 6 is not genuine.

For the interpretation of this line, and its significance for our
knowledge of Ter.'s handling of his original, see Introduction pp. 15ff.

7   **who's written it:**   i.e. written the Latin play.   It seems that this
information, and the fact that the original was by Menander, was
already known, perhaps through notices posted by the aediles (which
may eventually have provided the basis for the production notices).
By contrast, some of Plautus' prologues imply that the audience did
not know the author's name, nor who had written the original, nor
even the title of the play.   However that may be, nowhere in his
prologues does Ter. mention his own name, and he names the author
of his (principal) original only twice (*An*. 9; *Eu*. 20).

11   **an advocate, not a prologue−speaker:**   In a sense this is true of all
the prologues, since none of them deals with the plot, but all
undertake some form of special pleading (see Introduction p. 11).
However, here and in the second prologue to *Hec*. − where the word
orator "advocate" is again used (9:   "I come before you as an
advocate in the guise of a prologue−speaker") − the speaker's task is
more than usually delicate; cf. 1−2n.

12   **made you the judges:**   Cf. *Ad*. 4:   "you will be the judges."

16   **spiteful individuals:**   Luscius Lanuvinus and his associates;   see
Introduction p. 12.   It is likely that there were several such critics,
and that Ter. is referring to them as a group here, while singling out
their leader later on (22).   But none of the associates can be
identified, and they were probably insignificant supporters of Ter.'s
one real opponent.   A less likely possibility is that no such associates
existed, and Ter. is using the plural here for rhetorical exaggeration.

17   **messed about with many Greek models:**   The verb translated "mess
about with" ("sully", "spoil", "mar"), *contaminare*, appears in a
similar context in *An*. 16 (*contaminari non decere fabulas* "that it is
not right for plays to be messed about with") and in a more general
usage in *Eu*. 552 (*ne hoc gaudium contaminet vita aegritudine aliqua*
"for fear life should sully this joy with any anguish").   There has
been great argument about what the word means when used with
reference to the adaptation of Greek plays into Latin, but it is far
from certain that it has any specific reference when so used.   It is
more likely to be a deliberately vague description intended to cover
all forms of alteration in adaptation.   See Introduction pp. 13−14.

Except in the unlikely event that Ter. used several originals to
produce his previous plays (*An*. and the unsuccessful *Hec*.), the
reference to "many" Greek models must be exaggeration, either by

Luscius or by Ter. in describing what his critic had said. See
Brothers 105.

20 **good playwrights:** Presumably, but not necessarily, those whom Ter.
calls his *auctores* "models" at *An.* 18−19, Naevius, Plautus and
Ennius. See Introduction pp. 5−6 and 14.

22 **a spiteful old poet:** Luscius Lanuvinus again, this time singled out;
cf. 16n. Reference to his age is Ter.'s way of hitting back at
someone who regarded him as a young upstart.

23 **the poetic art:** The Latin adjective used here, *musicus*, means
"pertaining to the muses", and therefore to the arts over which they
preside. When so used, it is frequently applied to poetry; cf. *Ph.* 17
and *Hec.* 23.

all of a sudden: The clear implication is that Ter. turned his
attention to writing at too early an age and without adequate training;
see Introduction pp. 9 and 12−13. If he was born *c.* 185 B.C., he
would have been 22 when *Hau.* was produced, and 19 when he put
on *An.*

24 **relying on his friends' talents:** For these "friends", see Introduction
p. 11.
[*amicum* is gen. pl. The early Latin 2nd declension gen. pl. ending
−*um* (or, earlier, −*om*; cf. *iniquom, aequom* 27) is related to the
Greek 2nd decl. gen. pl. ending −ων (−*ōn*). It was later largely
replaced by −*orum*, formed after the pattern of the 1st decl. gen. pl.
−*arum*, which was itself related to the Greek 1st decl. gen. pl.
−αων (−*aōn*) or −ῶν. See L.R. Palmer, *The Latin Language*
(London, 1954), 243 and W.M. Lindsay, *The Latin Language*
(Oxford, 1894), 401−2.]

25 **your verdict, your view:** See Introduction p. 13. Ter. is on the
horns of a dilemma; to admit the charge would be professional
suicide, while to deny it too vehemently might offend his influential
friends. His solution is this vague appeal to the audience's
judgement. In dealing with the same charge in *Ad.* 15ff., when his
reputation is more firmly established, he is bolder, calling it "the
greatest compliment" to have found such favour − though again he
does not specifically confirm or deny the accusation.

28 **give them a chance to get on:** Ter. repeats this plea for
advancement in his career at the end of the prologue to *Ad.* (24−5:
"make sure your open−mindedness increases the poet's application to
his writing"), where, in view of his death shortly thereafter, it has a
certain irony.

29 [**novarum ... spectandi ... copiam:** This seemingly strange construction
occurs also in Pl. (e.g. *Capt.* 852, 1008, where see W.M. Lindsay's
edn (London, 1900)), once in Lucretius (5. 1225, where see C.R.
Bailey's edn (Oxford, 1947)), several times in Cicero, and occasionally
elsewhere. It appears to be a cross between one using a gerund,

novas ... spectandi, and one using a gerundive, *novarum ...
spectandarum*. In the majority of instances the noun (here
fabularum, understood with *novarum*) is plural, and so this
construction avoids ugly repetition of the gen. pl. ending, here *−arum
... −arum*; and the noun governing the gerund is most often either
copia "chance" or *potestas* "opportunity".]

30 **that chap:** Luscius again, though it is hard to see how his scene
constitutes a "fault" (cf. 33); the stock character of the "running
slave" (cf. 37) often threatens anyone who gets in his way. One of
the best examples, though admittedly with an element of parody, is
Mercury in Pl. *Am.* 984−5: "make way and withdraw everyone, get
off the road, and let nobody be so rash as to get in my way", while
the character obviously appealed to Ter. (Davos at *An.* 338ff.; Geta
at *Ph.* 179ff., 841ff.; Geta at *Ad.* 299ff.). The point seems to be
that Ter., himself criticized for lack of originality in that others
assisted him, counters that Luscius exhibits no more originality in
portraying hackneyed scenes showing stock characters up to their usual
tricks. However, when it suits his purpose differently (*Eu.* 35ff.),
Ter. defends such a course.

32 **Why should our author ...?:** With the traditional punctuation of a
colon after *populum* "crowd", it is difficult to make sense of the
following words *quor insano serviat?* "Why should he serve a
madman?" when they have to be related to what has gone before.
The subject of *serviat* is held to be either *servus* "slave" ("what is
the point of the slave serving a mad master?"; so Eugr.) or *populus*
"crowd" ("why should the crowd indulge the whim of a madman?"; so
some scholia); but in neither case, as far as we can tell without
knowledge of Luscius' scene, does it seem that any great point is
being made. The alternative is to put a full stop after *populum* and
construe *quor insano serviat?* in the light of what follows. The
subject of *serviat* then becomes the same as that of *dicet* "He'll say"
in the next sentence, i.e. Ter. himself, and the sense will be "Why
should our author do a service for a mad poet like Luscius (instead
of exposing his faults)?". For *servio* in this sense, cf. 50 ("serve
your interests") and *Hec.* 224; for the interpretation, see further H.
Gelhaus, *Die Prologe des Terenz* (Heidelberg, 1972), 76−7, n. 19.

33 **He'll say more ...:** Compare further disparaging references to
episodes in Luscius' plays at *Eu.* 9ff. and *Ph.* 6ff., and similar threats
to expose such faults at *An.* 22−3 and *Eu.* 16−19. See Introduction
p. 12.

35−6 **Pay attention ... without interruption:** A plea for attention and
silence particularly closely echoed at *Ph.* 30 (*adeste aequo animo per
silentium* "pay attention without interruption), and, rather less closely,
at *Eu.* 44 and *Hec.* 55.

36 **contains more talk than action:** A translation for *stataria* (*sc.*

164

fabula), a play which involves little vigorous action, and is conducted mainly through the dialogue; the involved intrigue of *Hau.* necessitates just such long dialogues which make it *stataria*. The same adjective is used of actors in such plays, and orators who speak with a minimum of gesture (Cic. *Brut.* 116, 239). (Don. on *Ad.* 24 gives the opposite of *stataria* as *motoria*, presumably a play full of action, and adds a third type, a mixture of the two.)

37–9 **the running slave ... and the grabbing pimp:** Some of the stock characters of Roman comedy, two of whom, the slave and the parasite, appear in another such list of characters (and situations) at *Eu.* 36ff. As might be expected, the most colourful examples of the characters are found in Pl. (e.g. for the pimp, Ballio in *Ps.*, Labrax in *Rud.*); but most of them also appear in Ter. in a less extreme form. For the running slave, see 30n.; for the angry old man, Chremes at 915ff., Simo at *An.* 859ff.; for the greedy parasite, Gnatho at *Eu.* 232ff.; for the grabbing pimp ("dealer in female slaves" might be more accurate), Dorio at *Ph.* 485ff.

swindler: A translation for *sycophanta*, Greek *sūkophantēs*. From its original application to an unscrupulous bringer of prosecutions, the usage of the word is extended in Latin to any swindler or impostor who preys on credulous victims; cf. Latin *calumniator*, similarly used both literally (Cic. *Caec.* 65) and more widely (Sen. *Dial.* 9.3.2). In *An.* Crito is afraid of being thought a *sycophanta* of this type (815), and is indeed called such (919); but the character is not very common in existing *palliatae*, though one appears (unnamed) at Pl. *Trin.* 843ff.

44 **they run to me:** As leader of the company; see Introduction p. 7. The speaker seems proud of his position, but, since he twice refers to himself as an "old man", he is also aware that he is not the vigorous actor that he once was; cf. 1–2n.

46 **talk that is natural and unaffected:** A translation for *pura oratio*; the reference is appropriate for a play which depends for its effect on what is said in it rather than on the action; cf. 36n. Though the meaning of *oratio* here is disputed, it seems always in Ter. to refer to the content of what is being said, not to the style of writing; it is specifically contrasted with *stilus* "style" in *An.* 12, and with *scriptura* "composition" in *Ph.* 5. See further Marouzeau I 44, n. 2 and D.A. Kidd, 'Terence *Heaut.* 46', *CR* 62 (1948), 13. *pura* means "unelaborate", "unembellished", as in Caesar's famous description of Ter. (Suetonius, *Life* 7) as *puri sermonis amator* "a lover of unaffected speaking"; but there the similarity to Caesar's words ends, since he is talking of Ter.'s Latin, not the content of what he says.

47 **in either line:** i.e. in a play of quiet dialogue as well as in one of vigorous action.

48–50 **[If I've never been ... as much as I can,]:** These lines are the

165

same as *Hec.* 49−51, and perhaps fit better there, later in Ter.'s career; 48−9 are not in A. It seems unlikely, though not impossible, that Ter. would have used the same lines in two prologues, since the prologues were written with a view to each performance. On the other hand, the sentiment expressed is not particularized, and there are other points of similarity between different prologues (cf. 35−6n.) − though admittedly never as large as this one would be. On balance, we should reject the lines here and assume they were introduced to smooth over what was wrongly considered an awkward break between 47 and 51.

51 **to please you rather than themselves:** i.e. to take note of the tastes and wishes of the audience, instead of pursuing fashionable artistic trends. Artists of all sorts have always been the objects of such complaints.

ACT ONE SCENE ONE

With the scene set in a township in Attica (unspecified in Ter., but see 61ff. n.), the 'traditional' side exits (see Introduction p. 8) hardly need modification; that to the audience's left leads out into the countryside, that to their right to the centre of the township and/or to Athens itself (cf. 191n.). There is no need to suppose that the stage set is not the 'normal' one of fronts of houses (see Introduction p. 7); the land Menedemus works is nearby (54), not on stage, and the exertion of 88ff. is not actual hoeing, but carrying the hoes. Phania's house is only used once, but is on stage (cf. 169: "Phania, my neighbour here", and see G. Jachmann, *Plautinisches und Attisches* (Berlin, 1931), 249ff.).

The text does not indicate from where the two men enter; but Menedemus is clearly coming home at the end of the day (168−70, 248), and Chremes has also been away (179), and does not know that his son has brought Clinia to his house in his absence (182−3). The setting is correctly pictured by W. Beare, *Hermathena* 74 (1949), 35−6.

53ff. **Though this acquaintance …:** Chremes' whole opening speech has the air of a prepared piece; in particular the first long and pompous sentence (53−60) seems like a carefully rehearsed excuse for his inquisitive and patronizing interference in the personal affairs of a virtual stranger. His words show that, though he has had little to do with his new neighbour (55) and can only guess at his age (62−3), he has been closely observing him (67ff.) and been thinking up replies to his imagined explanations (71−2). By the time he ends with an astonishingly presumptuous piece of unsolicited advice (73−4), we have a clear picture of the unhealthy interest Chremes takes in other people.

It is probable that a fragment of a dramatic hypothesis found at Oxyrhynchus (*POxy* 2534) is of Men.'s original. It appears to contain, as other such hypotheses do, a citation of the first line of his play corresponding to 53 — parts of two words meaning "has been brief" — and the presence later in the fragment of the word νουθετῶν "warning" (cf. 58: "give you a ... warning") may mean that the citation goes further than that. See R.A. Coles and J.W.B. Barnes, 'Fragments of dramatic hypotheses from Oxyrhynchus', *CQ* n.s. 15 (1965), 52—7, esp. 55.

61ff. **In the name of gods and men ...:** We possess some five lines of the Greek original at this point (= Körte II 56, fr. 127):

πρὸς τῆς Ἀθηνᾶς, δαιμονᾷς, γεγονὼς ἔτη
τοσαῦθ'· ὁμοῦ γάρ ἐστιν ἐξήκοντά σοι
... καὶ τῶν Ἅλῃσι χωρίον
κεκτημένος κάλλιστον εἶ, νὴ τὸν Δία,
ἐν τοῖς τρισίν γε, καὶ τὸ μακαριώτατον,
ἄστικτον.

"In Athene's name, you're insane, when you're so old. You're roughly sixty ... And, of the people of Halae, you've acquired the finest piece of land among the three, by Zeus, and, best of all, unmortgaged."

The passage is made up of two fragments, the first specifically from Men.'s *Heautontimorumenos*, the second merely from Men. They have been correctly joined by comparing Ter.'s text, and the short gap between them has been variously filled, again by comparison with Ter.

Ter. has removed the special oaths, the place name "Halae" and the technical term "unmortgaged", probably because they would mean little to a Roman audience. He has also removed "among the three", and it is interesting to speculate whether Men. referred to the three farms of Menedemus, Chremes and Phania. H. Oppermann (*Hermes* 69 (1934), 274—5n.) defends Ter. against Jachmann's earlier charge that, besides removing superficial detail, he had lost more essential items in the characterization of Chremes.

We can now see that Men.'s play was set in Halae. There were two settlements of this name in Attica, Halae Araphenides on the east coast due east of Athens, and Halae Aexonides on the south coast, half way between Athens and Sunium. But it would be enough for Ter.'s audience to know that the scene was in Attica, or even merely somewhere vaguely in Greece.

65 [**servos compluris:** Supply *habes* from *habet* in the previous line.]

66 [**officia:** As in Pl., *fungor* is usually constructed with an acc., not an abl., in Ter. (cf. 580); the one exception is *Ad.* 603.]

69—70 **In short ...:** Is *denique* connected with what precedes ("or at any rate carrying something about. You don't relax ..."), or with what follows ("or carrying something about. In short, you don't relax ...")? Kauer—Lindsay follow Cicero and Don. in the former; but

167

Cicero quotes in isolation, and Don. is aiming to find a parallel for *Ph.* 121 (which is, in fact, a very different case). In *An.* 147 and *Eu.* 40, 432 and 444 *denique* as last word in the line definitely belongs to what follows, with the force "in fact" in a summary; so here, it introduces a summary of the preceding details about the length and nature of Menedemus' exertions.

70 **don't show any consideration for yourself:** Menedemus will quote these words back at Chremes when their situations are reversed towards the end of the play (919).

71−2 **"But," you'll tell me ...:** How much should be enclosed in quotation marks? Is "but" part of Chremes' quotation of Menedemus' objection with "I'm not satisfied", or part of his own comment with "you'll tell me"? There is little to choose between them, but I marginally prefer the one not favoured by Kauer−Lindsay.

75−6 **Chremes, have you got ...:** Menedemus addresses Chremes by name immediately for the benefit of the audience; but it is only in 159 that Menedemus' own name is revealed. His justifiable resentment at Chremes' interference is expressed in words as brief and to the point as Chremes' were long and involved. It is hard not to sympathize with his reaction; see Introduction p. 20.
Varro (*R.* 2.11.11) cites Menedemus as an example of the comic character engaged in farm work appearing dressed in the Greek *diphthera*, a leather jerkin; cf. Men. *Dyskolos* 415 and E.W. Handley (ed.), *The Dyskolos of Menander* (London, 1965), 32.

77 **I'm a human being ...:** One of Ter.'s most celebrated 'quotable' lines (like *Ph.* 203: *fortis fortuna adiuvat* "fortune favours the brave"), this is discussed at length by Jocelyn, *passim*. It has too often been cited out of context as an example of true human sympathy − it is, for example, the motto of the London Hospital Medical College − but it is more correctly to be seen as Chremes' attempt to justify his interference, and serves further to characterize him as a busybody (Greek *polupragmōn, periergos*; Latin *curiosus*), especially when viewed alongside passages such as 168ff. and 498ff. See further M. Delcourt, *Collection Latomus* 44 (1960), 257−62. Jocelyn also points to Chremes' pretensions to amateur philosophy (cf. 151ff., 192ff., 208ff., 439ff.), adding (27) that there is "something ludicrously incongruous about an old farmer spouting philosophical phrases". On this showing, any discussion of the serious philosophical import of the line will be largely misdirected. On the other hand, it is nowhere specifically stated that Chremes *is* a farmer, and he may be more educated than Jocelyn allows.
It is not surprising that, with such a 'proverbial' saying, various passages of Men. have been suggested as its source. Webster (144) accepts Körte II 164, fr. 475, from an unidentified play:
οὐδείς ἐστί μοι

ἀλλότριος, ἂν ᾖ χρηστός· ἡ φύσις μία
πάντων, τὸ δ' οἰκεῖον συνίστησιν τρόπος.
"Nobody is a stranger to me, if he is a good man. There is one
nature for us all, and it's character that brings about intimacy."
However attractive this identification seems, there is no proof; and it
can be argued that the absence of the second sentiment in Ter.
makes such identification hazardous.

79 [**rectum est ... non est:** As printed, this must be equivalent to *si
rectum est ... si non est* (cf. *Eu.* 252). But possibly Bentley and
Marouzeau are right to print *rectum est? ... non est?*]

81 **torment himself:** The English, like the Latin *se ... cruciet*, translates
Men.'s title. Cf. Hor. *S.* 1.2.20−2: "such that the father whom
Terence's play depicts having lived in misery when he banished his
son did not torment himself (*non se ... cruciaverit*) worse than he."

82 [**laborist:** = *laboris est*, which most MSS write in full in violation of
metre. (*laboris* is gen. after *quid*: "if there is any distress (for
you)".) As −*us est* has sometimes to be scanned −*ust* (cf. *periocha*
4 etc.) and −*us es* −*u's* (cf. 580 etc.), so −*is est* must sometimes
be scanned −*ist* and, perhaps, −*is es* −*i's* (cf. *An.* 702); this is said
to be prodelision or enclisis of *est* or *es* after −*us* or −*is*. See D.S.
Raven, *Latin Metre* (London, 1965), 28; W.M. Lindsay, *Early Latin
Verse* (Oxford, 1922), 74ff., and Laidlaw 30ff.]

84 **Don't cry:** Chremes seems to feel some genuine concern now that
Menedemus has broken down under his relentless probing. But
Jocelyn points out (29) that it is too easy for a reader to retroject
this concern into his appreciation of 77, when an audience could not.
[**ne lacruma:** *ne* and imperative for a 2nd person prohibition is
regular in early Latin; cf. 85, 89 etc. It appears in later verse as an
archaism (e.g. Verg. *A.* 2.48), but is rare in later prose.]

86 **I'll assist:** Hunter 100 thinks it absurd of Chremes to promise help
before he knows Menedemus' situation; but such general offers are
often made by people who are as yet ignorant of the facts.

87 [**qua:** For *quam*; attraction of the relative into the case of its
antecedent, *causa*.]

88 **those hoes:** The *rastrum* (pl. *rastri*, masc.) was properly a
drag−hoe, a type of mattock used, among other things, for breaking
up clods of earth left after a plough had passed or the entire surface
of the ground in areas too inaccessible for ploughing. Such uses
necessitated its notorious weight (cf. 92, Verg. *G.* 1.164 etc.); see
K.D. White, *Agricultural Implements of the Roman World*
(Cambridge, 1967), 52−6 and plate 5.

89 **exerting yourself:** The reference is to carrying the hoes, not using
them; see the introductory note to the scene.

93 **I have an only son:** The exposition proper begins here. Suggestions
that Ter. has lengthened this by inserting details from Men.'s prologue

seem questionable. We know from fragments corresponding to 61ff. that in the original Chremes protested at (and thus presumably did not know the reason for) Menedemus' self−inflicted toil, and so we should expect that ignorance to be made good in the Greek as in the Latin; we also possess a fragment which may correspond to 124ff. To judge from parallels in Men., the prologue is more likely to have introduced some characters, set the scene (which we miss in Ter.; cf. 61ff. n.) and hinted at the outcome; this hint may have concerned Antiphila's origins and/or the eventual reversal of roles of Menedemus and Chremes. Some subtleties in the plot may thus have been lost to the Roman audience, but an element of surprise may have been gained. Was a liking for surprise the reason for Ter.'s removal of the explanatory prologue?

94 **But why did I say ...?:** Emendation to *ah* "ah", which has no direct MS support, seems unnecessary, especially since *at* "but" makes good sense and is well attested in the tradition.

95ff. **I'll tell you:** Lit. "You shall know". Menedemus' account is vividly written, and his self−critical frankness arouses sympathy and admiration for his honesty. See Introduction p. 19.

96 **a stranger here from Corinth ...:** It was not the poverty of Antiphila's (supposed) mother which was the principal bar to marriage between Clinia and Antiphila − though, other things being equal, the absence of a suitable dowry would have been serious enough − but the fact that she was Corinthian, i.e. non−Athenian. Over a century before Men.'s dramatic career began, the Athenian statesman Pericles had passed a law which restricted Athenian citizenship to children both of whose parents were themselves Athenians. Therefore any offspring of a union between Clinia and Antiphila would not be citizens, and this was a situation which no self−respecting Athenian father· could contemplate in the matter of his son's marriage. Citizenship was a prize and a privilege, and, in a society where the continuation of the family in the male line was all−important, such an alliance would have been quite impossible in Menedemus' eyes, the more so because Clinia was his only son (cf. 93). Though the detailed background of all this would probably not have been known to Ter.'s audience, they would doubtless have grasped the main point − that citizens could only marry fellow−citizens.

98 **considered her as his wife:** The essential point here − so important that it is repeated at 104 − is that Clinia regards Antiphila, supposedly a foreigner from Corinth, as his wife; this arouses sympathy among the audience, and even foreshadows eventual marriage. Compare Pamphilus' attitude to Glycerium in *An.* (145−6, 215−6, 273), and contrast Clitipho's attitude to Bacchis in our play. [**clam me:** Most often in Ter. *clam* as a preposition governs *me* (cf. 118) or *te*. But *Hec.* 396−7 (*clam ... patrem atque ... omnis*

170

(= *omnes*)) shows that *me* and *te* are acc. not abl.   See *periocha* 4n.]

101   **the hackneyed way of fathers:**   Hunter 99 says of this passage and of
439:   "By thus assimilating his behaviour to a familiar pattern of
stage action, Menedemus allows us to understand much about the
history of the relationship between himself and Clinia which need not
be expressly stated."   It is also possible that Ter. is here gently
poking fun at his own trade, as he does more obviously at the end of
Hec. (866—7):   "I'd like this not to happen like it does in comedies,
where everybody gets to know everything".
[There is effective alliteration of *v* in *vi et via pervolgata*.]

102   **What?:**   The Latin word so translated, *hem!*, is discussed at length by
G. Luck, *Über einige Interjektionen der Lateinischen Umgangssprache*
(Heidelberg, 1964), 13.   He calls it "the expression of a person who
has not heard correctly or who acts as if he had not heard correctly";
he argues that the interjection has an interrogative force, and
regularly prints *hem?*.   However, R.H. Martin, in his commentary on
Ad. (Cambridge, 1976, 139 on line 224) says that there are occasions
when "What!" is a more appropriate translation than "What?", and
that the word "most commonly expresses astonishment at the
unexpected, whether pleasant or unpleasant".   I have usually translated
"What?" (102, 128, 340, 654, 706, 906) or "Eh?" (311, 517), but
have felt "Ah!" more appropriate for Syrus' expression of exaggerated
pleasure at 757.

105   **Clinia:**   The name of Menedemus' son is slipped in for the first time
casually and naturally.   But the audience still does not know the
name of the father who is speaking.

110   [**istuc aetatis:**   Equivalent to *istac aetate*, *aetatis* being partitive gen.
after *istuc*.]

111   **to Asia:**   i.e. Asia Minor.   In Men.'s youth many Athenians must
have fought under Alexander the Great (died 323 B.C.) in his
campaigns of conquest; later in Men.'s life there were frequent wars
between Alexander's *diadochoi* "successor generals", who fought for
their share of his empire and, in many cases, founded dynasties.
Serving in these armies as mercenaries was the stock course for young
Athenians who were impoverished (Menedemus) or crossed in love
(Clinia, 117).   The wars continued for so long that it was perfectly
possible to envisage a father and his son both taking part, and the
Athenian (though not the Roman) audience would have known enough
to be able to imagine Menedemus fighting under Alexander himself
and Clinia taking part in the wars of his successors.   See 117n.
In keeping with his respect for the spirit of his originals, Ter. has
kept the allusion, though he may have cut out some details; cf. *Eu.*
125—6, where Thais talks of Thraso serving in Caria.

112   [**armis belli:**   *belli* is locative "at war", not gen. after *armis*; cf. Pl.
Am. 647 and *Epid.* 442.]

171

113 **things reached a critical point:** Lit. "the matter came to such a point"; cf. 980: *adeon rem rediisse ut ...* "To think that the matter has come to such a point that ...".
117 **for the King:** One of Alexander's successors; cf. 111n.
118 **What!:** As Don. remarks (on *An.* 137) *quid ais?*, lit. "what are you saying?", is the comment of someone not so much asking a genuine question as expressing astonishment; cf. 182, 702.
119 **You're neither of you ...:** This impertinent and insensitive remark of Chremes is either wisely ignored by Menedemus or not noticed in his distress.
124ff. **I sat down:** Ter. uses short, simple sentences and clauses which help to convey the hurry and bustle and produce a very vivid impression; cf. 140ff., 274ff. and Simo's description of Chrysis' funeral in *An.* 127−9: "Meanwhile the funeral procession moved off; we followed; we reached the tomb; she was laid on the pyre; there was weeping."
A fragment of Men.'s original (= Körte II 56, fr. 128: λουτρόν, θεραπαίνας, ἀργυρώματα "a bath, servant girls, silver plate") may correspond to part of this passage. Other possibilities are 140ff. or 451−2.
129 [**solius:** This is the only time the gen. sing. of *solus* appears in Ter. On the evidence of Don.'s note on the only appearance of the gen. sing. of *nullus* (*An.* 608: *tam nulli consili sum*), and because pronominal adjectives sometimes took noun declension forms in gen. and dat., especially in early Latin, Kauer−Lindsay print *soli* for the *solius* of all MSS. Such an unsupported alteration seems questionable, especially with *unius* in 205 and *alterius* in *An.* 628. Whatever its form, the gen. agrees with the gen. implied in *mea*.]
130 [**vestiant:** Kauer−Lindsay accept the minority reading *vestient* (fut. indic.), presumably to make all three questions in 128−31 (*sunt ... vestiant ... faciam*) indicative. But there seems no reason why the first should not be indicative, and the other two subjunctive (deliberative), even granted the close connection between them evidenced by *tot ... tot ... tantos*.]
134 **through my own unfair behaviour:** Here as elsewhere (e.g. 158) Menedemus is disarmingly candid and objective about how wrong his attitude to Clinia was.
139 **by toiling ...:** The Latin line contains many long syllables (four spondees, two iambi); the heavy, toilsome effect highlights the painful effort of Menedemus' activities.
140ff. **That's what I did:** The Latin again has short, simple sentences (varied by one longer one 142−4) to add vividness to the description and convey the haste with which things were done.
141 **a cushion:** *vestimentum* can refer to rugs, blankets etc. used as coverings for furniture as well as to clothes (cf. 903, where it is used

of making up a bed); such a meaning is more appropriate here when related to the contents of the house. "Not a cup nor a cushion" attempts to capture in English the alliteration in the Latin *nec vas nec vestimentum*.

144 **put the house on the market:** Lit. "advertised the house for sale." But since *mercede* (here translated "for sale") can also mean "at a rent", Bentley and some other editors follow Eugr. in assuming that Menedemus is letting his house, not selling, intending to repossess it on Clinia's return. However, it is much more in keeping with his mood that he sells the house, as he does all his other unnecessary possessions. (The editors of *OLD* seem inconsistent on the point; under *inscribere* 1b they interpret the passage as referring to selling, but under *merces* 3 as referring to letting.)
[*proscribere* is commoner than *inscribere* in this scene, but cf. Pl. *Trin.* 168: *aedis venalis hasce inscribit litteris* "he's put up a notice offering this house for sale"; as *venalis* helps to make the meaning clear there, so does *mercede* here.]

145 **about fifteen talents:** A considerable sum; compare the fact that Chremes thinks two talents an adequate dowry for his only daughter (838, 940). See further Jocelyn 22, nn. 56 and 59.

151ff. **I think you've got ...:** Chremes' second comment on Menedemus' story is as insensitive as his first (119—20). After a moderately considerate opening (151), he implies that Menedemus did not know how to handle his son, tells him what he did wrong and what he should have done instead, and ends with the observation that it could all have been avoided. This may be true, but as a response it could hardly be more unsubtle and unhelpful. One senses how pleased with his analysis Chremes will be when in 158 Menedemus agrees and in his misery admits the error of his ways. But Menedemus has already done this (cf. 134n.), and it seems that Chremes is merely turning the screw.

154 **When people don't live their lives truthfully:** More homespun philosophy from Chremes. For parallels on the *vera vita* "the life that is true" in Roman comedy, see Jocelyn 26, n. 86, and cf. especially *Ad.* 986—7: "so that I could show you that that did not come about as a result of a life which was sincere (*ex vera vita*)."
[*qui*: "how"; cf. 362, 492 etc.]

155 **You never showed ...:** Menedemus will find himself giving the same advice to Chremes when the tables are turned (925ff.); cf. 70n.

159 **But I expect ...:** For differing ways of viewing Chremes' remarks here and at 161ff. and 167—8, see Introduction p. 19.
Menedemus: This is the first mention of Menedemus' name and it is quite casual; such long delays in naming major characters are rare. As the Greek stage was usually careful of its conventions on naming, Terence may have omitted to translate an earlier mention, or in the

173

original the naming may have occurred in an explanatory prologue. But as no third character has yet appeared to confuse the issue, no difficulty is caused.

161 [**faxint:** The old Latin future indicatives and subjunctives formed by adding $-s-$ to the root of the verb gradually fell out of use. Even in Pl., half the examples are parts of *faxo* (*fac−s−o*), indic., and *faxim* (*fac−s−im*), subj., and in Ter. there are not many examples apart from these, nearly all used in set expressions like this one and *cave faxis* (187). Cicero uses this one as a religious archaism (e.g. *Att.* 16.1.6: *di faxint*).]

162 **the Dionysia here today:** "here" confirms that, as is to be expected when the play is set in a township in Attica, the Rural or Country Dionysia is meant. This was a festival held in the month of Poseideon (roughly our December) at various places all over Attica; but it "was not tied to a single date, but was celebrated according to the choice of each neighbourhood" (H.W. Parke, *Festivals of the Athenians* (London, 1977), 100). Since Menedemus is a new arrival in the area, and has been living the life of a recluse, Chremes has to explain that today is the day the festival is being celebrated in their particular community. For the festival, see Parke, *op.cit.* 100−3, who mentions (102) performances of comedies at it. Perhaps Men.'s original was first produced on such an occasion, possibly even at Halae (cf. 61ff. n.); certainly he wrote too many plays for them all to have been put on in Athens itself.
Here and at 733 Ter. keeps the Greek name of the festival, there being no true Roman equivalent. However, in the case of Greek deities, which all had their Roman counterparts, Ter. habitually changes the Greek names he (presumably) found in his originals to the corresponding Latin ones; cf. 256, 1036.

164 **would want:** Lit. "wants".

165 [**hinc pepulerim:** The line is incomplete, most MSS reading *inpulerim*. Since the reduplicated perfect of *impello* is not found elsewhere, Bentley's *hinc pepulerim* is more likely a conjecture than Kauer−Lindsay's *inpepulerim*.]

167 **Good−bye, then:** Since Chremes says good−bye first, we should expect him to be the one to leave, whereas in fact Menedemus goes while he stays. This further characterizes the two old men; Chremes the extrovert forces the words of farewell out of Menedemus by 'getting in first', and the latter rather unenthusiastically replies as he leaves the stage.
He's brought me to the verge of tears: Lit. "He's forced tears from me."

168 **But, seeing what hour of day it is:** After only a few words of sympathy for Menedemus, Chremes quickly becomes immersed in his own affairs, fussing (unnecessarily) over his supper invitations.

174

169 [**tempust:** The phrase (= *tempus est;* cf. 82n.) is in no MSS, but most editors follow Bentley in inserting it; it is easy to imagine how it fell out after *tempus est* at the end of 168. But, however correct this may be, it seems that no evidence for its existence can be found in the scholia Bembina — see Mountford 56.]

Phania, my neighbour here: From the evidence of parallels (e.g. 1001), this phrase seems to prove that Phania's house was on stage; see the introductory note to the scene.

170 **to supper:** Körte (II 58 on fr. 133) thinks that in Men. the meal was lunch (Greek *āriston*, Latin *prandium*), not supper (Greek *deipnon*, Latin *cena*), and that Ter. has altered the nature of the meal and inserted a night—interval between 409 and 410, not wishing to offend Roman susceptibilities by portraying a drunken meal (cf. 457ff., 518ff.) at midday. His evidence is: (i) mention of *āriston* in fr. 133; (ii) the meal in Men.'s *Epitrepontes* and *Perikeiromene* is *āriston*; (iii) there is no parallel for two—day action in Greek New Comedy. Arguments (ii) and (iii) are weak (*deipnon* is the meal in *Samia*, and there appears to be a precedent for two—day action in *Epitrepontes*); but (i) seems persuasive. If Körte were correct, it would follow that all mention of supper, as here, or of approach of evening (248) are points where Ter. has changed his original. See further 410n.

170−1 *He walks across:* The stage direction embodies what I envisage happened in Ter.'s play and says nothing about what may have happened in Men. It is likely that a choral interlude or, more possibly, a deferred prologue, occurred in the Greek at this point (see Introduction p. 17); but that is no reason to suppose, as do Kauer—Lindsay, that a *saltatio convivarum* "dance of supper—guests" occurred as a sort of choral interlude in Ter.'s play. After all that has been written on this famous problem, what probably happened in Ter. and how it related to what probably happened in Men. is neatly summed up in a single paragraph by J.C.B. Lowe (*Hermes* 111 (1983), 450−1). R.L. Hunter (*ZPE* 36 (1979), 27−8), like Lowe, favours a prologue rather than a choral interlude in the Greek at this point: "The clear parallel of [Men.'s] *Aspis* [94−6; 149ff.] makes it all but certain that the coming and going of Chremes at this point marks the omission of the divine prologue which stood here in the Greek play."

171 **He had no need ...:** Chremes' needless fussing is emphasized, characterizing him further.

172 **I'm told:** Lit. "they tell me", "they" being the slaves in Phania's house.

173 **But why this creaking ...:** By convention, in both Greek and Roman comedy, the doors of the stage set made a noise when they were being opened from inside; an actor on stage could therefore draw

175

attention to this and alert the audience's attention to the emergence of a character from one of the houses. 613 provides a close parallel; advance notice of people coming out, but without mention of noise, is given at 510, 561, 722, 1000 and 1023. In practice ancient doors were noisy affairs, with their elaborate system of locks, bars and bolts, and with the heavy door-leaves themselves swinging on pivots set into sockets in sill and lintel; the stage convention would thus appear fairly natural, but there is no need to expect it to reflect real life exactly. For the difficulties this matter has caused (including suggestions that stage — or even real — doors opened outwards, and the noise was a warning to people passing in the street!), see Beare 285ff. and Duckworth 116-7.

ACT ONE SCENE TWO

175 **There's nothing for you to be afraid of ...:** It is another common convention of this type of drama that characters emerging from a house talk back to people still inside, thereby connecting events and personalities off stage with what the audience can see happening; cf. Menedemus talking back to Clinia (842-4), and see Duckworth 125-6. Longer examples can be found at *Hec.* 76-80 and *An.* 481-5; the forced nature of the latter is put to good use dramatically when Simo thinks the words have been spoken outdoors for his benefit.
Clitipho's cryptic remarks would arouse interest; in particular, the audience would be intrigued by the mention of Clinia, who they had been led to believe (117) was in Asia.
they: Dromo ("the messenger"), Antiphila ("her") and Syrus (cf. 191); not Bacchis, who is not known to be coming until 311.

178 **Who's my son talking to?:** Chremes' question is meant as an aside, but is overheard by Clitipho. It might seem an odd question, since Chremes has heard his son address Clinia by name (175) and knows who Clinia is (105). But its dramatic purpose is to identify the newcomer for the audience; "my son", not "who ... to", are the important words. The relationship between the two is further stressed when Clitipho twice refers to Chremes as his father in the following line.

179 **how convenient:** Clitipho's primary motive for coming outside is presumably to wait for Syrus, Dromo and Antiphila; it is an added bonus that, while waiting, he can take the opportunity to tell his father what has been happening in his absence.

180 **Very well:** An exaggerated claim on the strength of one conversation, however long and intimate it may have been. But it is in character for Chremes to wish to be thought a close friend of as many people as possible, and he certainly would not want his son to think that he

176

did not know his own neighbour. He might also think that his long and close observation of Menedemus' habits (cf. 53ff. n.) did mean that he knew him well.

183–4 **a friend of his ever since we were boys:** The long and close friendship of the sons contrasts with the fact that their fathers were strangers until recently (53), and this has led to suggestions of clumsiness in adaptation by Terence. But fathers do not always know about their sons' friends, and we must remember that until recently Clinia and Menedemus lived some way away from Clitipho and Chremes. See further Brothers 102, n. 45.

185 **How I wish I'd been more insistent ...:** Lit. "How I would wish that Menedemus had been more (strongly) invited to be with us."
more insistent in inviting: The meaning if the comma is placed after *amplius* "further", "more", not before it where it is placed by Eugr., the scholia Bembina and Kauer–Lindsay. The meaning with their punctuation is neither so clear nor so natural, though it is in keeping with Ter.'s style to place at the end of one line a word which grammatically belongs to the next (cf. 61, 69, 71 etc.).
For Chremes' eagerness to be first to tell Menedemus the news, cf. 410ff. and see Introduction p. 19.

187 [**cave faxis:** *cave* with subjunctive is commoner than *cave ne* with subjunctive for a prohibition in Ter. and Pl.; cf. 826, 1031, 1032. For *faxis,* see 161n.]

188 [**se:** abl.; cf. *quid illo facias* 317, *quid faciet sua* 333.]

191 **his slave:** Dromo. The diminutive of the word for "slave" used here, *servolus,* appears three times in *Hau.,* each time referring to Dromo (cf. 471, 530). Diminutives are sometimes used contemptuously in Latin, and the choice of word may be deliberate, belittling Dromo in contrast to the magnificent Syrus. At any rate, Clitipho appears to have thought it wise not to entrust the mission to Dromo alone, since he has sent Syrus along too.
into town: Athens itself is meant by the use of the word *urbs* "city" in Ter. here, not the country township where the play is set (cf. the introductory note to Act One Scene One and 61ff. n.). This is presumably where Menedemus lived before he moved and where Clinia met Antiphila (and also where Clitipho met Bacchis).

194 **He's got his parents ...:** Chremes may merely be producing a conventional list of "blessings". He certainly knows nothing of Clinia's friends (except Clitipho and Antiphila), nor of his relatives. Moreover, the plural "parents" seems odd, since Clinia's mother is never mentioned in the play; indeed, the phrase "to satisfy just me" (129) perhaps implies that Menedemus is a widower or divorced.

195 **these are possessions:** More pompous philosophical moralizing from Chremes.

197 [**ill':** Scansion of *ille* with the final −e dropped (cf. 515) seems

177

necessary to avoid a badly divided anapaest $-\breve{e}$ $f\breve{u}\bar{u}t$ in the second foot. See Laidlaw 28.]

[Rather confusingly, *ill'* here refers to Menedemus, *illum* (198) to Clinia, and *illicine* and *illi* (199) to Menedemus again, with Clinia becoming *hunc*.]

199 **Menedemus?** (*Aside.*), **I'll bite my tongue:** Chremes' suppression of his first impulse to tell Clitipho of Menedemus' true feelings is not as "useful" as he thinks, but merely prolongs his neighbour's misery; see Introduction p. 19.

[Fleckeisen's conjecture *illicine* is preferable to the *illene* of all MSS; the latter poses serious metrical problems, since (i) it entails a dactylic word as the first foot (which is, at best, extremely rare in iambic lines in Ter.; see Laidlaw 44), and (ii) it involves the highly unlikely scansion *rēprimam* later in the line (cf. the unlikelihood of *dūplici*, 6n.) It is easy to imagine how a copyist ignorant of metre could change *illicine* to the more obvious *illene*; the latter possibly started life as a marginal note on the rarer form.]

[*illicine* = *illic* + *ne*. When *−ne* follows, *i* is inserted; cf. *illancin* (= *illanc*+*n(e)*) 751 and *huncine* (= *hunc*+*ne*) 203 etc.; also *sicin(e)* (= *sic* + *n(e)*) 166, 691. *illic* itself is *ille* strengthened by the enclitic *−ce*; cf. *istic* (380, 562, 579, 593), the strengthened form of *iste* (731).]

200 **What's that you're muttering?:** Clitipho hears his father's aside (cf. 178n.), but not well enough to be able to understand its content, and Chremes can thus change his approach.

[**mansum ... oportuit:** Supply *esse*, as at 247, 635 etc. Here *mansum* is impersonal passive, lit. "it ought to have been remained (by him)"; cf. *An.* 239: *nonne prius communicatum oportuit?*, lit. "ought it not be have been communicated (to me) first?".]

201 **than the boy would have liked:** The word *lubido* (= *libido*) has two allied but separate meanings: desire in general (here and 216) and desire specifically sexual (573).

203 [**huncine:** See 199n.]

206 **They don't want ...:** Visiting "prostitutes" (i.e. slave girls kept by *lenones* "pimps" or "slave−dealers", or more mature professional 'ladies' like Bacchis) and attending dinner parties (cf. e.g. *Eu.* 539ff.) are the standard pastimes for free−born young men in this type of comedy, just as the standard means for fathers to prevent excess in these directions is to keep their sons short of money (cf. Chremes' advice to Menedemus, 870−1). Much of the intrigue (e.g. by Syrus in our play) is therefore directed towards securing money to enable the young men to continue such activities.

209 **it's inevitable, Clitipho ...:** Clitipho's name is mentioned for the first time, casually and after some delay (cf. 105n., 159n.); but the important fact of his relationship to Chremes was made clear

178

immediately he appeared (cf. 178n.).

[The jingle *consilia consequi consimilia* is of the heavy type more common in Pl. than Ter.]

210 **The clever course** ...: After concluding his lecture to Clitipho with more moralizing (208−9), Chremes sums up with a pithy maxim. But it is a maxim he will be unable to put into practice himself at the end of the play (915ff., esp. 928−31), where it is clear that Menedemus' mistakes have not taught him how errant sons should be treated.

[The evidence for *face* (= *fac*), accepted by Kauer−Lindsay, is much weaker than that for *facere*. Moreover, to read *face* here would destroy the very close metrical correspondence between this line and Clitipho's quotation of it substituting *facito* at 221.]

211 **So I imagine:** The reason for the distinct lack of conviction in Clitipho's reaction will become clear very soon.

to see what we've got ...: Chremes presumably knows what is on the menu at his own supper−party, but this natural remark − many people say "let's go and see what's for supper" when they already know − is put into his mouth to motivate his exit and leave the stage to Clitipho, whose remarks in the next scene he must not hear. It also further illustrates Chremes' tendency to fuss (cf. 168n., 171n.).

[Kauer−Lindsay's adoption of a conjecture only slightly different from the reading of A is ingenious, but may be nothing more. *in cena* is an odd phrase for "for supper", whereas the partitive gen. *cenae* after *quid* (most other MSS) seems natural.]

ACT TWO SCENE ONE

Since the act−divisions are later additions to our text (see Introduction p. 24), there is no certainty that Ter. found one in the Greek original at this point. Indeed, since the end of the previous scene makes it clear that Clitipho stays on stage after Chremes has left, such a division is unlikely to have stood here. The only places where we can with some certainty suspect that an act−division occurred in the Greek are 170−1 (if a chorus, not a prologue, came there), 409−10 (the night interval), 873−4 (Menedemus' exit and re−emergence), and possibly where 723−48 now stand.

213 **What unfair judges** ...: The monologue is a prominent feature of this type of comedy. We have already seen a shorter example from Chremes at 167ff., and there will be others from Chremes (410ff.), Menedemus (420ff.), Syrus (668ff.) etc. This one is in two distinct parts, Clitipho's reflections on Chremes' words (213−21) joined by a 'link−line' (222) to news of an unexpected new development (223−9) − which Gaiser (1052) thinks was explained in the prologue in Men. A precisely similar arrangement is found in Davos' monologue at *An.*

179

206ff.: reflection (206—14), and fresh news (215—24), with 225—7 introducing the following scene.

Körte (II 57) thinks that fr. 131 (πᾶς πατὴρ μῶρος "every father is foolish"), quoted in the scholia Bembina alongside 440—1 (Mountford 68), fits more suitably here; it certainly seems more suited to a son's tirade against fathers than to a conversation between Menedemus and Chremes, but more than that we cannot say.

217 [ne is here the affirmative particle "indeed", not the negative adverb and conjunction; cf. 222, 556 etc.]

218 **finding and forgiving:** With the jingle *cognoscendi et ignoscendi* "of recognizing and pardoning", compare *Eu*. 42: *qua re aequom est vos cognoscere et ignoscere* "for which reason it is right for you to recognise and pardon".
[In early Latin *ignoscere* takes an acc., not a dat. (cf. 647: *istuc factum ignoscam* "I'll forgive what you've done"), so a construction employing its gerundive (which is passive) *ignoscendi ... peccati locus* "scope for wrongdoing being forgiven" is satisfactory. Failure to appreciate this led to *ignoscendi* being construed as a gerund (which is active), and to alteration of *peccati* to *peccatis* in the scholia Bembina and Σ MSS.]

219 **someone else:** Clinia; Clitipho is well aware that he was meant to apply his father's remarks on Clinia to himself.

220 **When he's had a drop too much:** The implication that Chremes, for all his moral posturing, sometimes drinks a little too much recurs in Syrus' comments on his master's behaviour at the supper—party (518ff.).
what escapades of his own ...: It is a commonplace in this type of comedy to contrast the current actions and attitudes of the old men with the way they had behaved in their youth. Thus, for example, at Pl. *Ps*. 436ff. Callipho criticizes Simo for being angry with his son Calidorus when he himself had been no better in his younger days. See also *Ad*. 100ff.
[perii is sometimes a mere exclamation, as here, but sometimes (e.g. 246) has the more literal meaning "I've had it", "I'm done for".]

221 [facito: 2nd sing. fut. imperative; cf. 550, and *credito* 577, *narrato* 702 etc.]

222 **how deaf I am:** 'Talking to the deaf' was a common proverbial expression in Latin poetry; cf. Hor. *Ep*. 2.1.199—200, Prop. 4.8.47, Verg. *Ecl*. 10.8 etc.

223 **the words of my mistress:** The sudden introduction of this new element into the plot would stimulate the audience's interest. The attentive among them would already have realized that Clinia's return signalled the beginning of the end of Menedemus' troubles; the news of Clitipho's affair would alert them to the fact that Chremes (of whom they had probably already formed an unfavourable impression)

was riding for a fall and would from now on be the focus of attention in the play. The abrupt introduction of this development is made more natural by Clitipho's explanation in 229.

226 **well and modestly brought up:** This description, verified by Syrus' account at 274ff., is designed further to arouse sympathy for Antiphila, and to lay the way open for eventual marriage; cf. 98n.

227 **Mine's grand and grasping ...:** In contrast to Antiphila, Bacchis is unsympathetically treated from the start; she is Clitipho's mistress (*amica* 223) and a 'professional' (*meretrix*, by contrast with Antiphila, 226), and the audience will not therefore be surprised when at the end of the play she is unceremoniously dropped, and Clitipho agrees to marry an acceptable bride.
The string of adjectives which make up the description has a pseudo—solemn ring about it.

228 [*recte* often appears "in a reply, implying that the matter is of no consequence and used esp. to avoid giving a direct answer" (*OLD* 1585, *recte* 10b); cf. 518.]

ACT TWO   SCENE TWO

230 **If things were going well:** Clinia is getting worried and impatient. Clitipho left the house at 175 and has not returned with any news, so against advice (cf. 235) Clinia comes out to see for himself where "they" (cf. 175n.) have got to.
Gaiser (1041) thinks that Men.'s second act began here, with Clitipho going indoors at 229 and now re—emerging talking to Clinia.

232 **to increase my fears:** There seem to be no parallels for *animus* in the meaning "fear", though it can be used for other emotions such as courage and wrath. But the virtual unanimity of the MSS, and the fact that the meaning given to the word is a natural extension of a more normal usage, should discourage arbitrary emendation.

235 [*etiam caves:* The impatient question is equivalent to a command; cf. *etiam taces? Ad.* 550, and see 813n.]

239 **it's quite a way away:** Further evidence that the party is coming from Athens, not the local town; cf. 191n.

240 **a year's gone by:** Humorous exaggeration on a topic which is still a source of joking today. Less exaggerated are Chaerea's remarks on the old man who waylaid him (*Eu.* 341): "While he was telling me this, an hour went by."

241 **here comes Dromo:** It is quite common for characters to look off into the 'wings' and claim to see characters advancing along the street, thereby informing the audience of the identity of a new arrival; cf. 375, 804. The audience would be expected to realize, by recalling Clitipho's words at 191, that Dromo was the name of Clinia's slave.

[**eccum** =/ *ecce* + *hum*, where *hum* is acc. masc. sing. of *hic* without the enclitic −*ce*. *ecce* governs the acc., and sometimes, as with *Dromonem* here, there is a second acc. as if in apposition; cf. *eccum me* 829.]

ACT TWO SCENE THREE

242ff. **Really?:** The scene opens with a good example of the convention whereby an actor or group of actors can be unaware of the presence of another actor or group on the stage at the same time. In 242−50 Syrus and Dromo are ignorant of the presence of Clinia and Clitipho, though the latter have seen the former, and in 251−5, after Dromo's departure, Syrus is still unaware of the other two, not catching sight of them until 256. This convention enables one of the parties to overhear and comment upon the conversation (or thinking aloud) of the other, and is facilitated by the wide and shallow stage; see Introduction p. 7, and cf. Syrus and Clinia listening to Bacchis and Antiphila 381−402, Chremes and Syrus listening to Sostrata and the nurse 614−21 etc.

It is another common convention that characters enter halfway through (or, as here, at the tail end of) a conversation; cf. Sostrata and the nurse 614ff., Clitipho and Menedemus 954ff., Sostrata and Chremes 1003ff. Like the 'talking back' convention (cf. 175n.), it is designed to connect events on stage with the wider world beyond its confines. See Duckworth 124−5.

while we've been chatting away: Lit. "while we've been chopping up the conversation". This strange and unique Latin phrase is explained by the grammarian Priscian (*G.L.* 3.323) as a literal translation of a Greek idiom *koptein ta rhēmata.* Presumably Ter. took it straight from Men. See 457n.

244 **I'm quite restored:** Clinia is as happy as he was miserable (234), but his happiness will be short−lived (246, 247, 250 etc.). See Introduction p. 22.

245 **It's not at all surprising:** To ascribe these words to Dromo on the evidence of the second hand in only one MS seems prompted chiefly by a desire to give him something more to say. But, as is clear from his only other appearance in the play (743−5), his speaking role is minimal.

The humour here lies in the devastating effect that the slaves' conversation, and, later, Syrus' musings, have on Clinia.

246 **Don't ask me:** Lit. "Are you asking me?"

250 **Get a move on:** Dromo is slow to react. We are told elsewhere that he is "pretty stupid" (545), and he is altogether a great contrast to the quick−thinking, quick−acting Syrus. See Introduction p. 20.

Such high hopes, and now ...: Lit. "From what high hopes have I

182

fallen."

252−3 [**quam ... reliqui:** The antecedent of *quam* is *ei* or *illi*, to be supplied with *esse*.]

255 **What a lot they'll eat!:** Syrus' fears are well grounded; cf. 455ff.

256 [**video eccos:** *eccos* = *ecce* + *hos*; cf. 241n. Here the word is further strengthened by *video*.]

Oh, Jupiter: See 162n.

Clinia has now reached such depths of despair that he is even prepared (262) to give Antiphila up; but see 267−8n.

257 [**loci:** Partitive gen. after *interea*, the whole phrase meaning "meanwhile". Cf. Pl. *Capt.* 385: *adhuc locorum* "up to now".]

259 **very disobedient:** Lit. "not very obedient", a polite understatement.

260−1 [**quoius nunc pudet me et miseret ...:** There are two constructions, *me pudet* + gen. of the person in whose presence Clinia is ashamed (cf. *Ad.* 683) and *me miseret* + acc. and inf. (cf. 750). *me* belongs to both, but the *quoius* of the first construction does duty for the *eum* with *monuisse* of the first acc. and inf. of the second.]

262 [**gratum** means "something by which one wins gratitude" (G.W. Williams, *CQ* n.s. 9 (1959), 158); cf. *ingratum* 934.]

267−8 **there's nothing in the world I'd like more ...:** As is usual with lovesick young men in comedy, Clinia very quickly goes back on his rejection of Antiphila at 262 when hope is once more offered him.

269 **the old girl ...:** The important piece of extra information about the "old lady of pretty slender means" first mentioned in 96, namely that she was not Antiphila's mother, lays the way open for Antiphila's eventual recognition as a free−born Athenian and thus able to marry Clinia; the audience would have been expected to pick up this further pointer to the outcome. Chremes, however, is left thinking that she is the old woman's daughter (cf. 602) until the very moment he finds out she is his own. The old woman's death is dramatically convenient; cf. the death of Chrysis before the action of *An.* starts (*An.* 104−5), and of Chremes' Lemnian wife in *Ph.* (*Ph.* 750).

271 [**alterae** is dat. fem. sing., as at *Ph.* 928 and Pl. *Rud.* 750; cf. *solae* from *solus* at *Eu.* 1004 and Pl. *Mil.* 356. Ter. and Pl. use *alteri, soli* for the masc. form, *alterae, solae* for the fem. For a later instance, see Caes. *Gal.* 5.27.5: *alterae legioni.*]

272 **Who's the other one?:** There is no reason why Clitipho should be interested in the other woman, as he has no reason to suspect she is Bacchis and is very surprised when he finds out (311) that she is. His question is a dramatic device, written with a view to 311, to ensure that the mention of the other woman, who will be so important later, does not go unnoticed.

274 **First of all ...:** Another passage where the short, simple sentences bring the picture vividly to life; cf. 124ff. n., and the similar passage

at *Ph.* 100ff.

280 **the way:** Lit. "with what zeal".

285 **We found the lady herself ...:** The scholia Bembina at this point (Mountford 61) preserve the corresponding fragment of Men.: ἐξ ἱσταρίου γὰρ ἐκρέματο φιλοπόνως πάνυ (= Körte II 57, fr. 129, though he accepts Meineke's suggestion of δ' for γάρ) "for she was very industriously occupied with her loom". For the sentiment — that the life described is honourable, the alternative being the *vita meretricia* "life of prostitution" — see *An.* 74ff. on Chrysis.

287 [**anuis** is gen. sing. of 4th declension. Nonius (p. 494M) quotes a parallel in a fragment from *Cato de liberis educandis*, one of Varro's lost *logistorici: anuis enim ut sanguis deterior, sic lac* "for as an old woman's blood is weaker, so is her milk". The authenticity of the form is attested by Priscian (*G.L.* 2.268) and, for other 4th decl. nouns also, by Gellius (4.16.1−4). The latter quotes Varro and Nigidius as always using the forms *senatuis, domuis, fluctuis*, and adds that early grammarians therefore held that the gen. was formed by adding −s to the dat. − as *caedi, caedis* in 3rd decl., so *senatui, senatuis* in 4th.]

289 **not finished off:** All MSS have *esse expolitam*, which cannot be right, since *esse* is quite out of place in the construction after *offendimus* (285). Of the several emendations proposed by editors, none is really satisfactory; Dziatzko's *os expolitam* "finished off on the face" is nearest to the MSS, but very un−Terentian. It is possible that a line has dropped out.

The metaphorical use of *expolire* (cf. Pl. *Poen.* 221) is derived from the basic meaning of polishing a surface or finishing off a wall to a smooth surface with plaster (cf. Pl. *Mos.* 101). Modern English humour about women's make−up often seems to run along similar lines.

290 **spread out:** *passus* "spread out" is the reading of the Σ MSS (and of MS V of Don. where he quotes this passage at *Ph.* 106); *pexus* is the reading of A (and of all other MSS of Don. at *Ph.* 106). The meaning "spread out" seems more appropriate for a context of mourning, and goes well with *prolixus circum caput reiectus neglegenter* "flowing round her head and carelessly thrown back"; by contrast, all parallels for *pexus* imply hair carefully groomed (see *OLD* 1371), which would not suit what follows. Moreover, this conventional picture of a woman in mourning can be compared with the description of Phanium at *Ph.* 106−7: *capillus passus, nudus pes, ipsa horrida, lacrimae, vestitus turpis* "her hair was spread out, her feet were bare, she herself was dishevelled, in tears and with unsightly clothes", where all MSS have *passus*.

In Greece women cut their hair short as a sign of mourning; in Rome they left it long. Don. (on *Ph.* 91) indicates that in that play

Ter. omitted the cutting of Phanium's hair "in order not to upset the Roman audience by mention of strange customs". It is possible that he has made a point of describing Antiphila's hair as long here for the same reason.

291 **that's all there is to it:** A translation for *pax*, a word which has nothing to do with the Latin noun meaning "peace", but is a transliteration of the Greek interjection πάξ. Signifying that there is nothing more to be said ("Enough!", *OLD* 1315), it has two meanings: "I've said it all", as here, or "Don't say any more", "Shut up", as at Pl. *Mil.* 808. The word occurs only once more in Ter., at 717.

293 **wool for the loom:** The Latin noun used here, *subtemen*, refers strictly to the weft, the threads passed horizontally through the vertical threads set up on the loom, the warp. The old woman is supplying this for Antiphila, who sits at the loom (cf. 285). The role of the "single servant girl" is less clear; she could be assisting Antiphila, or herself weaving at another loom.

there was just a single servant girl: The scholia Bembina (Mountford 61) again provide the corresponding fragment of Men.'s original (= Körte II 57, fr. 130):

καὶ θεραπαινὶς ἦν μία·
αὕτη συνύφαινεν ῥυπαρῶς διακειμένη.

"and there was just one servant girl; she was weaving along with her, in a filthy state". Though our lack of knowledge of how the Greek text continued makes certainty impossible, it seems likely that Ter. has greatly expanded the two words ῥυπαρῶς διακειμένη "in a filthy state" to *pannis ... illuvie* "all covered ... with grime".
It is worth noting that this is the last part of Ter.'s play with which a Greek fragment can definitely be associated.

295 **Clinia, if this is true ...:** In their excitement Clitipho and Clinia do not bother to stop and ask who or what is the reason for the maids and the baggage if it is not a change of lifestyle by Antiphila. But that will soon become clear by other means.

297 **shabby and scruffy:** In the Latin jingle *sordidatam et sordidam*, the first term refers specifically to dress, the second to general cleanliness.

306 **tears poured all down her face:** Lit. "she covered her entire face with tears."

308 **Heaven help me:** Clinia is once more on top of the world. In less than 80 lines, he has gone from despair to joy, back to despair and on to joy again.

309 **[scibam:** In early Latin, 4th conjugation imperfect indicatives are found in −*ibam* (as with the other conjugations in −*abam* and −*ebam*), as well as in −*iebam*, though these early forms later tended to fall out of use. Ter. always uses the older ones; cf. *Eu.* 113,

700, 1004 etc.   Cf. 824n. on early forms of 4th conjugation futures.]

310 **tell us who ...:**   The fact that Clitipho has already asked this question before and been rebuffed means that the audience is alert at its second asking; cf. 272n.

311 **your Bacchis:**   She has not been named before, but "your", addressed to Clitipho, makes it obvious who she is.

It is clear from Clitipho's reaction that, though he has asked for Syrus' help in his affair with Bacchis (cf. 330), he was not expecting such a seemingly foolhardy step.   Syrus has secured Bacchis' agreement to come along by undertaking (cf. 723−4) that this time Clitipho will indeed pay her the sum of 1,000 drachmas or 10 minae (cf. 601, 724) which he has already promised her (cf. 329, 823).   In return for getting the money, Bacchis has agreed to pose as Clinia's, not Clitipho's, and has been "well schooled" (361) in what to do. Syrus explains (364ff.) how he managed to persuade her to agree to all this.   (No wonder the party took so long to arrive!)   Antiphila, being the 'nice girl' she is, presumably acquiesced in Syrus' plans, wanting only to be with Clinia.   Though almost all this information is to be found in the text, it has to be looked for; the audience, however, swept along by the action, would not even have time to ask any of the appropriate questions, let alone start searching for the answers.   Ter. wrote his play to be enjoyed in the theatre, not dissected in the study, and he knew just how much (or how little) of such detailed explanation he needed to include.

312 **You villain:**   At this critical point, as the excitement mounts with the sudden news, the metre changes from the spoken iambic senarius to the musical trochaic septenarius.   Exactly the same thing happens at 940 (when Chremes hits on his plan to pretend to disinherit Clitipho) and, in reverse, at 908 (when Chremes finally realizes that Bacchis is his son's mistress.)

313 **[inpudentem audaciam:**   Acc. of exclamation; cf. *hominem felicem* 380.]

317 **What would you do with him?:**   Clitipho turns away from Syrus and addresses these words to Clinia, but before Clinia can reply, Syrus interrupts with "But indeed ...", playing for time while thinking up something to say.

320 **Yes indeed; I can't keep quiet:**   Syrus has now marshalled his arguments, and the stammering prevaricator of 318 launches into the attack, finding an unexpected ally in the fair−minded Clinia.   His words are a rejoinder to Clinia's "come to the point": "Yes indeed (come to the point I shall; the fact is) I can't keep quiet about it because ..."

321 **[potis es:**   = *potes*; cf. *potis est* = *potest* 659.   *potis* (or *pote*) itself is indeclinable in these early forms.]

322 **You want to love her ...:**   The Latin line is very close to the

popular Latin verse—form known as the *versus quadratus* "four—part verse". In terms of English 'stress' metre it would read something like "(You) wánt to lóve her,/wánt to háve her,/wánt cash gót to/gíve to hér."

323 **The wisdom you show in this** ...: A wordy translation for the pithy oxymoron *haud stulte sapis* "you're not stupidly wise"; cf. 628: *damno auctus* "increased by a loss".

329 **as for your having promised her money:** This refers back through 322 ("you want money to be got") to Clitipho's general lament about having nothing to give his grasping mistress at 223ff.; but nowhere has it been said that there is a problem about Clitipho having promised Bacchis a particular sum. Since, however, the audience knows the sort of financial difficulty into which young men in comedy commonly get, and is already aware that Bacchis' demands are unending, the transfer from the general to the particular would not surprise them.
in the same way: i.e. by having Bacchis as well as Antiphila stay in Chremes' house. From this statement, and from his stated intention (332—3) of pretending that Bacchis is Clinia's girl, it is clear that Syrus is already devising some sort of plan (cf. 327). But it is equally clear (cf. 513n.) that the plan is not yet fully worked out.

332 [*cedo* is 2nd sing. imperative, formed from the particle *ce* (the same as is used enclitically in pronouns like *hic*) and the root of *dare* "to give". Its plural, *cette*, is found in Pl., but not in Ter. The basic meaning "give me" is common in Pl; in Ter. the derivative meaning "tell me" is more usual, as here, 597, 846 — but see 493n.]

333 [*faciet:* In this textually very complicated line, no editors apart from Kauer—Lindsay claim to be able to distinguish *faciat* as the original reading in A, where Iov. has rewritten the last five words in an erasure.]

335 **to your mother:** i.e., in the Greek situation, to the separate women's quarters in the house (cf. 614ff.). The implication is that Bacchis' different status allows her to mingle more freely with the men, and subsequent descriptions of the supper—party (455ff., 567—8) confirm this.

It's a long story ...: Where Antiphila is sent is essential to the dramatist for reasons quite unconnected with Syrus' plan. Her presence in Sostrata's quarters is vital dramatically, in order for her true identity to be swiftly revealed. The dramatist knew that the swiftness of this recognition would render it unnecessary for him to make Syrus explain how Antiphila's whereabouts fitted into his plan, and so he could afford to have the slave give only the vague assurance that there was "a very good reason" (336) for his action — an assurance which would at the same time further enhance the audience's opinion of the slave's confident bravado. See Introduction p. 20.

336 **There's a very good reason:** It is preferable to follow Iov. and the Σ MSS in ascribing the Latin words *vera causa est* to Syrus; while refusing to explain further, the slave assures Clitipho that nevertheless "there's a very good reason" for his actions. If one follows A and ascribes the words to Clinia, they will mean something like "He's got a good case", "That's a good point", and Clinia will be supporting Syrus' refusal to go into details.

339 **Certainly:** It seems the obvious and natural choice that Syrus, who is about to provide an alternative suggestion, should say "Certainly" in agreement with Clitipho's request just before he explains what it is (so the Σ MSS), rather than that Clinia should say "Certainly" to reinforce Clitipho's instruction to his slave (so A).

340 **meet them and tell them:** By talking of "them" (i.e. Antiphila as well as Bacchis), Syrus cleverly ensures that Clinia will support his original plan, as indeed he does in the sentence split up between 343, 345 and 347.

341 [faxo: See 161n.]

343 **sleep easily on either ear:** For the expression, cf. the exchange in Pl. *Ps.* 123−4, where the fact that the phrase is parodied is a sure sign of its proverbial nature: Pseudolus: "As far as that's concerned, you can go to sleep on either eye." Calidorus: "Eye − or ear?" Pseudolus: "Oh, my version's less hackneyed." The same expression can be found in Men. (Körte II 121, fr. 333, 1−2 from the *Plokion*.)

343 [quid ago nunc?: The indicative is not uncommonly used instead of the subjunctive for vividness in deliberative questions in Pl. and Ter.; cf. e.g. *Ph.* 447.]

349 **He's warming to it:** Syrus' words could be an aside, or addressed to Clinia.

351 **I entrust myself:** Syrus' threat (340) has ensured Clitipho's total surrender; see Introduction pp. 21−2.

356 **scolding ... flogging:** For a precise parallel for the alliterative jingle *verba ... verbera*, lit. "words ... lashes", see Cic. *Tusc.* 3.64. Chremes' threats at 949ff. will be exactly along these lines. The slave in comedy often compares his fate to that of his young master or mistress in this way; cf. Geta (*Ph.* 219−20) and Parmeno (*Hec.* 335).

357 [neglectu from *neglectus*, a very rare 4th declension alternative to *neglegentia*; cf. Plin. *Nat.* 7.171. The form *neglectu* is rare dat. sing. for more usual *neglectui*; cf. *Ad.* 62−3: *quor ... vestitu nimio indulges*? "why are you so excessively generous about his clothes?", Sal. *Jug.* 6.1 *luxu*, not *luxui* etc.]

358 [scilicet: Here used, as often in early Latin, with acc. and inf., in accordance with the derivation of the word from *scire licet*; cf. 856−7, 892.]
   You can be sure: Clinia's immediate agreement to help Clitipho is

endearing; see Introduction p. 22. But later (699, 713), when he is asked to continue the pretence after it has been found that Antiphila is Chremes' daughter (and thus able to marry him), he is not so keen.

365 **a soldier:** Probably the same soldier whom Bacchis mentions in 733. We are reminded of Thraso, the soldier who features much more prominently in *Eu.* as Phaedria's rival for Thais' attentions.

369 [**sis** = *si vis* "please"; cf. 374.]

372 **double – entendres** ...: As well as containing the play on words *inversa* ... *eversas* (cf. 218, 297, 356), the Latin line is rich in alliteration and assonance.

376 **Where are they?:** At the announcement of Bacchis' approach, Clitipho – predictably – immediately forgets his high – sounding assurances of 374.

379 **At least let me say hullo:** Lit. "At least hullo", with some such phrase as "let me say" to have followed in the part of Clitipho's sentence which is cut short by Syrus' interruption. [The word *salutem* has its last syllable standing in hiatus. Failure to realize this led Iov. and the Σ MSS to substitute *salutare* "at least to say hullo", with "allow me" understood, which can be scanned without hiatus; this version ignores the effective jingle *saltem salutem*.]

380 **He'll be staying:** Though Syrus will not let Clitipho stay to see Bacchis, he lets Clinia stay to meet Antiphila, when in theory he should insist that he has nothing to do with her since the pretence is to be that Bacchis, not Antiphila, is his. This is done (i) to make Clitipho's situation more humorously unfortunate, and (ii) because the audience would be much more interested in the reunion of Clinia and Antiphila after a long separation than in a meeting between Clitipho and Bacchis (who are never actually shown together in the play). The literal – minded spectator or reader could also add that there would be less danger to Clinia than to Clitipho if Chremes caught him embracing a strange women outside his house.

ACT TWO SCENE FOUR

There are good grounds for thinking that this scene was not in Men.'s play, but has been written in by Ter., who wanted to depict the reunion of Clinia and Antiphila on stage, and at the same time took the opportunity to put into Bacchis' mouth a speech designed to enhance the audience's opinion of Antiphila's good character; see Introduction pp. 16–17 and Brothers 108ff., 117ff.

The scene falls naturally into two distinct sections. The first (381–97), in trochaic septenarii, consists of Bacchis' long speech (381–95) and a conventional reply by Antiphila (396–7). The second (398–409), in iambic metres, consists of a discussion about Antiphila between Clinia and

Syrus, the (brief and strangely delayed) reunion of the lovers and the departure of everyone into Chremes' house; in this section Bacchis takes little part, only asking four short questions of Antiphila, which the latter makes no attempt to answer.

381ff. **My goodness, Antiphila my dear ...:** This speech, the object of which is to stress Antiphila's virtuous lifestyle and her devotion to Clinia during his absence, is extraordinary in one particular respect, the picture of Bacchis which it gives. We have been told (227) that she is typically "grand and grasping, full of airs and graces, extravagant, and high and mighty", and this picture will be confirmed by Chremes' account of her conduct at supper (455ff.); but her words here show a very different person, with a detached and reflective turn of mind and a philosophical resignation which make her anything but typical. The fact that the picture given here is out of line with that given earlier and later is perhaps evidence for the Terentian origin of this part of the play.

Though it is quite usual for the audience to hear the ends of conversations which characters just entering have begun off−stage (cf. 242ff. n.), it is not common for the conversation to be as long as it is here. More evidence for Terentian workmanship?

382 **your character matches your beauty:** Each person has an appearance corresponding to his or her (true) rank and character, and so the free−born woman has not only a character but also an appearance which differs from that of the professional mistress or the slave−girl; cf. *An.* 122−3, where Glycerium, later to be found to be of free birth just like Antiphila, is described as *forma ... honesta ac liberali* "of honest and ladylike appearance", and *Eu.* 682, where Chaerea (who is free−born, but disguised as a eunuch) is said to be *honesta facie et liberali* "of honest and gentlemanly looks".

384 **your conversation made quite clear to me ...:** In the scholia Bembina at this point (Mountford 65) appears the Greek line ἀνδρὸς χαρακτὴρ ἐκ λόγου γνωρίζεται "a man's character is recognised from his speech" and another brief and mutilated Greek fragment. The fact that two passages of Greek are being cited perhaps suggests that they are parallels from elsewhere in Greek literature and not quotations of Men.'s original. Indeed, the full line is elsewhere quoted as from Men.'s *Arrēphoros*, and is so listed by Körte (II 36, fr. 66), who rejects the view that the saying is sufficiently proverbial to have appeared in both plays, as has sometimes been suggested. Further, the presence in the line of ἀνδρός "a man's" seems odd in a conversation between two women, and adds yet more weight to the idea that it is not from Men.'s version of *The Self−Tormentor*. Therefore, if this line is the original of, and not a mere parallel for, the sentiment here, and if it appeared only in Men.'s *Arrēphoros*, we have further evidence of Terentian workmanship, with Ter. borrowing

from another of Men.'s plays. But they are two big 'if's.

390 **faded:** This, the reading of A, *imminuta* "diminished", is preferable. As often, Iov. and the Σ MSS have altered it to something more obvious, *immutata* "changed".

392 **But once you've decided to spend your days with one man:** G.W. Williams, 'Some aspects of Roman marriage ceremonies and ideals', *JRS* 48 (1958), 16−29, esp. 23, sees passages such as this, which stress the ideal of marriage to one husband for a lifetime, as specifically Roman in tone, and he compares Pl. *Cist.* 76ff. and *Mer.* 824ff.

393 **[quoius ... hi:** For the switch from sing. to pl., cf. *An.* 626−8 and *Eu.* 1−3.]

398 **So, Antiphila my love ...:** Clinia and Syrus have eavesdropped on the conversation between Bacchis and Antiphila, and now react to what they have heard.

400 **[tui:** *careo* takes the gen. only here in Ter.; it takes the abl. in 137, 257 and *Hec.* 663, and the acc. in *Eu.* 223.]

401 **[ingenium:** The acc. (A) should be preferred to the abl. (Σ) as the more difficult option, despite the fact that *fruor* takes the abl. in 149 and elsewhere in Ter.; cf. *fungor* with the acc. in 66 (where see note), and *fruor* with the acc. in Lucr. 3.940. The whole sentence is acc. and inf. of exclamation; cf. 503, 630, 751 etc.]

402 **[duras:** Supply *partes* (cf. *Eu.* 354) or *res*.]

403 **Who's this young man ...?:** Bacchis at last sees Clinia and draws Antiphila's attention to him. Because of the length of Bacchis' opening speech, the reunion of the lovers is awkwardly delayed, and the devices of eavesdropping and of failure to notice the presence of others are heavily overplayed.

408 **you who I've longed for:** *exoptatam* "longed for" is supported by those MSS which read *exoptata*. *exspectatam* "waited for" should be rejected as having crept in under the influence of *exspectat* (409) and the *exspectate* which some MSS insert in 406.

409 **my master's been waiting ...:** Syrus' words are just an excuse to clear the stage. It would be over−pedantic to ask precisely how he knew that Chremes had been informed of the women's arrival.
If it is correct that this scene is Terentian, then some such exit line as this must have stood in Men.'s original at a point corresponding to 376 of Ter., to shepherd everyone into Chremes' house immediately the women arrived; Ter. will have altered the end of the previous scene to enable it to lead naturally into this one.
The stage is now empty, and time has elapsed before the action resumes. It is highly likely that in Men. a choral interlude occurred to 'mask' the arrival of the women and to indicate the passage of time. See Introduction p. 17.

ACT THREE SCENE ONE

410 **Daybreak already:**   It is made clear immediately that a night has passed since 409.   But was this also the case in Men.?   Körte (cf. 170n.) felt there were no precedents for two—day action in Greek New Comedy; Gomme and Sandbach, however, argue (325—6) that the action of Men.'s *Epitrepontes* could well be just such a case.   K. Gaiser (*WS* 79 (1966), 197—201) thinks that the action of Men.'s original of our play also extended over two days; he disposes of Körte's argument from the mention of *āriston* "lunch" in fr. 133 (argument (i) in 170n.) by referring that passage not to 455ff. of Ter., but to somewhere in Act Five, such as 902ff.   Hunter 36 concludes that "there are no good reasons for believing this [the spread of the action over two days] to be a Terentian change to the Menandrian model".

Many of the characteristics exhibited by Chremes in Act One, before the audience knew about Clitipho's affair with Bacchis, are shown again in this scene, so that they can be relished afresh in the light of the new knowledge.   Thus we get further evidence of his eagerness to be first to give Menedemus good news (411—12), his unsure judgement in not revealing Menedemus' true feelings (to Clinia 436; cf. to Clitipho 199), and his tendency to preach and moralize (439ff.), to give advice (469ff.), to have recourse to philosophical maxims (483ff.), and to be fussy and self—important in his dealings with friends and neighbours (498ff.).

[**luciscit hoc iam:**   Cf. Pl. *Am.* 543, *Cur.* 182 and *Mil.* 218.   The verb is, strictly speaking, impersonal, but appears in these phrases to have *hoc* (possibly sc. *caelum*) as its subject.]

Why don't I knock ...?:   Lit. "Am I hesitating to knock?"   Cf. 757: *cesso hunc adoriri?*, lit. "Am I hesitating to accost him?".   i.e. "Why don't I tackle him?".

411 **so I can be first to tell him:**   For Chremes' motives in wishing to be first with the news, see Introduction p. 19.

412 **the young chap doesn't want me to:**   The "young chap" is Clinia (cf. 433).   Chremes is not going to respect his wishes, and proceeds to justify his failure to do so.

420ff. **Either I've been born ...:**   The picture of Menedemus' continuing misery arouses the audience's sympathy, the more because they know that Clinia has spent the night in the house next door to his father's, and that the continuation of this sorry state of affairs is unnecessary.   The misery contrasts with the happiness Menedemus is shortly to experience.

422 **time takes away men's sorrow:**   A common sentiment; for an example from Men., cf. Körte II 207, fr. 652:   "Time is the healer of all necessary ills; and it will even heal you now."

192

429ff. **You haven't heard ...:** The succession of short, eager questions and simple, direct answers (five of each in four lines) is a highly effective contrast to the longer speeches preceding and following. The questions accurately capture Menedemus' incredulous excitement; the anwers perhaps exhibit a certain smug satisfaction on Chremes' part.

436 **Didn't you tell him ...:** Chremes' refusal to reveal the truth about Menedemus, though justified in his own eyes (437−8), is again ill−judged; cf. 199n., and see Introduction p. 19.

439 **harsh enough as a father:** See 101n.

439ff. **Oh, Menedemus:** Chremes pours cold water on Menedemus' new−found joy by delivering him a long lecture; it contains at the start more half−digested philosophy, this time about the Golden Mean.

440 **too extreme in each direction:** For the Greek which appears in the scholia Bembina at this point, see 213n.

442 **[in eandem fraudem:** *fraus* is here used in the older meaning, preserved in later legal Latin, of "harm", "mischief", "danger" (*OLD* 732); cf. *An.* 911.]

447 **began to look for a living ...:** The same slippery slope from the virtuous life to prostitution is described in the case of Chrysis at *An.* 74ff. Here, of course, Chremes is mistaken, since what he describes as Antiphila's changed lifestyle is in fact a picture of Bacchis, whom he believes to be Clinia's girl.

451 **more than ten maidservants:** The most precise description in the play of the size of Bacchis' retinue.

452 **a sheik:** The Latin word used is *satrapes* "a satrap", the title held by provincial governors in the Persian empire. Satraps had great power in their own provinces, being in effect vassal kings of the supreme monarch, and were proverbial for their wealth. This system of government was continued by Alexander after his conquests. Here we have further evidence (cf. 111, 117) of the familiarity of Men.'s Athenian audience with conditions on the other side of the Aegean. Earlier this century the terms "nabob" and "pasha" might have captured the spirit of "satrap" more completely.

455ff. **I've given just one supper ...:** Körte (II 58) and Webster (145) associate with this passage Körte's fr. 133:

ἐγὼ μετ' ἄριστον γὰρ ὡς ἀμυγδάλας
παρέθηκα καὶ τῶν ῥοιδίων ἐτρώγομεν.

"After lunch I served almonds and we nibbled at some pomegranates." It is the mention of "lunch" here that has led to the suggestion that Ter. has introduced the night interval into the play (cf. 170n., 410n.). But the meal could be breakfast or lunch on the second day, and Gaiser (cf. 410n.) associates this fragment with Menedemus' description (902ff.) of what went on in his house after Bacchis and her maids had transferred there − even though a meal is not specifically

193

mentioned in Ter. at that point. In either case, the identification is extremely tenuous and assumes that Ter. has removed all the detail in his version; cf. the omission of detail from Körte's fr. 127 (61ff. n.).

457 **by tasting:** Lit. "by spitting out", i.e. the tasted wine, as is customary in wine−tasting. The verb Ter. uses, *pytisso*, is found only here in Latin (though a noun, *pytisma* "wine spat out", occurs in Juv. 11.175); the word is taken direct from the Greek *pūtizō*, and its meaning could be understood from the context and from the appropriate spitting gestures by the speaker as he uttered the onomatopoeic word.

Ter. uses far fewer of these Greek words than Pl., who clearly liked their humorous effects; but cf. *pax* 291n. It should be remembered that, because of the influx of Greeks into Rome, Greek words must have been increasingly common in Latin at this time, much as French words are common in English. See further Sandbach 124.

459 **father:** It is easy to imagine Chremes' disgust at Bacchis' over−familiarity and lack of respect for her host in addressing him in this way.

[**sodes** = *si audes* "please", "if you don't mind"; cf. 580.]

460 **I opened all my jars and all my bottles:** The verb translated "open", *relino*, literally means "unsmear", referring to the practice of making the containers airtight by smearing the stopper and the top of the neck with pitch.

Strictly speaking, both the *dolium* (here translated "jar") and the *seria* (here "bottle") were large earthenware vessels for storing wine, oil, grain etc. But a *seria* was "apparently smaller than a *dolium*" (*OLD* 1743).

463−4 **I do feel sorry for your finances:** Chremes is very much concerned for Menedemus' material wealth (cf. 480, 486 etc.), as he will be later for his own (e.g. 909, 930−1).

465 **let him take, spend and squander:** The Latin consists of a *tricolon* (three−unit word−group) with asyndeton *sumat, consumat, perdat*; such *tricola* are a characterstic of early Latin verse and rhythmical prose; cf. 592: *servas, castigas, mones* "you watch, reprimand and admonish".

468 [**ut ne** is a pleonasm for *ne*, used with no apparent difference in meaning. It is found occasionally in all periods of Latin, but not in certain authors such as Caesar and Livy.]

470 [**ut des** depends on *fac* or *facias* understood from *faciam* 469.]

471 [**techinis:** Ritschl's suggestion for the *technis* of the MSS is proved correct by an entry in the Abolita glossary (see Introduction p. 25). Latin tended to insert vowels (usually *i* or *u*) into words borrowed from Greek which contained combinations of consonants which the Romans found hard to pronounce; as *techina* from Greek *technē* here, so *mina* from *mnā* 475, *drachuma* from *drachmē* 601, *Aesculapius*

194

from *Asklēpios Hec.* 338 etc.]

472 **they're on to it:** Lit. "they are there" (*illos ibi esse*); cf. 983: "I'm on to something", lit. "I'm there" (*ibi ... sum*).

473 **[Syrus cum illo vostro:** The verb is plural by a perfectly understandable construction according to the sense, as if the Latin were *Syrus et ille voster*.]

475 **a whole talent this way than a mina that:** There were 60 minae to the talent.

477 **of how we can give it:** It is a nice touch to have Chremes change, within the space of eight lines, from using the second person singular "arrange that *you* give" (470) to the first person plural "of how *we* can give" here. He is gradually taking over, and, no longer content merely to give advice, becomes an active participator.

483 **We're all of us worse ...:** Another of Chremes' philosophical maxims.

484—5 **A man will want ... he'll go for it:** Several editors have followed Bentley in excluding these lines, believing them to be a later critic's illustration of the sentiment expressed in 483. But they are in all MSS and are commented on in the scholia Bembina; and if it is right to picture Chremes as an incompletely—educated amateur philosopher, then the laboured explanation of his own maxim comes rather well from his lips.

493 **[cedo** is here used in its literal meaning "give me"; cf. 332n.]

498ff. **There's just one little bit of business ...:** Some editors have found this passage so puzzling and awkward that they have questioned its authenticity or assumed ill—disguised alteration by Ter. at this point; see Introduction p. 17.

Those who suspect the authenticity of the passage point to the fact that there is a serious problem with the text, since in all MSS 498—508 follow 509—11. But once the lines are rearranged in their present order (Bentley was obviously correct in doing so, since 509—11 must come at the very end of the scene), the passage reads perfectly naturally provided it is correctly understood. Kauer—Lindsay are probably right in believing that 498—508 were removed by an early critic to shorten the scene and later put back in the wrong place.

Those who assume that Terentian alteration has rendered obscure a passage which in *Men.* would have had more point (e.g. Marouzeau II 50, n.1 and Radice 96) cite the mention of Simus and Crito (498), who have no other connection with the play, and the impossibly short time that Chremes is off stage (502—7) considering what he claims (508) to have done while he was away. But an incident where Chremes rushes off to postpone business with two neighbours in order to deal with the more pressing problems of another pointedly highlights his fussing over his dealings with other people (cf. his

195

concern over his supper−guest Phania, 169−70) and his self−important pleasure at getting involved in their affairs. And Chremes' brief absence can be explained by reference to a not uncommon (but here rather overplayed) dramatic convention; see 508n.

500 **chosen me to arbitrate**: Lit. "taken me as arbitrator." It is Athenian legal procedure which is pictured here. In Greek states settlement of disputes by arbitration was a common practice, and in Athens there were two types of arbitrator (*diaitētēs*), public ones, citizens over 60 appointed from each tribe, and private ones, chosen for the occasion by the parties to the particular dispute; Chremes is clearly an example of the latter type. Although Ter.'s audience would not know these details, the general drift of the passage would have been clear enough. Cf. *Ad*. 123 where Micio, exasperated by his brother Demea's criticisms and complaints about how he is bringing up Aeschinus, tells him "either stop it or produce an arbitrator".

502 **I'll be back here right away**: Chremes' remark is perhaps designed to make his very brief absence (502−7) seem less incongruous.

503ff. **to think that human nature's so arranged ...:** The irony in this remark would not be lost on the audience. Menedemus is speaking of his own case, but the audience knows enough about the situation to realize that Chremes is an even better example of those who "can see and decide about other people's problems better than their own". In time, Menedemus will realize this too (cf. 922−3).

508 **I've got myself out of it**: It is clearly impossible to believe that in just over five lines Chremes has really had time to find Simus and Crito, explain the situation to them, secure their agreement to a postponement of his arbitration, and return. But it is a common convention in this type of comedy that events taking place off stage can be telescoped into a very short space of time − indeed into practically no time at all; see Marouzeau II 13−14. Thus between Chremes' exit into his house at 558 and his return at 562, he has had time to discover Clitipho and Bacchis together and to drag Clitipho outside; and between 948 and 954 Menedemus has had time to go indoors, explain to Clitipho about Chremes' plan to disinherit him and to bring the young man outside; cf. also Gnatho's impossibly brief stay in Thais' house (*Eu*. 283−5) and Hegio's impossibly short visit to Sostrata (*Ad*. 507−10). However, it must be admitted that here the convention is overplayed. In all the other instances cited, the characters are absent in one of the houses on the stage set; but here Chremes has gone off stage by one of the wing entrances and the 'telescoped' events are thought of as having taken place some way away.

510 **Someone's coming out**: See 173n.

511 [**congruere**: Metre demands that this, the reading of all MSS, is scanned *congruēre*, from *congrueo*, 2nd conjugation. This is the only

instance (except for a variant reading *congruet* at *Ph.* 726) where the 2nd conj. form occurs; the 'normal' form is *congruo*, 3rd conj. Those editors who feel unable to accept the unique 2nd conj. form have variously emended the line. For 2nd/3rd conj. alternatives, cf. *subolat*, 3rd, 899 and *subolet*, 2nd, *Ph.* 474.]

ACT THREE SCENE TWO

512 **Run here, run there:** The scene opens with a good example of the 'eavesdropping' convention (cf. 242ff. n.).

513 **a trap laid for the old man:** By the "old man" Syrus means Chremes, as is made clear by his consternation (517) when he discovers that his master has overheard his remarks; it is equally clear that Chremes, recalling his own earlier remarks to Menedemus in 471ff., thinks that the "old man" of whom Syrus is speaking is Menedemus.

It is, of course, natural that Syrus would at this stage be intending to deceive his own master; it is only the golden opportunity offered by Chremes' advice that he help Dromo defraud Menedemus (546−7) which makes him direct his attentions to his master's neighbour.

Syrus' remarks here make it clear that he has not yet fully worked out his plan for getting money out of Chremes (cf. 329n.), and it is presumably this fact which inclines him to take the unusual step of attempting to get it from Menedemus rather than from his own master.

515 **a bit on the slow side:** Cf. 545: "He's pretty stupid" and see 191n., 250n.

[**ill':** See 197n. But here dropping of the final −*e* of *ille* is the only (not the preferable) way of scanning the line.]

[**Cliniai** (−$\overline{ai}$) is archaic gen. sing. of 1st declension for *Cliniae* (which appears in all MSS). Though common in Pl., this older form is found in Ter. only here and at *An.* 439 (*hospit$\overline{ai}$*).]

516 **the mission's been transferred:** The phrase Ter. uses here, *tradere provinciam*, is distinctively Roman. It means strictly "to hand over the magistrate's task or function", and hence is used of a provincial governor handing over his province (*provincia*) to his successor. In a transferred sense, often with humorous overtones, *provincia* is used for any more mundane task or mission, as here; cf. *Ph.* 72−3: *o Geta, provinciam cepisti duram* "Geta, you've taken on a tough job", and Syrus' use of military phraseology which is distinctively Roman at 668ff.

519 **seeing you drank so much:** See 220n.

521 **your 'eagle's years':** Lit. "the old age of an eagle." Eugr. explains this by saying that the beak of an old eagle grows so incurved that it cannot eat its prey's flesh but only drinks its blood (cf. Plin. *Nat.*

197

10.15), thus referring the words to Chremes' drinking at the party; but it is unlikely that the audience would be familiar with such a technical piece of natural history, even if it were true. Nevertheless, it does indeed look as if Ter. is referring to Chremes' drinking prowess; but equally the words *quod dici solet* (lit. "as is customarily said") show that the reference must be to a well—known proverb — undoubtedly the Greek one ἀετοῦ γῆρας κορύδου νεότης "the eagle's old age is as the lark's youth", which refers to the eagle's (and thus Chremes') continued vigour, and not specifically to Chremes' drinking. For Men.'s audience, only the first part of this proverb was necessary (much as we might say "least said" without adding "soonest mended"), but for Ter., who elsewhere too seems to have had difficulty understanding Greek proverbs, it was a different matter. G.B. Townend, '*Aquilae senectus*', *CR* n.s. 10 (1960), 186—8, argues that Ter., not knowing the proverb, wrongly associated the "eagle's old age" he found in his original with the Roman "habit of connecting heavy drinking with equalling the years of some long—lived creature". It was thus due to Ter. that the association with drink crept in here, and this explains the forced and fanciful nature of Eugr.'s explanation.

524 **Not like they were in the old days ...:** Syrus is ingratiating himself with Chremes by implying that young women were better looking when he was young. This nice touch gives more point to the line than the other possible interpretation, "Not so good as she (Bacchis) was when she was younger, but, considered as she is now, still pretty good."

526 [**avidum ... aridum:** For the play on words, cf. 218, 356, 379.]

529 [**quid ... ni:** = *quidni* "why not?"; "also written as two words, which may be separated" (*OLD* 1552); cf. *Ad*. 662: *quid illam ni abducat?* "Why shouldn't he take her away?"]

530 **The fellow deserves a spell in the mill:** Chremes refers to Dromo, who in his eyes deserves to be punished for his lack of inventiveness in extracting money from Menedemus. But Syrus (as his remark "Syrus, I was terribly afraid for you" at 531 makes clear) thinks that Chremes is referring to him because of the rude remarks he has just made about his master's neighbour.

To be sent to grind corn in the mill on the master's country estate or farm was a customary punishment for town slaves in comedy; cf. *An*. 199 and 600, *Ph*. 249, Men., *Hērōs* 3 and the many references in Pl., who liked jokes about the punishment of slaves. Conditions for country slaves were in any case worse than those for their town counterparts (whose lot was regarded as comparatively easy); but working in the flour—mill was regarded as particularly harsh, even by the standards of the country slaves. Compare Demea's decision (*Ad*. 840ff.) to take Ctesipho and his music girl to the country, and put

198

the girl to work in the mill.

534 **the young man would have something:** Chremes (and Menedemus) think that it is Clinia who wants money for Bacchis, but it is Clitipho.

536 **[oportebant:** The verb is sometimes used personally in early Latin; cf. *oportent An.* 481. Here, as there, MSS tend to change to the commoner impersonal form which is found at e.g. 546, 562.]

537 **do you approve of slaves ...?:** For the audience, Syrus' question is a pointer to the fact that before the end of the play Chremes will be deceived by his own slave, Syrus himself; cf. 550ff. n.
In the right situation ...: If Chremes were honest, he would say "*In the case of other people*, yes, I do." He would not be (and, later, is not) so broad−minded when he himself is the object of the deception.

542 **to have a bit more fun:** The "cunning slave" of comedy is always on the look−out for situations where he can display his talents. For Syrus to hear Chremes criticizing Dromo for inaction and admitting that on occasions slaves should deceive their masters is almost too good to be true (cf. 559−61), and he thinks his master's words give him further scope for his favourite activity.

545 **He's pretty stupid:** See 515n.

546 **you ought to give him a helping hand:** Despite Chremes' earlier advocacy of "the life that is true" .(154n.) and his later claim "Pretending isn't my way" (782), he is here actively encouraging his own slave to do the exact opposite. As at 210, his preaching and his practice do not coincide.

549 **It's not my way to tell lies:** These words refer to Syrus' boast (548) that he is skilled in deception, and are equivalent to "I'm not one to be falsely modest"; Hunter's suggestion (100) that Syrus is protesting at being asked to be deceitful is surely wrong.

550ff. **make sure you remember these words:** If the audience missed the pointer to the later tricking of Chremes given in 537 (where see n.), they would surely notice the one given here. The discussion about Clitipho getting into Clinia's (supposed) situation and about Syrus' ability to trick Chremes occupies eight lines; the audience knows (despite Syrus' denial, 554) that Clitipho *is* in that situation, so can guess that Syrus *will* trick Chremes. The point is further driven home by the triple mention of 'need arising' (553, 556, 557).

554 **[quicquam illum senserim:** Supply *facere* from *faciat* 552.]

555 **if he does, then don't:** Lit. "if (he does) anything, don't (you forget) anything (of what we've said now)"; "forget" in "don't (you forget)" is supplied from "make sure you remember" (550).

560 **and there's never been a time when:** Lit. "nor when." There is a slight anacolouthon in the sentence, as if it had begun "There's never been a time when I heard ..."; cf. Pl. *Mos.* 157−8: "My goodness,

199

I haven't enjoyed a cold bath more for a long time, nor (is there a time) when I think I've been better cleaned up, Scapha my dear."

ACT THREE SCENE THREE

562 **What's all this, then?:** For Chremes' swift return, see 508n.

563 **Did I see you just now ...?:** It never occurs to Chremes that the reason for Clitipho's behaviour is that Bacchis is really his, rather as it never occurs to Demea in *Ad.* that the music girl is really Ctesipho's, not Aeschinus'. Such obtuseness emphasizes the extent of Chremes' self−deception and highlights his folly in presuming to give advice to others.

564 **It's all over:** Syrus' doubts about Clitipho's ability to keep up the pretence that Bacchis is Clinia's (369ff.) are amply justified, and he fears (cf. 584) that his young master's indiscretions will mean the collapse of his plans.

567 **That's true:** Lit. "That's what happened." Syrus was of course present at the party (cf. 519), and saw what went on.

570 **[novi ego amantis; animum advortunt graviter:** Paumier's conjecture for *novi ego amantium animum; advortunt graviter* "I know the minds of lovers; they take offence" of all MSS and Eugr. The difficulty with the MSS reading is that in Ter. (and Pl.) *advortere* does not mean "to notice" without *animum* as its object (cf. 656) − though it can do so in later Latin. The conjecture is the more attractive because we can see how the MSS version arose from it. A scribe, mistaking *amantīs* (acc. pl.) for *amantĭs* (gen. sing.), assumed that it depended on *animum* and that *advortunt* by itself meant "they notice", in accordance with later Latin usage; he then changed *amantis* to *amantium* because there were two lovers, not one. Those who accept the MSS reading argue (e.g. Marouzeau II 55) that the proximity of *animum* as object of *novi* before the semi−colon allows it to be understood with *advortunt* after it.]

573 **lovers:** Lit. "sexual desire". For the meaning of *lubido*, see 201n.

574ff. **there's not one of my friends ...:** Chremes seems more concerned with his standing in the eyes of others than with the actual morality of his conduct. This preoccupation with his reputation is seen again at 1035−7, where his principal objection to Clitipho's "disgraceful conduct" ⸗is that it might earn him (Chremes) "an infamous reputation". See also 797n.

579 **What's he saying?:** Syrus, having taken no part in the conversation (his comments at 564 and 568 being asides), comes across and interrupts with this question. It is addressed to Clitipho, and *istic* "he" is Chremes; although he has heard what has been said, Syrus pretends to ask what Chremes' lecture was about.
Damn it!: Clitipho is annoyed to discover that Syrus is present and

200

will therefore know that he has disregarded the slave's instructions of 369ff. Chremes himself would regard the exclamation as one of more general annoyance, or as an admission of guilt.

is this how I've been telling you to behave?: Syrus is referring to the instructions he gave at 369ff., but to Chremes the words would relate to the general moral instruction which Syrus, as Clitipho's *paedagogus* (cf. 594n.), has been giving Clitipho since childhood.

580 [**functu's** = *functus es*. See 82n.]

581 **Syrus, I'm sorry:** As twice in 579, these words mean different things to each of the other two people on stage. To Syrus, they are a specific apology for breach of the instructions of 369ff.; to Chremes, they are a general apology for bad behaviour.

582 **it's really annoying for me:** Again, these words would have a specific meaning for Clitipho, and a more general one for Chremes.

583 **is there only one way ...:** i.e. "Can't you go near them without making advances to Bacchis?"

584 **That's done it:** Syrus makes his general expression of gloom at 564 more specific, explaining why the situation is so serious. Following Chremes' advice of 546−7, he has formed a plan to get money out of Menedemus (cf. 597). But this plan, too, depends upon the original pretence of 332−3 that Bacchis is Clinia's girl, and Clitipho's recent behaviour is likely to prevent that pretence being kept up.

585 **stupid though I am:** A false show of humility by Syrus, to ingratiate himself with Chremes and incline him to accept his slave's advice. Earlier (548) Syrus had boasted about his cleverness.

589 **Blast you:** Lit. "May the gods destroy you root and branch."

589−90 [**extrudis! SY. at tu pol:** Craig's simple emendation of the reading of A (*CQ* 29 (1935), 42) − to transfer *at* from the beginning of 590 to the end of 589 − is fully in keeping with Ter.'s style; cf. 185n.]

591 **Is that what you really think?:** Syrus' question refers to Chremes' "I think so too" (588). With Clitipho gone, he asks Chremes for his true opinion.

What do you suppose ...?: Lit. "What would you suppose ...?"

592 **watch him, reprimand him and admonish him:** For the Latin *tricolon* (three−unit word−group) *servas, castigas, mones*, see 465n.

593 **keep an eye on him *now*:** Syrus' stress on *nunc* "now" is a response to Chremes' use of the future tense *curabo* "I'll be taking care ...".

594 **he's less and less obedient to me:** This remark shows that Syrus was once Clitipho's *paedagogus* (Greek *paidagōgos*) "child−escort". This was a slave specially attached to one of his master's sons, whose duties included taking the boy to and from school, but also extended to general supervision of his upbringing (cf. 579n.). The slave would remain attached to the son when the latter grew up, though, as Syrus complains here, his charge would by then be less inclined to follow

201

his advice. Many of the slaves in Syrus' position in comedy are former *paedagogi*; cf. e.g. another Syrus' words about Ctesipho and Aeschinus (*Ad.* 962): "I've looked after them both carefully for you ever since they were boys."

595 **a little while ago:** 546ff.

598 **in the right order, point by point:** Lit. "as one thing follows from another."

599ff. **This mistress of his ...:** Syrus' first attempt to get money for Clitipho to give to Bacchis begins here. He makes three attempts in all, the first two aimed at getting the money out of Menedemus, the third aimed at getting it from Chremes. The first is thwarted by the discovery of Antiphila's identity, and the second by Chremes' refusal to cooperate; the third succeeds. The story which Syrus tells here about Bacchis, Antiphila and the debt is central to the first and third attempts, but has no part in the second. See further Introduction pp. 20−1.

The beauty of the story is, of course, that for all Chremes knows it could be true. But for the audience there is early confirmation of its falsity (602), when Syrus says that Antiphila is the Corinthian woman's daughter − a fact which he has earlier said (270) is untrue. Since this 'fact' is the crucial element of the story (as Syrus first tries to employ it), it follows that the whole thing must be nonsense.

600 **an old woman from Corinth:** Since there must have been many Corinthians living in Athens in Men.'s day, it is not surprising that Chremes does not connect this old woman with the one Menedemus mentioned to him in 96, even though both are said to have daughters.

601 **a thousand drachmas:** There were 100 drachmas to the mina, so the 1,000 drachmas of the supposed debt, for which Antiphila is said to be surety (603), are exactly the 10 minae which Syrus has promised on Clitipho's behalf (724) to give to Bacchis.

[**drachumarum ... mille:** In early Latin and occasionally later (e.g. Liv. 25.24.1), *mille* is treated as a noun followed by a gen. (like its pl., *milia*), not as an adjective. This usage is retained particularly with phrases like *mille nummum* 606.]

603 **security for the money:** The situation envisaged here conflicts with the generally accepted view that from the time of Solon it was forbidden at Athens to make loans on the security of the person. Yet − assuming that Ter. is faithfully following his original − this is not the only instance of such a situation in Men., since a similar one appears to be pictured in *Hērōs* (18−36 and hypothesis 3−4), a play which is also set in Attica. See Gomme and Sandbach 390−1 (cf. 385), who suggest that such situations can be reconciled with Solon's ban by supposing that "in practice the laws do not cover all situations and are not always obeyed". A different explanation is given by

202

G.E.M. De Ste Croix, *The Class Struggle in the Ancient Greek World* (London, 1981), 163: "we must remember that all Menander's plays were produced in the generation following the destruction in 322 of the fifth/fourth−century Athenian democracy, when forms of debt bondage could well have crept in and even received at least tacit legal recognition." Yet another explanation might be that, as Corinthians, Antiphila and her (supposed) mother were not protected by the ban; cf. Gomme and Sandbach, *loc. cit.*: "It may be that the law of Solon admitted exceptions, perhaps regarding non−citizens".

604 [**ea quae est:** *ea* looks as if it is *eam*, the antecedent, attracted into the case of its relative (cf. 724), a rarer form of attraction than the other way round (as at 87). But the whole phrase *ea ... tuam* could be parenthetical.]
inside with your wife: Cf. 335.

605 [**illam illi ...:** Supply "she says" from *orat*. *illam* is object of *daturum* 606; supply *se* (i.e. Bacchis) as its subject.]

606 [**daturum:** This old Latin indeclinable fut. inf. in −*urum* (without *esse*) is discussed by Gel. 1.7.1−15 and Priscian in *G.L.* 2.475−6. Later it was declined (like the fut. participle) and *esse* added to form the inf. Cf. Pl. *Cas.* 671, 693 (where see W.T. MacCary and M.M. Willcock's edn (Cambridge, 1976)); there, as here, some MSS change −*urum* to the later −*uram*.]
[**nummum:** With this particular word, the old gen. pl. (cf. 24n.) was often retained, even in later Latin, esp. after *mille* or *milia*.]
the thousand drachmas: Lit. "a thousand *nummi*." Until about 190 B.C. (and in Pl.), the word *nummus* was used as equivalent to two drachmas, but afterwards as equivalent to one (*OLD* 1204). See further H. Mattingly and E.S.G. Robinson, 'The date of the Roman denarius and other landmarks in early Roman coinage', *PBA* 18 (1932), 211−267, esp. 260: "This [*Hau.* 606] is probably the earliest extant use of *nummus* (by itself) in the sense of denarius − the equivalent of the Attic drachm."

608 **I'll go to Menedemus:** The real meat of Syrus' first plan comes here.
abducted from Caria: As Caria, in S.W. Asia Minor, had a long coastline, the audience would probably assume the pretence to be that Antiphila was captured by pirates − a not uncommon motif in comedy; but the pretence could equally be that she was captured in one of the wars between Alexander's successors (such as that in which Thraso served; cf. *Eu.* 125−6). See 111n.

609 **a handsome profit:** Presumably by selling her as an accomplished slave, or back to her family in Caria.

612 **You'll know very shortly:** In fact Chremes is never told why there is "no need" (611−2) for Menedemus to buy Antiphila. Since the discovery of her identity would ruin Syrus' plan, the dramatist knew

he would not have to explain this remark. As with the episode at 335, his object is merely to increase the audience's opinion of Syrus' ingenuity. See Introduction p. 20.

613 **noisy creaking:** See 173n.

ACT FOUR SCENE ONE

Since Chremes and Syrus stay on stage, it is most unlikely that an act—division occurred at this point in Men.'s original; cf. the introductory note to Act Two Scene One.

614 **Unless my mind's playing tricks ...:** The scene opens with good examples of the conventions of characters entering in the middle of a conversation (see 242ff. n.) and of eavesdropping.

615 **the one my daughter was exposed with:** Exposure was the practice of abandoning unwanted babies in the open to die, which could apparently be done with impunity if the child had not gone through the ceremony of acceptance into the family (cf. 627n.). In a male—dominated society, baby girls (often drains on the family finances, since they had to be provided with dowries) were particularly liable to be exposed. But a 'token' was often left with the abandoned child — some item of the family's material possessions which might identify it if it somehow survived and the giving of which served to salve the parents' conscience (cf. 650−3). So we learn here, and more fully later, that Sostrata give her ring to the old woman who was to expose her daughter, with instructions to leave it with the child.

For discussion of the practice in the ancient world, see Gomme and Sandbach 34−5 and A.R.W. Harrison, *The Law of Athens* I (Oxford, 1968), 70ff. It is difficult to tell how frequent it was; but its occurrence in myth (e.g. Oedipus) and, particularly, as a motif in comedy shows that it cannot have been extremely rare. It was, of course, a godsend to comic poets, since it (along with themes such as the capture of small children by pirates) could lead to a 'recognition scene' such as we have here, where a girl of supposedly low estate could be found after all to be a suitable partner for someone to whom marriage would otherwise have been impossible.

Rings are frequent 'recognition tokens'; cf. *Hec.* 574, 811, 821ff.

617 [ut ... **contemplata** ... **sis:** Supply *vide*.]

618 **Go indoors at once, and tell me ...:** The nurse never returns with the news; the line is written solely to motivate her exit, once she has fulfilled the task of being an interlocutor for Sostrata.

622 (*mockingly imitating her*): For Chremes' treatment of Sostrata, see Introduction p. 19. For Sostrata, see Introduction p. 22.

626 [me **gravidam:** Bentley was right to remove *esse* which occurs in all MSS between these words. If allowed to remain, it would have to be

scanned with its final −e dropped, which is unprecedented in Ter.; on the other hand, it is easy to see how it could have crept in to fill out the construction.]

627 **if I had a girl:** See 615n.

to be accepted into our family: Lit. "to be lifted up". After birth, the baby was placed on the floor near the family hearth, and the father formally accepted it into the family by picking it up; refusal to do so meant rejection of the child, which often led to exposure (cf. 615n.). The verb *tollere* "to lift up" is frequently used in this context (cf. 628, 665, *An.* 219 and *Hec.* 571) and therefore comes to mean "to acknowledge, accept (a child)".
It is clear that Chremes had refused to acknowledge the baby and expected it to be exposed. Why he did not ensure this was done is not explained. Thierfelder (144, n.13) supposes that he was away at the time; but he may more simply have been about, but refused even to come near his unwanted child, leaving it to others to carry out his orders.

628 **got the bonus of a thumping loss:** Lit. "increased by a loss" (*damno auctus*), a nice oxymoron (cf. 323n.). Syrus means that Chremes will have to provide a dowry for the girl (cf. 838). [The Latin line also contains a neat chiasmus *domina ego, erus damno.*]

629 **an old lady from Corinth:** The alert spectator, recalling 96 and 600, would now realize the inevitable outcome of the conversation.

635 **the child should have been killed:** Chremes is not necessarily being as heartless as to suggest that Sostrata should have actually put the child to death; he merely means that she should have seen to it that it did not survive.

640 **earn a living on the streets:** "on the streets" is not in the Latin. In the ancient world, since women did not take paid employment, for one to "earn a living" would obviously entail prostitution; but in English some such phrase must be added to clarify the meaning. At 447, Latin and English are closer: *victum volgo quaerere* "to look for a living among the public at large".

be put up for public sale: In a slave−market; it seems that exposed babies who were discovered alive by strangers were frequently kept as, or sold as, slaves.

643 **[melius peius, prosit obsit:** i.e. *utrum melius an peius sit, utrum prosit an obsit.*]

644 **Chremes my dear:** Sostrata knows when to give in to her husband, and when to hold out against him (as at 1003ff., 1009−11).

645 **your mind is more sensible because of your years:** Lit. "your mind is more sober by its age." Such an expression is more usually applied to a person than to his mind, but the transference is understandable.

650−1 **wretchedly superstitious:** For Sostrata's superstitious piety, see also 1015 and 1030. Her self−deprecatory approach here again shows her

205

skill in handling Chremes.

659 **That's done it!:** Syrus' growing discomfiture as he listens to the conversation between Chremes and Sostrata would amuse the audience. At 628 he was merely worried at the prospect of being saddled with another mistress, but at 654 the first mention of Antiphila in connection with the ring began to alarm him. Now he at last realizes the consequences if Antiphila is found to be Chremes' daughter — he will no longer be able to use her (cf. 608ff.) as a means of getting money out of Menedemus.

662 [**Philterae:** Gen. agreeing with *mulieris*, the construction of Chremes' question being carried over into Sostrata's answer.]

663 **That's the one:** The name of Antiphila's supposed mother has not been mentioned before, but Syrus obviously knows it (cf. his familiarity with everything about her at 269ff.). He therefore realizes the truth before Chremes and Sostrata have confirmed it for themselves, sees that it entails the collapse of his plan, and can start working on another immediately the other two have left the stage.

667 **Now's the sort of time ...:** Evidently Chremes could not afford to bring up a daughter at the time Antiphila was born (cf. 615n.); even now he is to complain (835ff.) of the expense of doing so.

ACT FOUR SCENE TWO

668 **Unless my mind's playing tricks ...:** It is amusing to see Syrus repeating Sostrata's agitated words of 614; he is equally agitated himself now.
His monologue is meant to impress the audience with his inventiveness; see Introduction p. 20. It contains some distinctively Roman military phraseology (669n., 672n.), and Syrus himself — like other slaves in comedy, e.g. Toxilus at Pl. *Per.* 753ff. — is likened to a general fighting a campaign. The stress on the slave's role, coupled with the Roman terminology, may mean that Ter. has expanded the scene; but he will not have invented it, since in Men. too Syrus must have thought up a new plan before Clinia comes outside at the start of the following scene.

669 **my resources are pushed into a very tight corner:** Lit. "my troops are forced into a very narrow space", a military metaphor of an army being forced into a narrow pass or defile; the punning double—entendre is assisted by the fact that in Latin *copiae* can mean both "resources" and "troops". For more extended use of military metaphor by slaves, cf. Pseudolus at Pl. *Ps.* 578ff.]

670 **the old man tumbling to the fact that this woman is his son's girl—friend:** Is "the old man" Chremes, "this woman" Bacchis and "his son" Clitipho? Or is "the old man" Menedemus, "this woman" Antiphila and "his son" Clinia? The former seems more likely

206

because (a) in general terms, there would be more trouble if Chremes discovered that Clitipho was involved with Bacchis than if Menedemus found out that Clinia was involved with Antiphila; and (b) the Latin of the line is echoed at 690 *nequid de amica nunc senex* and, particularly closely, at 697 *senex resciscet ilico esse amicam hanc Clitiphonis*, both of which refer to Chremes, Bacchis and Clitipho. There are, however, also considerations which might incline us to the opposite view: (i) from Syrus' point of view at this particular moment, it is in his interests to ensure that Menedemus does not find out about Clinia and Antiphila, since the slave's plan depends upon everyone (including Menedemus) believing that Clinia is devoted to Bacchis; (ii) *hanc* "this woman" is an odd word to use of Bacchis when she has not been mentioned since 606, and would be more appropriate for Antiphila, who has been the centre of attention for the whole of the previous scene; (iii) "the old man" should be the same old man who is the object of *fallere* "to trick" in 671, i.e. Menedemus. On balance, the argument from the close parallels in 690 and 697 seems decisive in favour of the fact that this line refers to Chremes, Bacchis and Clitipho, though some doubt must remain; perhaps the points of reference were clearer in Men.

672 **it'll be a triumph:** The concept of a victorious general being awarded a triumph is distinctly Roman; cf. Pl. *Bac.* 1072−3 where another slave 'general' (cf. 668n.) says: "But, spectators, don't now be surprised that I'm not having a triumph."
with my flanks protected: There are two meanings here. One continues the military metaphor and refers to the flanks of Syrus the general's army; the other refers to the flanks of Syrus the slave's body and is equivalent to "without getting a flogging". Webster 144, n.48 associates with this line Körte II 58, fr. 134 (ταῦτά σοι καὶ Πύθια καὶ Δήλια "these are your Pythian and Delian [? moments]", supposedly a proverb relating to a person's final hours or actions). But, though the words are attested as coming from the original of our play, the connection with this line is, to say the least, tenuous.

673 **from my lips:** Lit. "from my throat."

675 **Nothing's so tough …:** Some have seen Körte II 268, fr. 935 (ἅπανθ' ὁ τοῦ ζητοῦντος εὑρίσκει πόνος "the searcher's labour finds out everything") as the original of this line. But the passage is not even definitely by Men., and others think it belongs more properly to tragedy.

676−7 **What if I start off …:** We are not, of course, told what the rejected ideas are, because the dramatist never bothered to work them out. The picture of Syrus thinking up and dismissing a succession of schemes is simply meant to accentuate the difficulty of his task in order to highlight his ingenuity and tenacity.

207

677 [**optumam:** Supply *rationem* from *ratio* 674.]

678 **I'll catch that runaway money:** The verb translated "catch" (*retrahere*) is frequently used of recapturing escaped slaves, and the adjective translated "runaway" (*fugitivus*), when used as a noun, means "runaway slave". It is amusing to find a slave using such words of his own hunt.

[A contains two words, *ego* "I" and *hodie* "today", not in any Σ MSS. Kauer—Lindsay accept these and, with slight rearrangement of order, produce two shorter iambic lines (678, 678a) to end a scene of iambic octonarii. But the two extra words are of the sort likely to creep in later for clarity, and acceptance of the reading of the γ MSS gives a single iambic octonarius, making all lines in the scene of the same type.]

ACT FOUR SCENE THREE

679 **From now on ...:** In the short time since Chremes and Sostrata entered their house (667), the excitement inside has alerted Clinia to the good news.

684 **here with them all through:** i.e. with Chremes and Sostrata during their conversation of Act Four Scene One.

688 **it's your turn now, Clinia:** Syrus sets to work on his newly—devised plan (the second; cf. 599ff. n.). Like the first, it is designed to extract money from Menedemus, but, unlike it, it does not turn on the story of the debt. But it depends entirely on Clinia's cooperation, and it is some time before Syrus can calm him down sufficiently to listen to it.

690 [**nequid de amica ...:** Supply e.g. *resciscat*; cf. 670, 697.]

691 **going to marry me:** Clinia has not yet, of course, made any formal moves towards a marriage, but he realizes that all obstacles to it are now removed.

693 **the life of the gods:** A common sentiment from young men in comedy who are successful in love; cf. Pamphilus at *An.* 959—60.

696 **If you move out ...:** Syrus realizes that Clinia no longer wants to continue the pretence he agreed to at 358—9, but wants to abandon Bacchis, move to his father's house and hasten forward his marriage to Antiphila. But since the slave's present plan depends upon the old pretence being kept up, Syrus must at least persuade Clinia to cooperate in that; he does not, however, go so far as to try to prevent him leaving Chremes' house, provided (698) that he takes Bacchis with him when he goes.

698 [**celabitur:** The subject is *amici ... res* 695.]

700 **How shall I have the face to speak to ...:** Lit. "with what face shall I address ..." [For *os* "the face as showing or failing to show signs of shame", see *OLD* 1273, *os* 8b, and cf. *Ph.* 917, 1042.]

208

709 **This is my prize—winning plan:** Lit. "To this plan I award the palm [of victory]." Like many a "cunning slave", Syrus is not modest (cf. 549n.), and the idea of pulling off a coup by actually telling the truth appeals to him greatly.

718 **what if my father finds out?:** It is difficult to decide whether *pater* "father" here means "my father Menedemus" (Shuckburgh, Marouzeau), who would be angry if he found out that Syrus was trying to get money from him when his son was not in fact attached to Bacchis, or "his father Chremes" (Radice, Ashmore), who would be angry if he found out that Bacchis was Clitipho's, not Clinia's. Since Clinia is the speaker, the former is perhaps more likely.
Like many young men in comedy, Clinia is timorous (cf. 720), and not keen on taking risks.

719 **What if the sky falls in?:** A proverbial phrase for a dreadful possibility, but one so remote that it is not worth bothering about; Shuckburgh compares Arr. *An.* 1.4.8, where the Celts tell Alexander that their greatest fear is "that heaven should fall on them", i.e. they fear nothing.

ACT FOUR SCENE FOUR

Just as Ter. probably wrote Act Two Scene Four into Men.'s play, so he probably wrote this scene in too, and was thus responsible for introducing the whole of Bacchis' contribution to the action. If this is so, then in Men. Clinia will have retired into Menedemus' house (cf. 729n.) after he had agreed (722) to Bacchis' transfer, and Syrus will have gone into Chremes' house to supervise the move. It follows that Syrus' words in 722 ("She's coming outside ...") will also be Terentian, designed to lead up to the new scene. In Men. the place of the scene will have been taken by a choral interlude, designed to 'mask' the transfer of Bacchis and her maids. See further Introduction p. 17 and Brothers 112−6.

723 **Syrus has been ...:** Lit. "Syrus' promises have enticed me here shamelessly enough." This is the passage which, according to Suetonius (*Life* 4), Nepos said had been written by C. Laelius; see Introduction p. 11.

724 **the ten minae:** The sum is the same as the thousand drachmas of 601, where see note. Syrus presumably gave the promises when he went to see Bacchis as he describes at 364ff.
[**decem minas:** Attraction of the antecedent into the case of its relative; cf. 604n.]

724−6 **If he's misled me now, ...:** Punctuating with the comma after *deceperit* "he's misled", there are two possible interpretations, depending on whether *saepe* "often" is taken closely with *obsecrans* "begging" ("when he often begs me to come, he'll come in vain") or with *frustra veniet* "he'll come in vain" ("when he begs me to come,

209

he'll often come in vain"); I have preferred the latter. Kauer—Lindsay, however, punctuate with a comma after *veniam*, thereby attaching the phrase *saepe obsecrans me ut veniam* "often begging me to come" to *deceperit*, not to *frustra veniet*; the meaning would then be "If he's misled me now when he often begs me to come, he'll come in vain."

727 [**in spe pendebit animi:** For *animi pendeo* "I am on tenterhooks", see *OLD* 1322, *pendeo* 12, and cf. Pl. *Mer.* 166: *nimis diu animi pendeo* "I've been on tenterhooks for far too long". In these phrases (as in *periocha* 3, *Eu.* 274, *Ph.* 187, *Hec.* 121 and *Ad.* 610) *animi* is best taken as locative.]

728 **will give me the satisfaction ...:** Lit. "will pay the penalty to me with his back." Syrus will be flogged when Bacchis does not arrive, and she sees his punishment as satisfaction paid to her. [As well as alliteration in *poenas pendet*, there is punning of *pendet* with *pendebit* 727.]

729 **That's a really neat little promise ...:** These are Clinia's last words in the play, and it is odd that his final remark is part of such an insignificant aside. This is due to the Terentian authorship of this scene; in Men. his last contribution would have been much stronger — the assent to Bacchis' move (722). In both versions, his absence from the last third of the play is testimony to the shift of interest from him and Menedemus to Clitipho and Chremes; see Introduction p. 18.

It is also (and for the same reason) odd that there is no indication in the text of when Clinia leaves the stage — though the audience, of course, would see him go. He must have been in Menedemus' house for some time by 842, when Menedemus talks back to him as he comes outside. It is best to assume that he goes there with Bacchis and her maids at the end of this scene. This will be the first time that he enters his father's house since his return from abroad, and the fact that he does so so unobtrusively is further evidence of the shift in emphasis.

732 **to the right:** Assuming that Bacchis is facing the audience, she will be pointing to their left, i.e. (appropriately) to the country exit.

733 **celebrating the Dionysia:** There is no conflict between Bacchis' words here and Chremes' statement of the day before (162) "it's the Dionysia here today"; the soldier (presumably the same as the one mentioned in 365) is 'celebrating the Dionysia' in much the same way as we might 'spend Christmas' somewhere without implying that we were only there for Christmas day. The passage cannot therefore be seen alongside 162 as evidence for a Terentian origin for the night—interval (170n., 410n.).

737 **Then I'll wait:** It is difficult to show in modern English how the first word of Bacchis' *quin ego maneo* mockingly picks up Syrus' use

210

of the word in *quin est paratum argentum* "But the money's ready".
Shuckburgh translates: SY. "Why, the money is ready." BA. "Why,
then I stop."

739 **your party:** The Latin word employed here, *pompa*, was originally
used of solemn processions at festivals, funerals etc. That Syrus uses
it for Bacchis' retinue of maids is a humorous touch, exposing her
self—importance; cf. its use to describe Phaedromus' slaves in Pl.
Cur. 2.

742 **Then have I any more business ...?:** Bacchis' swift acquiescence in
Syrus' plan seems somewhat unnatural, and may provide further
evidence for the Terentian origin of this scene.

745 **make sure they bring out ...:** In the space of the next two lines,
Dromo must be supposed to enter Chremes' house, assemble Bacchis'
maids, get them to pack the luggage, and lead them all outside.
Such compression of the action may again point to Terentian
workmanship; but see 508n.

747 **what a great loss this little gain will bring him:** The "loss"
(*damnum*) is the same as the one which Syrus mentioned at 628 —
the sum which Chremes will have to provide as a dowry for
Antiphila. Syrus knows what Chremes at this point does not, namely
that Clinia genuinely loves Antiphila and will shortly ask to marry her
(cf. 691n.); he therefore realizes that the small amount Chremes
stands to gain by not having to entertain Bacchis and her retinue will
soon be more than offset by the two talents (cf. 940) which he will
be spending on his daughter's dowry.

ACT FOUR SCENE FIVE

749ff. **Heaven knows ...:** Chremes' speech clearly indicates how
completely he is deceived about the situation.

751 [*illancin:* See 199n.]

757 **Why don't I tackle him?:** See 410n.

759 **It looks as if ...:** Chremes correctly connects the departure of
Bacchis with Syrus' plan to extract money from Menedemus.

760 **a little while ago:** As at 595, the reference is to the conversation of
546ff.

It's a case of 'no sooner said than done' with me: Lit. "I've made
it said (and) done." The phrase *dictum factum* "said (and) done"
recurs at 904 where it means "it was done as fast as it can be said",
and is equivalent to our "in less time than it takes to say so.'

762 **giving you a pat on the head:** Lit. "stroking your head"; *demulceo* is
a rare word, used in Liv. 9.16.16. of stroking the back of a horse.
This unexpected show of affection by the master to his slave, like his
promise (763) to do him a good turn, contrasts with Chremes' later
threats against Syrus (950ff.) when he discovers that he has been

211

tricked.

[**adduxisse:** Supply *se* (i.e. Clinia) as subject and *eam* (i.e. Bacchis) as object of the infinitive.]

770 **Well done!:** Chremes' position is identical to that of Simo in Act Three, Scenes One and Two (459ff.) of *An*. Neither man can see the truth when it is told him; both are in such an unreal world that they cannot believe wrong of their sons when they are given the facts. It is the old story of "Don't tell a man a lie — he won't believe it — but tell him the truth and he'll think it's a lie."

Pardon?: Lit. "Say it (again), please." Either Syrus cannot believe his master's compliment and gets him to repeat it, or he pretends not to have heard it so that he can have the pleasure of hearing it again.

774 [**cupere:** Supply *se* as its subject from *sese* 772.]

777 **For the wedding he'll be given money:** The real meat of Syrus' second plan, hit upon at 677−8, is given here for the first time. All the slave's actions for the last hundred lines have been aimed at setting that plan in motion, but only now are we told precisely how the transfer of Bacchis, Clinia's revelation of the truth to his father, his request to marry Antiphila and Menedemus' approach to Chremes will be used to extract money from Menedemus. It is good theatre to keep the audience guessing in this way. Once again, of course, the money is really for Clitipho to give to Bacchis, though Chremes thinks it is for Clinia to give to her.

778 [**qui:** Instrumental abl., equivalent to *ut eo*; cf. *qui* equivalent to *ut ea* in 989.]

To be bought: In the Latin the verb is active (*comparet* "for him" — i.e. Clinia — "to buy"), but the order of the interrupted sentence (begun by Syrus, completed by Chremes) cannot be kept in English unless the verb is turned passive.

779 **But I'm not giving her:** Syrus' second plan now founders on the rock of Chremes' refusal to cooperate. He remonstrates with Chremes about this briefly, but gives way with a good grace (788), perhaps because he already sees the third possibility of getting the money.

The minds of the audience must by now have been reeling at the amazing rapidity of the unfolding of events. Only two lines after learning what the second plan actually is (cf. 777n.), they learn that it has failed, and only eleven lines after they learn that, they are hearing about Syrus' third plan (cf. 790n.). The audience is not necessarily meant to have digested all this as it occurs; carried along by the swiftly changing action, they are meant instead to be impressed by the slave's ingenuity (and, of course, by Ter.'s skill as a dramatist). See further Introduction p. 18.

782 **Pretending isn't my way:** Chremes appears to be living up to his avowed devotion to the *vera vita* "the life that is true" (cf. 154n.), but these sentiments contrast with his earlier encouragement of Syrus

212

to practise deception (cf. 546n.).

786 **you'd been urging:** *suaseras*, the reading of A; Kauer—Lindsay prefer *iusseras* "you'd been ordering", the perhaps more obvious reading of the Σ MSS. The reference is again to the conversation of 546ff.

788 **I regard your stand as fair and right:** A translation for the phrase *aequi bonique facio* which here means "I take it [your stand] in good part". See *OLD* 68—9, *aequus* 6b, and the parallels quoted there. [*aequi* and *boni* are gen. of price or value.]

790 **we must look for some other solution:** The way in which Syrus embarks on this third (and final and successful) plan to obtain the money shows him at his best. By following his words "we must look for ..." with "*But* what I told you ...", he makes it appear that he has temporarily shelved his search for another solution and has instead turned back to another matter altogether, the problem of the debt first mentioned at 600ff. This is cleverly contrived to put Chremes off the scent, since the words "But what I told you ..." in fact introduce the third plan. Moreover, this plan is extremely bold, since it involves a total change of tactics in aiming to get the money from Chremes, when the first two plans aimed at getting it from Menedemus; and it employs the old story of the debt, now put to good use in a different way, thus obviating the need for long explanations. Finally, not only does Syrus come up with this third plan incredibly quickly (only eleven lines after his second one collapsed at 779), but he foresees and counters (792ff.) any possible objections from Chremes.

791 **that old woman:** Does the Latin word *ista* "that woman" refer to Antiphila (Shuckburgh, Marouzeau) or to her supposed mother Philtera, the old woman from Corinth (Sargeaunt)? In fact, the woman from Corinth must be meant, since (i) it is she (even when dead), and not Antiphila, who supposedly owes the money to Bacchis, and (ii) whereas Syrus is unlikely to talk to Chremes about his newly—found daughter using the rather curt *ista* "that woman", he could perfectly well use such a word of Philtera.

793 [**quid mea:** sc. *refert.*]

796 **"Strictest law ...":** The same proverb appears in a slightly different form in Cic. *Off.* 1.33: "from which is coined that proverb now constantly used in talk "strictest law is greatest wrong" (*summum ius summa iniuria*)."

797 **I won't do that:** Chremes' delusion is now complete; having just refused to cooperate in a plan based on the truth, he falls in with one which is based on the total nonsense of the story of the debt.
if others can: Syrus has cleverly played on Chremes' preoccupation with his reputation in the community (seen again at 574ff. and 1035—7), thus ensuring that he will agree to pay.

798 **Everyone believes ...:** This line is corrupt in all MSS, and none of

213

the many emendations is satisfactory. There is no doubt, however, of its general meaning.

Note the not—uncommon sentiment that it is the wealthy who can afford to practise virtue, and, indeed, are expected to do so.

799—800 **Better tell your son to:** Syrus completes his triumph by persuading Chremes to let Clitipho take the money to Bacchis himself.

ACT FOUR SCENE SIX

806—7 **this walk of mine wasn't at all hard, but ...:** Lit. "My walk — how far from hard! — has reduced me to exhaustion." [*quam* is exclamatory, meaning "how!".] The walk is the one on which Clitipho was despatched at Syrus' suggestion at 589.

811 [**perduint:** Subjunctive, for *perdant*. This old form is used by Ter. only in this set oath; cf. *Ph.* 123 and *Hec.* 134. See also 161n. on other old forms of the subj. in Ter.; as with the phrase *di faxint* there, Cicero uses this one, too, as an archaism (*Deiot.* 21: *di te perduint*).]

813 **You can go to hell ...:** Lit. "Are you off from here to where you deserve to be?" The MSS are confused over the verb at the start of this phrase, which appears to be a question equivalent to a command. But again, the general meaning is clear.

814 **your brazenness:** Syrus refers to Clitipho's behaviour with Bacchis earlier that day (cf. 562ff.) and the night before (as described at 568ff.).

817 **You went off:** Clitipho means Syrus' journey into town to fetch Antiphila (cf. 191), during which he also collected Bacchis.

818 **That's me finished:** Clitipho, knowing nothing of Syrus' machinations during his absence, naturally sees the departure of Bacchis from Chremes' house as the ruin of his hopes.

824 [**experibere:** In early Latin, 4th conjugation futures are found in −*ibo* and −*ibor* (as with the 1st and 2nd conjugations in −*abo*, −*abor* and −*ebo*, −*ebor*) and in −*iam* and −*iar* (as with the 3rd conjugation in −*am*, −*ar*). The latter formation, which is akin to that of the subjunctive, did not oust the former until the Classical period, and Ter. uses both. For instance, the other form for *experibere, experiere*, occurs at *Ad.* 888; cf. *scibis* 996, but *scies* 95, 331 etc.]

825 **Then I really am a lucky fellow:** Like Clinia at 244, Clitipho swiftly changes his mood from despair to elation.

828 [**loquitor:** 2nd sing. fut. imperative of the deponent verb; cf. *utitor* 972. For *facito* (and *obsecundato* in 827), see 221n.]

ACT FOUR SCENE SEVEN

829 **Say "Here I am":** Predictably, here and at 831−2, Clitipho does not manage to show no surprise, as Syrus urged him at 826−7.

835−6 **My daughter's already got ...:** Chremes, thinking the ten minae is paying off the debt for which Antiphila was supposedly surety, regards the payment as a substitute for what he would have had to have paid if he had brought his daughter up himself.

836 **for her food and lodging:** A translation for *hortamentis*, a rare word found in some MSS and supported by Eugr. He connects it with the feeding of horses, and it is perhaps in character for Chremes, annoyed at the expense Antiphila is causing him, to stoop to the use of such an unfeeling term. But W.M. Lindsay (*CQ* 19 (1925), 34) merely calls it Chremes' "'horsey' language".

837 **another ten ...:** Apparently, when a female slave was bought, the price did not include her clothes and jewels, which were paid for separately, and usually cost ten minae (cf. Pl. *Cur.* 344 and *Per.* 669). In an equally unfeeling way, Chremes now regards the cost of acquiring Antiphila as little more than the purchase of a new slave, and imagines that Bacchis will demand a further ten minae for her wardrobe.

838 **another couple of talents:** Antiphila's dowry is actually fixed at two talents by Chremes (940).

ACT FOUR SCENE EIGHT

842ff. **I consider ...:** The 'talking−back' convention (cf. 175n.) is put to good use dramatically. The words "my boy" (843) tell the audience who Menedemus is talking to, and the content of what he says shows that Clinia has carried out the instructions which Syrus gave him at 702ff. See also 729n.

844 **How wrong he is!:** The irony in these words, coming as they do from Chremes, is unmistakable.

845 **the saviour of my son ...:** Very shortly (941) Chremes will find himself making much the same appeal to Menedemus.

849 **the conversation we had together:** At 469ff.

851 After this line Kauer−Lindsay insert an extra line 851a: *erravi? acta est res? quanta de spe decidi!* "Have I been wrong? Is it all over? From what high hopes have I fallen!". No trace of this is found in A, but it occurs in some Σ MSS in a slightly different order from Kauer−Lindsay's; in others only the first part of it occurs, with the rest in the margin; the last part also occurs in 250. The most telling argument against it is that in 852 Menedemus is still claiming that his version of events is correct, and it is not until 856 that Chremes' explanation of the use to which the money will be put convinces him

that he is wrong; only then (857) does he give way to despair.

853 **That's what they tell you:** There seems much more point in giving these words (lit. "so they say") to Chremes with A, than to follow the Σ MSS in ascribing them to Menedemus ("that's what they're telling me"), where they are weak and otiose.

854 **when I've betrothed my daughter to him:** So the Σ MSS (*desponderim*); A has "when you've betrothed your son to her" (*desponderis*), probably under the influence of the other nearby second person singular verb *des* "(so that) you'll give" in 855. (The object of the verb is not expressed in the Latin and must be supplied.) It is Chremes who is betrothing his daughter, not Menedemus who is betrothing his son. Cf. *desponsam* (sc. *Antiphilam*) in 866 "that she's engaged to him" and 891 "that Antiphila was engaged to your son", where Antiphila is the subject of the passive verb; so here she, not Clinia, is the object of the active one.

857 **Oh, dear me:** It is ironic that Chremes — full of confidence in his own wisdom, yet actually himself the one who is deluded — brings unnecessary pain and disappointment to the person he is trying to help, when that person is in fact in possession of the truth.

861 **You're much too lenient with him:** Chremes is still lecturing Menedemus.

866 **say that she's engaged:** Chremes seems to be doing exactly what he said (779) he would not do. He takes a different line with his friend and equal Menedemus than he would with his slave Syrus; and he makes it clear that the engagement is only a pretence.

873 At the end of the scene both men go into their houses, and the stage is left empty for the first time since 409−10 (but for Men.'s play see the introductory note to Act Four Scene Four). As R.L. Hunter points out (*ZPE* 36 (1979), 38): "An act−break at this point in the Greek original, during which the events which Menedemus proceeds [884ff.] to relate took place, may be regarded as certain." Whether in Ter. the pause (either here or at 409−10) was filled by e.g. music from the piper is impossible to prove one way or the other.

ACT FIVE   SCENE ONE

For discussion of the possibilities of Terentian workmanship in this final act, see Maltby, *passim*.

874 **I know I'm not all that clever ...:** The opening words of Menedemus' monologue make it clear that he has discovered the facts and knows that Chremes has been duped. Accordingly, the audience will realize that the tables will soon be turned, and so can appreciate to the full the complete reversal of roles as Menedemus reveals the truth to his self−appointed "helper, counsellor and guide" (875). This reversal is highlighted again and again as the scene unfolds.

216

879 **Oh, wife ...:** The fact that Chremes is still being rude and overbearing to Sostrata serves to heighten the audience's anticipation of his coming discomfiture.

882 **But why's my son hanging about ...?:** Syrus had said (834) that Clitipho and he had no reason to remain in Menedemus' house for very long, and their prolonged absence mystifies Chremes. This puzzlement will eventually make him more ready to see the truth of what Menedemus has to say.

883 **Who do you say's hanging about ...?:** Throughout the early part of this scene, Menedemus derives quiet — though not vindictive — amusement from the irony of the situation; such amusement gradually increases, and is seen especially clearly at 897−8, 907, 910, 911 and 913−4. However, as soon as he realizes the dangers inherent in Chremes' reaction to the truth, he stops poking gentle fun at him and tries to calm him down (919) and to give him sound advice (924ff., 932−4).

887 **The scoundrel counterfeits ...:** Right to the last, Chremes is so certain that he is right that he can find an explanation to suit his views.

890 **Wait a moment:** Chremes' interruption of Menedemus' attempt to tell him the truth serves several dramatic purposes. It further shows how he persists in his deluded views (cf. 887n.), it prolongs the suspense for the audience's enjoyment, and it produces, in Menedemus' answers to his questions, some vital facts which help finally to bring home the truth.

897 **I've no idea why that was:** For once in his life, Chremes is at a loss for an explanation, and Menedemus cannot resist the obvious rejoinder.

898 **did a remarkable job on your son:** The Latin verb used here, *finxit*, is the perfect tense of *fingit* (translated "counterfeits") in 887. By using the same word as Chremes had used to describe Syrus' activities, Menedemus mockingly pretends to go along with the improbable explanation which Chremes had offered on the earlier occasion.

904 **In less time than it takes to say so:** A translation for *dictum factum*; cf. 760n.

908 **Then Bacchis is my son's mistress:** Chremes, who has been getting increasingly worried (905, 906), is finally convinced of the truth. This significant moment is marked by a change of metre from the musical trochaic septenarius to the spoken iambic senarius; cf. 312n.

909 **My property's barely enough ...:** As at 930−1, Chremes' major concern is for his own financial well−being; cf. 463−4n. Fathers in this type of comedy are frequently pictured as preoccupied with their own wealth.

910 **[quid? istuc times ...?:** Cf. 1017: *quid? metuis ...?* "What? Are

you afraid ...?"; the close parallel makes such a punctuation more likely than Kauer—Lindsay's *quid istuc times ...?* "Why are you afraid ...?"]

910–11 **friend ... girl—friend:** The Latin contrast *amico ... amicae* is neater than any possible English translation.

913 **as to let his mistress, under his very eyes ...:** The unpleasant word is tactfully suppressed; cf. 1041: "bringing indoors before my very eyes a ..." and *Eu.* 479: "As for that eunuch, even if I was sober, if it came to it I'd ...".

915 **It's myself I'm angry with now:** Chremes' despair of 908–9 gives way to rage, as he becomes the typical angry old man of comedy; cf. 37–9n.

920 **Aren't I sufficient warning to you?:** i.e. of the perils of undue severity to one's son. Here, as at 928ff., Chremes is unable to learn from the examples of others, despite his earlier advice to Clitipho (2i0) to do just that. Even Menedemus' specific remarks at 932 are ignored.

922–3 **Don't you think it's a disgrace ...?:** Menedemus puts Chremes' problem in a nutshell.

924 **What you kept telling me ...:** At 153–6.

931 **It's really and truly a life with the hoe for me:** Lit. "This business really comes to hoes for me." Chremes refers to the hoes which Menedemus was carrying in Act One Scene One; but, he implies, whereas Menedemus chose life on a farm voluntarily as a self—imposed penance, he himself will be forced by Clitipho's extravagance to sell up and work for his living on the land, whether he wants to or not.

934 **it won't be appreciated:** Lit. "it will not earn gratitude." [For the meaning of *ingratum* here, see *OLD* 907, *ingratus* 2, and cf. the meaning of its opposite, *gratum*, 262n.]
As you wish, then: Menedemus gives up trying to prevail on Chremes, and turns to the matter of his son's desire to marry Antiphila. Since both men now know the truth, they realize the sincerity of Clinia's intentions.

937 [**filio:** Dat. after *dixisse* ("appointed for my son"), not after *dicam*; cf. *dixisse illi* "appointed for him" 942.]

938 **Why the silence?:** Menedemus thinks that Chremes' failure to reply is due to his reluctance to provide a dowry for a daughter he has only just found, and therefore says (938–9) that he does not wish to press the point. But, as will shortly be made clear (940–2), Chremes is silent only because he is working out a plan, which mention of the dowry has suggested to him (cf. "Dowry?" 938), to protect his fortune from Clitipho's extravagant demands.

940 **two talents:** Cf. 838. Again, the decisive moment when Chremes hits on his plan is marked by a change of metre, this time from

218

iambic senarii back to trochaic septenarii; cf. 312n., 908n.

941 **the salvation of myself** ...: In just under 100 lines, the situation of the two men is completely reversed; Chremes is appealing to Menedemus in terms almost identical to those in which Menedemus appealed to him in 845.

945 [**luxuria et lascivia:** Note the effective alliteration; cf. also *deridiculo ac delectamento* 952.]

946 **take the edge off ... and bring ... back:** A *dicolon* (two−unit word−group) with asyndeton, formed of two similar and alliterative words *retundam, redigam*; cf. the *tricolon* (three−unit word−group) 465n.

947 **let me please myself** ...: Menedemus had made a similar appeal to Chremes in 861−2.

948 **to fetch his wife:** The reference is to the ceremonial fetching of the bride from her father's house to her future husband's, a part of the wedding ritual technically known as *deductio*, from the verb *deducere* "to bring home in procession as one's bride" (*OLD* 497, *deduco* 10b). The verb used here, *accerso* (= *arcesso*) is used in the same sense at 1047−8: *quor non accersi iubes filiam?* "Why aren't you giving the orders for my daughter to be fetched?" and, of the same ceremony, in *Ad.* 903−4, where Demea asks Aeschinus: *quor non domum uxorem accersis?* "Why aren't you fetching home the bride?".
At the end of this line Menedemus goes into his house to see that Chremes' instructions are carried out; cf. 950n.

949ff. **This son of mine will be put in his place** ...: The contrast between the punishments proposed for Clitipho and Syrus is exactly what the latter foresaw at 356 − between a "scolding" and a "flogging" (*verba* and *verbera*).

950 **But as for Syrus:** So A (*Syrum quidem*); but Kauer−Lindsay follow the Σ MSS and Don., where *quidem* is replaced by *quid eum?*, given to Menedemus: "As for Syrus ..." ME. "What of him?" (*Syrum ...* ME. *quid eum?*). There are, however, a number of reasons for following A and against assuming that Menedemus has any words to say in this line: (i) there is no reason why Menedemus should be interested in Syrus' fate − for the rest of the play he is solely concerned with what is to happen to Clitipho; (ii) if he does ask the question "What of him?", he must stay on stage to hear Chremes' answer, and so cannot enter his house until 954, by which time he is due to come out of it again with Clitipho; (iii) by contrast, if we assume that he departs earlier, at 948, that departure is well−motivated (cf. 948n.). (Although his absence from the end of 948 until 954 is still impossibly short for him to explain everything to Clitipho, it nevertheless complies with the common convention described in 508n.; but an exit and an immediate re−entrance, both in 954, would not.)

951−2 **such a pretty sight, such a punchbag:** Lit. "so beautiful, so combed out." Although these expressions, employing *exorno* and *depecto*, seem unique, the simple forms of both verbs (*orno* "I beautify", *pecto* "I comb") are used elsewhere in comedy to mean "I give a thrashing"; cf. Pl. *Rud.* 730: *ita ego te hinc ornatum amittam tu ipsus te ut non noveris* "I'll send you away from here so beautified [i.e. with such a thrashing] that you won't know yourself", and Pl. *Rud.* 661: *leno pugnis pectitur* "the pimp is being combed [i.e. beaten] with their fists".

954 The scene ends part−way through a line, a thing which happens elsewhere in Ter. only at *An.* 580, *Eu.* 1049, *Ph.* 795, *Hec.* 767 and *Ad.* 81, 635 and 958. In four of these instances, as here, some MSS do not mark the start of a new scene, and this is an indication of the haphazard nature of such scene−divisions.

ACT FIVE   SCENE TWO

954 **Please ...:** For the convention of characters entering halfway through a conversation, see 242ff. n. Here the conversation shows that Menedemus has alerted Clitipho to the new situation.
[**tandem:** Used to emphasize the preceding *itane* (as at *An.* 492 and *Ph.* 231) "expressing a strong sense of protest or impatience" (*OLD* 1904, *tandem* 1).]

960 **There he is:** There is no clear indication in the text of when Menedemus returns into his house − as he must do, because Syrus speaks of him as off stage at 1001−2 and he re−emerges at 1045 (cf. 1046: "I'm on my way outside"). It is best to assume that he leaves the stage immediately after he has pointed Chremes out to Clitipho, not wanting the embarrassment of being present at the confrontation between father and son.
Why are you criticizing me ...?: Since *quid?* can mean "why?" or "what?", the meaning could equally be "What are you complaining of in me?", with *incusas* "are you criticizing?" having two objects, the person and the thing complained of, as at *Ph.* 914.

965 **the first person I should have given it to:** A father would naturally, under normal circumstances, leave his property to his only son.

966 **the relative who was closest to you:** Clinia, his (future) brother−in−law. This is made clear in the Latin, where the word "closest" (*proxumum*) is masculine singular. Since women could not inherit or own property, Chremes' fortune would go not to Antiphila, but to her husband as her legal guardian on her marriage; failure to appreciate this led some MSS to read *proxumos*, masculine plural, embracing both Clinia and his wife. Clitipho is being treated as an irresponsible person or a juvenile, who has to be placed in the care of relatives.

968 **clothing:** Webster 144, n.48 associates with this passage Körte II 58, fr. 135 (ἀλλ' ἦν χιτών σοι "But, look, a tunic [i.e. clothes] for you"); but the brevity of the fragment makes such an identification no more than a possibility.

970 **What a mess I'm in!:** Syrus' genuine distress at the trouble he has brought on Clitipho, like his attempt to intercede (973−4), endears him to the audience; see Introduction p. 21. Clitipho's remorse (971, 1043−4, 1049 etc.) is also endearing.

975 **a place of sanctuary:** Lit. "an altar", at which sanctuary could be sought. An altar stood on the stage, and it sometimes featured more prominently in the action than, as here, merely receiving a mention. See Introduction p. 8.

976 **someone to plead for you:** Nevertheless, this is just what Syrus intends to "line up" at 1001−2: "I'll go to our neighbour Menedemus, and get him lined up to intervene on my behalf". The same Latin word, *precator* "intercessor", is used on both occasions.
I'm not annoyed with you: Chremes does not seem to be acting as he said he would at 950−1, and this has led to suggestions of Terentian alteration at this point. However that may be, Chremes' assurances do not satisfy Syrus (cf. 1002n.), and at the end of the play (1066−7), Clitipho still feels he has to ask his father formally to forgive the slave.

977 Kauer−Lindsay's marking of a new scene after this line is not based on any MSS evidence, but on the fact that Chremes leaves the stage at this point. Some MSS, however, do mark a new scene after 979, where the metre changes from the trochaic septenarii which have lasted since 940 to the iambic octonarii which continue until 999. We thus have further evidence of the uncertain nature of these scene−divisions; cf. 954n.

978 [**und':** i.e. *unde*. The dropping of the final −*e* is dictated by the demands of the metre; cf. *ille* scanned *ill'* 197, 515.]

979 **renounced:** The verb used here, *alienavit*, literally means "he's declared us to belong to someone else"; cf. Sostrata's use of *alienum* "someone else's child" 1029.
[**tibi iam esse:** Supply *cibum* from 978.]

983 **I'm on to something:** See 472n. In this line and the next, Syrus plays for time while thinking up a plan to reconcile Clitipho (and therefore himself as well) to Chremes; he finally hits on one in 985. Compare Syrus' playing for time at 317ff., and his more protracted deliberations at 668ff.

985 **I don't think you're their son:** Syrus does not, of course, believe that there is any truth in his suggestion, as his remarks at 996−8 make clear. But, realizing that his ingenious tricks have only served to get Clitipho into serious trouble (970), he now proceeds to employ that same ingenuity one last time to get him out of it. He correctly

calculates that, when, at his prompting (994), Clitipho voices to Sostrata the suspicions which are now being planted in his mind, she — pious woman and devoted mother that she is — will be shocked into interceding with Chremes on their son's behalf. This final service which Syrus does for Clitipho shows the slave's real devotion to his young master, and proves his essential good nature; and it ensures that he remains the mainspring of the action until the end of the play, instead of fading into the background when 'the balloon has gone up'.

986 [in mentem est: This archaism (for which some MSS substitute the more obvious *in mente est*) may be equivalent to *in mentem venit* (cf. 997). It recurs in *Ad.* 528 (*nilne in mentem est*? "Hasn't anything occurred to you?") and several times in Pl., e.g. *Am.* 180 where the metre proves its correctness. It is paralleled by such phrases as *in potestatem esse* "to be in the power (of)", and is discussed by Gel. 1.7.16—20. See also W.M. Lindsay, *Syntax of Plautus* (Oxford, 1907), 89.]

988 [te: Here and at *Eu.* 222 *indulgeo* governs an acc., as in early Latin. But in 861 and *Ad.* 63 it governs a dat. in accordance with later practice.]

996 [quoius sis: So all MSS; but Kauer—Lindsay prefer to delete *sis* as an interpolation, presumably because they wish to scan *quoius* as two syllables rather than as one.]

997 [nam quam maxume ...: The text is very uncertain. A has a totally different version of the line from the Σ MSS, and Kauer—Lindsay ingeniously keep both — though with some emendations — by including an extra line, 997a. Their version reads: *nam quam maxume huic visa haec suspicio/ erit vera, quamque adulescens maxume quam in minima spe situs/ erit* "the fact is, the more these suspicions of his seem to him to be true, and the more the young chap is made to despair". They believe that copyists, confused by the repetition of *quam* and *maxume* in 997 and 997a and of *erit* in 997a and 998, have combined the two lines into one; but, in their attempt to disentangle them, they have to insert, without any MSS support, the word *vera* "true" at the start of their 997a.
I follow the many editors who make one line based on A, but without the word *adulescens* "young man", which is assumed to be an interpolation. These editors read *vana* "unfounded" for Kauer—Lindsay's *visa* "seem", the actual word in A being very unclear; they assume that the version of the Σ MSS started life as an explanation of the version of A, which later crept into the text and ousted the true line.]

998 on his own terms: In fact, Clitipho's "peace with his father" is finally achieved more on Chremes' terms than on his own; cf. 1054ff. The metaphor is taken from the conclusion of a formal pact or

treaty. [For *lex* meaning a "term" or "condition", see *OLD* 1022, *lex* 12, and cf. 1054: *ea lege* "on this one condition".]

999 **He may even find a bride ...:** This remark by Syrus anticipates, for the audience's benefit, the solution to Clitipho's present predicament which Chremes dictates to his son at the end of the play. There will be "no thanks for Syrus" because, once Clitipho has settled into a marriage, he will not be inclined to be grateful to his slave for any help received in his premarital adventures.

1002 **get him lined up to intervene ...:** Syrus has evidently not been reassured by Chremes' remarks at 975−6; see 976n.
[**fide:** Gen. sing., a form found not infrequently in Pl., and, as an archaism, in Hor. *Carm.* 3.7.4 and Ov. *Met.* 3.341.]

ACT FIVE SCENE THREE

1003 **Really, if you're not careful ...:** Once again the device of characters entering halfway through a conversation is put to good use dramatically. Sostrata's rebuke to Chremes immediately tells the audience that Clitipho has (in the usual unrealistically short time; cf. 508n.) voiced his suspicions about his birth to his mother − a fact which is confirmed by her words at 1014: "Our son suspects he's not really ours." As Eugr. saw in his note on 1014, it is natural that Clitipho has sought out his mother, as the parent likely to be more sympathetic to him; similarly it is his mother to whom he appeals at 1024ff.
Here, as elsewhere in this scene (1009−11, 1015−16), a more forceful side to Sostrata's character emerges; as well as knowing when to humour her husband (cf. 644n.), she also knows when to stand up to him. The audience is therefore being prepared for the decisive role which she is to play in assisting Menedemus to secure Chremes' forgiveness for Clitipho in the final scene (1045ff.).

1006ff. **Oh, still persisting ...:** As at 1010, 1015 and 1018ff., Chremes is still overbearing and inconsiderate in his treatment of his wife. Such behaviour not only highlights Sostrata's distress, but also prevents the audience from feeling too much sympathy for Chremes.

1008 **why I'm behaving like this:** So Iov., the Σ MSS and Eugr. (*quam ob rem hoc faciam*); A has "why you're behaving like this" (*quam ob rem hoc facias*). The former is correct, with the subject of *peccem* and *faciam* the same: "what it is I'm doing wrong ... why I'm behaving ..."; *facias* "you're behaving" probably arose under the influence of the adjacent *nescias* "you wouldn't know".

1010 **starting up all over again:** Lit. "returning to their original (starting) point."

1013 **Don't you see how much trouble you're stirring up ...?:** Sostrata's warning is similar to that of Menedemus at 932, but is similarly disregarded. Once again we see how Chremes fails to live up to the advice he gave to Clitipho at 210 about learning from the examples of others.

1014 **he's not really ours:** Lit. "he was substituted", i.e. as a suppositious child or changeling. Such fraudulent supplying of children to childless parents, or exchanging of a true child for another is, of course, a frequent motif in fiction.

1015 **Do you admit it, then?:** A singularly unfeeling remark for Chremes to make to his wife.

leave that sort of thing to our enemies: The pious Sostrata (cf. 650−1n., 1030n.) is shocked by Chremes' reaction, and seeks to "deprecate" the ill−omened words. For the sentiment itself, cf. Pl. *Mer.* 135a: "Keep that sort of opening remark for our enemies".

1018 **Because I've also discovered my daughter ...?:** Sostrata's naive innocence is well contrasted with Chremes' heartlessness. Despite her present worries over Clitipho, she is still overjoyed that she has managed to prove the identity of their long−lost daughter, and she therefore interprets Chremes' remark of 1017 as meaning that she will with equal skill be able to prove that Clitipho, too, is their child. Chremes, however, has a less kindly motive for what he has just said.

1023 **You'd think him so too, if you knew the facts!:** The meaning if one punctuates with a comma after *videas* only; *rem* "the facts" thus becomes the object of *videas* "you knew", and "him" must be supplied as object of *censeas* ("you'd think him serious"). Kauer−Lindsay, however, punctuate with a comma after *rem* as well as after *videas*, making *rem* the object of *censeas* and supplying "him" as object of *videas*. The meaning would then be "You'd think it was the case [i.e. that he is serious], if you were to look at him."

ACT FIVE SCENE FOUR

1024ff. **If ever there was a time:** Maltby (37) comments on the "high, almost tragic style" of Clitipho's appeal to his mother, as befits the description of him as "serious" in 1023. Compare Dido's appeal to Aeneas (Verg. *A.* 4.317−18): "if I have deserved well of you at all or if anything about me has brought you pleasure".

1025 **with the consent of you both, was called your son:** "your" in "your son" is singular, referring to Sostrata alone, whereas "your" with "consent" is plural, referring to both Sostrata and Chremes, and so is here translated "with the consent of you both". Clitipho is appealing directly to Sostrata (cf. 1003n.), so refers to her alone when calling himself her son, though he realizes that his mother's acknowledgement of himself as her child has always been dependent upon Chremes' consent.

1030 **As surely as I pray ...:** Lit. "So may you survive me and this man here, as you were born of me and him." To the pious Sostrata, this is the most solemn assurance that she can give, since a Roman parent could wish for nothing more devoutly than that his children should outlive him; cf. the similar oath in Pl. *As.* 16−18: "As you wish your only son to outstay your own life, safe and sound and living on, so I implore you ...". Conversely, for a child to die before its parents was regarded as a monstrous reversal of the ordinary processes of nature; cf. e.g. the pathos expressed in Verg. *G.* 4.477 (= *A.* 6.308): "young men laid on pyres before their parents' eyes".

1032 **And, if you've any respect for me** ...: Chremes, impatient of Sostrata's superstitious worrying, deliberately and mockingly employs much of the terminology which she has used in 1031 to put across a far sterner and less sympathetic message to Clitipho. Thus *cave* "make sure I don't" (cf. 187n.) appears in both 1031 and 1032, *si me amas* "if you love me" of 1031 is paralleled by *si me metuis* "if you've any respect for me" of 1032, *istuc verbum* "words like that" 1031 by *mores ... istos* "behaviour like that" 1032, *ex te* "from you" 1031 by *in te* "in you" 1031, and *audiam* "hear" 1031 by *sentiam* "see" 1032.

1034 [*crede ... credito*: A good example of the difference between pres. and fut. imperative (cf. 221n.): "Believe all this now, and believe hereafter that you are ours."]

1035−6 **If you'd been born out of my head** ...: Clitipho has just said that Chremes' words are not those of a true father, meaning that if Chremes were really his father he would not talk like that. Chremes replies "Even if I were your sole parent without a woman to help create you [i.e. if I were your father and mother rolled into one], I wouldn't find it any easier ..."
The reference is to the Greek myth of the birth of Athene − that the goddess sprang fully armed from the head of her father, Zeus, when it was cleft with an axe wielded by Hephaistos. To suit his Roman audience, Ter. has altered the deities' names to those of their Roman counterparts (Zeus/Jupiter; Athene/Minerva); cf. 162n. And it is probably for the benefit of the less cultured members of that audience that he gives the rather laboured explanation of the allusion to being born from someone's head "as they say Minerva was from Jupiter's". But Ter. must have been reasonably confident that most of his audience would have been familiar with the story; cf. the remarks on the use of Greek mythology by Pl., Sandbach 124−5.

1037 **to endure getting an infamous reputation:** As at 574ff. and 797, Chremes' chief worry seems to be about his personal reputation in the eyes of others; it might be thought that his main concern should be for Clitipho's moral welfare.

1039ff. **You're looking for what you've got** ...: In here admitting that Clitipho is of course his son, Chremes becomes both less angry and

225

more serious than in his previous ill—tempered remarks of 1033—4 and 1035—7. He puts his son's problem in a nutshell, and we, like the audience, must acknowledge the truth of his statement and admit that the criticism of Clitipho is accurate and justified. Clitipho, too, accepts the criticism, as his remarks of 1043—4 make clear. As the play draws towards its close, the evident correctness of Chremes' judgement and its acceptance by his son signify that the gulf between the two is being bridged and that the final reconciliation cannot be far off.

1041   **bringing indoors before my very eyes a ...:**   The sentence is unfinished, and some such word as *amicam* or *scortum* "lady—friend" or "prostitute" is suppressed; cf. 913n.   Also missing are some such words as *te puduit* "you were not ashamed" which can easily be supplied in the Latin from their later occurrence in 1042—3, but which have been included in the translation.

ACT FIVE   SCENE FIVE

Now that Clitipho is contrite, and looking for ways to "placate" his father (1044), reconciliation can be effected. But even so, it takes the combined efforts of Sostrata and Menedemus to persuade Chremes to drop his plan of effectively disinheriting his son (1048—53); we are reminded of the way in which Demea and Aeschinus join forces to persuade Micio to marry in *Ad.* 933ff. Sostrata and Menedemus also have to work hard to persuade Clitipho to accept his father's conditions for forgiveness (1056—9).   Once, however, everything concerning Clitipho has been settled, including the choice of a bride for him (1060—5), it is a comparatively easy matter for Chremes to be persuaded to forgive Syrus too (1066—7), and the conventional happy ending is assured. For the roles of Menedemus and Sostrata in this scene, see Introduction pp. 20 and 22.

As with other scenes in Ter. (and Pl.) which contain more than three speaking characters, those who believe in the strict application of the so—called 'three—actor rule' in Greek New Comedy (cf. Introduction p. 2) have speculated on which character Ter. has added here in his adaptation. Webster's suggestion (*Studies in Menander*[2] (Manchester, 1960), 86) that it is Menedemus is unlikely, since it seems probable that the self—tormentor of the title appeared in the last scene of the Greek original, and that that play ended, as it began, with a confrontation between the two old men. A more likely possibility is that, if a character has indeed been added, it is Sostrata. See further Maltby 38, and cf. 1060—1n.

There is considerable disagreement in our MSS about the ascription of words to speakers in the latter part of the scene (1056ff.); I have everywhere followed Kauer—Lindsay. See also 1065n.

1046   **to bring about some peace between them:**   In the Latin we again find language reminiscent of the formal striking of a treaty of peace;

cf. 998n.

1047−8 **for my daughter to be fetched:** See 948n.

1048 **the dowry I fixed on:** Not, of course, the two talents of 940, but the whole of his estate (cf. 942), which Chremes is still maintaining is what he has decided on as Antiphila's dowry.

1053 **Very well:** Chremes at last gives way under the combined pleading of the other three, but with rather a bad grace. However, he has a trump card still to play to ensure that Clitipho will not misbehave in future.

The Latin phrase here translated "Very well" (*quid istic?*) is, as Don. says when he comments on it at *An.* 572, "the words of a man who is making a concession and is, as it were, beaten" (*concedentis et veluti victi verbum*).

1056 **I'm telling you to choose a wife:** The abrupt way in which Clitipho is ordered (and eventually agrees) to forsake Bacchis in favour of a conventional marriage has seemed so unnatural to some scholars that they have seen in this passage clear traces of alteration by Ter. The assumption underlying such a view − that anything which seems (to modern critical judgement) to be a weakness or imperfection in a Roman comedy must necessarily be the responsibility of the Roman dramatist and cannot have appeared in the Greek original − is typical of the attitude which has until recently prevailed in the study of Roman drama. However, as our knowledge of Greek New Comedy has increased, a less extreme view has arisen, and, in connection with this passage at least, there are good reasons to believe that Ter. is accurately reflecting a situation which also occurred in his original. Firstly, it seems very much in character for Chremes to impose such a condition on his son; secondly, the passage has at least one parallel in Greek New Comedy or other Roman adaptations of it, e.g. in Pl. *Trin.* 1183ff., where Charmides hastily provides Callicles' daughter as a wife for his extravagant and wayward son, Lesbonicus; and thirdly, Plutarch (*Mor.* 712C) mentions just such a situation as this when stressing Men.'s decency in dealing with love affairs − indeed, he could almost have had the contrast between the treatment of Bacchis and Antiphila in mind as he wrote: "Affairs with *hetairai* ("courtesans"), if the women are headstrong and shameless, are cut short by some sort of chastening experience or repentance on the part of the young men, whereas, in the case of nice girls who reciprocate the love, either a legitimate father is found for them, or else additional time is given for the romance."

1058 **whichever course:** i.e. either to give up Bacchis and marry, or to continue seeing her and be disinherited.

1060−1 **I'll get you a bride:** Within the context of the Greek original at least, it might seem odd for the mother to be making suggestions (here and at 1063) for her son's bride, when such arrangements would be more readily thought of as the responsibility of the father. This is one of the principal arguments advanced to support the view that Ter. has added Sostrata to this scene; see further Maltby 38 and 41, n. 46. But we might have here a genuine Menandrian touch, evidence of the 'behind—the—scenes' influence of Athenian women in domestic matters.

1061 **That red—headed girl ...?:** Clitipho's rejection of the wife picked for him and his subsequent selection (1064—5) of a bride of his own choosing ensure an agreeable ending to what is, after all, a comedy. If a particular girl had been forced upon him, the play would have ended on rather a sour note. But his willingness to make the best of a bad job and actually nominate someone he likes "well enough" (1064) prevents the audience from feeling too sorry for him; they realize that, once he has settled into marriage, his future life will not be too unpleasant.

1065 **Now I *am* pleased with you, my son:** Of the several places where our MSS disagree over the ascription of words to speakers in this scene, the matter of whether it is Chremes or Sostrata who speaks these words is the most crucial. Does Chremes unbend sufficiently to express approval of Clitipho's acceptance of his instructions (so A)? Or does he remain unrelenting to the end, while it is left to the more sympathetic Sostrata to praise her son's compliance (so the Σ MSS)? In following A (and Kauer—Lindsay), I have thought it in accordance with the spirit of a comedy and with Chremes' swift forgiveness of Syrus in 1067 — and notwithstanding the fact that he has made a sarcastic comment to Clitipho as lately as 1063 — that a genuine reconciliation between father and son is expressly shown on stage at the very end of the play.

1066 **I want you to forgive Syrus:** Clitipho evidently still feels it necessary to make this request of his father, a move more in keeping with Chremes' threats to punish Syrus (950—1) than with his later statement that he is not angry with him (976—7). Whether or not there has been a genuine inconsistency in Chremes' attitude to Syrus in these earlier passages (cf. 976n.), it gives a final neatness and completeness to the happy ending to have the formal act of forgiveness spoken here.

1067 **Farewell, and give us your applause:** All Ter.'s plays end with this direct appeal to the audience, though in *An.*, *Hec.* and *Ad.* it is shortened to the single word *plaudite* "Give us your applause". In Pl. the appeal is often considerably more elaborate, e.g. *As.* 942ff., *Capt.* 1029ff. and *Cist.* 782ff. Since there was no curtain in the type of theatre at which the plays were originally produced (see Introduction p. 8), some such indication is required to signal that the performance is at an end. Such addresses to the spectators reflect the words which (as far as our evidence goes) appeared at the end of the plays of Greek New Comedy, appealing for applause and for success in the dramatic competitions at which the plays were originally produced; cf. Men. *Dysk*. 965ff., *Mis*. 463ff. and *Sam*. 733ff.

In all Ter.'s plays the words of this appeal are prefixed in the MSS by the symbol ω, Greek omega (ō), the last letter of the Greek alphabet. There has been much debate about what this symbol represents when so used. Bentley (on *An*. 981) thought it was a corruption of CA., the abbreviation for Latin *cantor* "singer" or "piper", and cited Hor. *Ars* 154−5: *si plosoris eges aulaea manentis et usque/ sessuri donec cantor "vos plaudite" dicat* "if you want an approving listener, who waits for the curtain [such as was used in later Roman theatres] and who will remain seated until the singer says "Give me your applause"." Don. nowhere comments on the appeal, but some MSS of Eugr. say that the words were spoken by a *recitator* "reciter", whatever that may mean. In Pl. the appeal is spoken by the whole troupe of players or by one of the actors, and the same may well have applied in the case of Ter. However, I have followed the traditional view about the *cantor*, though doubt must remain.